On 10 January 1987
Shops stopped busi
gathered, straining
within. The cathedral was full, the service relayed to St Mary
Clement and the City Hall.

All this was for a thanksgiving service for someone described
by himself and his wife as a very ordinary man – a back-bench
MP from a small political party, who had served just twelve
years in Parliament.

Politicians as a breed are not popular. Yet David Penhaligon
was more than popular. He was loved – not just in Cornwall,
but throughout Britain. This book does much to explain why
this was so.

It is a very personal book. It gives us his family's own lively
memories of David. It also gives us the recollections of his
friends and parliamentary colleagues, from cabinet ministers
and party leaders to those who knew him first in Cornwall as
an engineer or Young Liberal.

It illustrates too why people are prepared to devote their lives
to politics, despite its disappointments and its agonizing
frustrations – not just for MPs, but also for their families, who
suddenly find themselves left alone at home, and wondering if
the next election could put them on the dole.

Above all, it shows what it was like for an underrated,
inexperienced enthusiast to come from nowhere to win an
unwinnable seat, almost immediately to be called upon to play
a key role in the dramas of the Lib/Lab pact, and then to
become the most popular public champion of a new great
force in British politics.

David Penhaligon loved it all. He was the happy warrior of
British politics. He loved people and he loved challenges. This
book communicates that love.

PENHALIGON

ANNETTE PENHALIGON

BLOOMSBURY

First published in Great Britain 1989
This paperback edition published 1990
Bloomsbury Publishing Limited, 2 Soho Square, London W1V 5DE

Copyright © 1989 by Annette Penhaligon

A CIP catalogue record for this book
is available from the British Library

ISBN 0–7475–0616–7

10 9 8 7 6 5 4 3 2 1

Typeset by Scarborough Typesetting Services

Printed in Great Britain by
Richard Clay Ltd, Bungay, Suffolk

A NOTE ON THE AUTHOR

Annette Penhaligon was born in Cornwall in 1946, and has
lived there all her life.

After David's death, Annette was elected to Carrick District
Council for the first time, and is enjoying being involved in
local politics. Her interest in the local Social and Liberal
Democrats remains strong, and she still plays a very active
part in the running of the Truro constituency.

She is also proud to be a trustee of the David Penhaligon
Memorial Trust Fund, which was set up in 1987 by David
Steel and the then chairman of Cornwall County Council,
Julian Williams. The fund assists schoolchildren with learning
difficulties and helps provide retraining opportunities for the
long-term unemployed in Cornwall.

Matthew, now seventeen, is studying for his A levels at Truro
Sixth Form College, and Anna, twelve, attends a special day
school near Truro.

CONTENTS

FOREWORD

This is a very personal book. Matthew, Anna and I wanted to have our own record of David. We hope it will also give pleasure to others who knew him through his work and his appearances on TV and radio, but I think I should give a word of warning.

You will not find here the things we as a family have always taken for granted. I do not write about the love that sustained us all, because that is something that we do not need reminding of. Nor do I write of the laughter, though with David there was always that. He was incapable of pursuing any argument without reducing it to a joke. The love and laughter were part of his personality, and there is no danger of our ever forgetting them. What we have recorded are the incidents, the stories, the oddities that made him the ordinary and extraordinary man he was.

In this I have been helped generously by many of his friends, who have helped fill the background to the story. You will find their memories too within the book. In particular I would like to thank Malcolm Brown and Alan Beith, for reading the text before publication and for their advice, and Debbie Owen for her support throughout the writing of the book.

Most especially I thank David Blomfield, who interviewed over forty of David's friends and relations, then gathered together and edited their memories and opinions along with mine. His own involvement in politics has run parallel with ours. He was elected to Richmond-upon-Thames Council in 1971, as one of only three Liberals, and later became leader of the group. When he stood down from the Council in 1986, the Alliance held 49 of the 52 seats. Not only his editorial but also his political experience has proved invaluable.

ANNETTE PENHALIGON

> 'When he shall die
> Take him and cut him out in little stars,
> And he will make the face of heaven so fine
> That all the world shall be in love with night.'
>
> These words from *Romeo and Juliet* were
> inscribed on my wreath at David's funeral

1

BEGINNING

'I have always said that I only got elected because I was too naive to realize it was impossible.' – DP on *Desert Island Discs*, first broadcast the month after his death, January 1987

David was essentially a very humble man, but of one thing he was intensely proud – that an 'ordinary' little couple like us could succeed in politics, when all that we had were enthusiasm and a passionate belief in our cause. I hope, as David would have hoped, that this book will show that, if they believe sufficiently in their cause, any man and any woman can get to Westminster as he did, regardless of their background and regardless of where they start their journey.

David's own journey, he believed, began not so much in his own city of Truro but unexpectedly in the ancient town of Bodmin, some twenty-five miles closer to the River Tamar. With its granite-faced and brownstone buildings, Bodmin has all the quiet dignity expected of a peaceful Cornish country town. Yet, incongruously, it was in Bodmin in November 1963 that, for the last time in Britain, two men were jointly condemned to death for murder. At their trial, David, then a nineteen-year-old student, was chief witness for the defence.

The circumstances of that trial were extraordinary, and for David they were crucial to the career he was to choose – work totally, even obsessively, devoted to serving the people of Cornwall. They were also to be crucial to me, though I did not realize it at the time, for it was with that work and with the rest of Cornwall that, first as his girlfriend and then as his wife, I was to share him for the next twenty-three years.

David's father, Charles Penhaligon, owned and ran a garage and a caravan site with some seventy caravans on the outskirts of Truro. He was a well-known, well-respected local businessman. The caravan site was well-known too, but much less well-respected. You could say that Kenwyn Hill Caravan Site had a certain 'reputation', because it housed a fairly mixed bunch of people. There were those who had, from choice, decided to live in a caravan, happy to tend their pretty gardens and enjoy the freedom of a fairly easy-to-run home. There were newly married couples too, patiently awaiting the chance of a council house or the purchase of a house of their own. There were also some who had just got work in Truro and needed a base for house hunting. None of these caused trouble. There were others there who did, however. They were the even more transient tenants, mostly employed as casual labourers. They were the ones that gave the caravans a dubious name and kept the local police occupied.

It was in the summer of 1963 that two of these transient tenants, Russell Pascoe and Dennis Whitty, were arrested for a particularly brutal murder of a reclusive farmer from the small Cornish village of Constantine. The arrest was an awful shock for the other residents, and of course for the

Penhaligons. Charles Penhaligon was himself an inspector in the special constabulary, and accustomed to coping with petty criminals, but this was no petty crime. They all watched with amazement as the police checked the contents of Whitty's caravan, article by article, each meticulously and painstakingly sealed and labelled in a plastic bag before being removed for further investigation. Then, to add to the drama, David was called on to appear as a witness for the defence.

He was asked to recall an occasion when he had seen Whitty in the throes of an epileptic fit. This had occurred some time before, late one Saturday evening when David was studying at the Penhaligons' bungalow, close by the caravan site. He was asked for help by some passers-by who had found a man they thought had been knocked down by a car. When David went to see what had happened, he recognized the man as Dennis Whitty; he seemed to be unconscious and had scratches and bruises on his face. An ambulance was summoned and Whitty was taken to hospital. A few days later, Whitty called at the bungalow to thank David for his help. He suffered from epileptic fits, he said, which made him cut and bruise himself. This was why he had looked as if he had been knocked over by a car.

Whitty's defence at the trial was that he became uncontrollably violent when attacked by epilepsy, that he had been seized by such a fit while robbing the old man and that this accounted for what was clearly an extraordinarily frenzied attack. As David was the only person available who had seen Whitty in a fit (apart from the defendants' girlfriends), his evidence was crucial. The defence, however, failed and both men were hanged.

David was shocked by the trial. It was not that he thought

3

Whitty should have been found not guilty. He had quite clearly committed the most horrific murder. However, David felt strongly that Whitty was not wholly responsible for his acts. He was clearly immature and suggestible, and it was very probable that his medical condition could have affected him.

Years later, in a programme recorded just before his death, David recalled the way in which the experts dealt with the possibility that Whitty might have acted under the influence of hysteria. 'After I gave my evidence, which was clearly key to it all, a series of these eminent psychiatrists came in. The first one took an hour to say he didn't know. The second one took about three quarters of an hour to say – well he thought he could have done. The third one took about four minutes to say "Garn, he's having you on." The third one was believed.

'I've often wondered if I gave precisely the same evidence as David Penhaligon, chartered engineer, forty-two years of age, Member of Parliament, as opposed to David Penhaligon, nineteen-year-old fitter-and-turner apprentice, whether it would have made more impression. You remember these things.'

2

BACKGROUND

*'He wouldn't consider university. He felt it was essential to have **practical** knowledge.'* – David's mother

David gave his evidence at Bodmin on 31 October 1963. It was the first, and in many ways the most agonizingly frustrating, of many occasions when he was to find himself in disagreement with so-called experts. It was also the first of an even greater number of occasions when public duty interfered with his private life and with mine. We had booked 31 October as the occasion of our first date!

The weekend before, I had been staying with my grandmother and aunts at Tregony, a village some eight miles east of Truro. I was then seventeen and living and working in Truro. However, I had spent the first twelve years of my life in Tregony and I was either related to or friends with everyone there. Ever since my parents had moved our home to Truro, I had come back regularly to see my friends and relations, and as I got older I came back even more regularly because of the Saturday dances.

At that time the dances in Tregony's village hall attracted the young for miles around. Many of my old schoolfriends came from Truro, generally by taxi, though occasionally the odd boyfriend would have a car and we would travel in fairly rickety style, without (anyway in my case) letting our parents know our mode of transport. I had been out with a number of boyfriends but none for long and never remotely seriously. I liked having boyfriends but if one gave the least hint of being serious, I had no idea how to handle the situation. That is how I met David.

I had gone to the dance with a boy I had been seeing for about six weeks and I had decided to drop him. I did so that evening, in an appalling way, telling him a terrible lie instead of the truth – I am not sure I knew it anyway – and then returning to the dance so as not to spoil *my* evening. On my return, David asked me to dance. I did not know David at the time, although I recognized him as someone I had seen around. He was tall, fairly heavily built, dark-haired – not really good-looking but with a great deal of confidence. We had a number of dances, then he walked me back to my grandmother's. We made plans to meet during the next week.

My sister, Claire, two years younger than me, was disgusted with my choice. I had given up someone quite good-looking, she said, for what she described as a 'great bear'. A few days after our meeting, to my great surprise, the great bear turned up at my parents' house. Most of my previous boyfriends would never have called without being invited. They would have telephoned instead. David, as I was rapidly going to discover, was unusually self-assured for his nineteen years. He certainly needed to be self-assured, as he had to explain that he was going to be late for our first date. Still, he did have a dramatic excuse to offer. I had never before had a boyfriend who had been called to give evidence in a murder trial. I was impressed.

Looking back, I am not sure that otherwise I was so very

much impressed by David at this time, but there were a number of plusses. He had a car. He was respectable – my parents seemed happy to have him around and my sister was quickly won round when he began to help her with her homework. He was conventionally dressed, nearly always in a suit and tie, which in later life I could never wean him from, even on visits to the beach. He was not particularly short of money and he was *never* short of conversation. In fact, he talked all the time! He was jolly, not 'serious' – what a relief! – and confident to a point that some people might have considered a minus.

I have no idea what he thought of me. He never said. Neat, I suppose; quiet – I expect he noticed that, though he seemed quite blind to how shy I was; respectable – I could be taken home; certainly not pushy or making any demands on the relationship.

I had been working for about a year when we met. I had attended the local grammar school at Truro but my academic career had not been impressive: I had left with only two 'O' levels and no ambition to improve the score. There was no threat of unemployment then. My father worked on the clerical side of the Post Office and I found a job there as a telegraphist. Other friends went to work in solicitors' or accountants' offices, more often than not jobs found them by their fathers. We obviously were not the wise ones. They continued into the sixth form and went on to teacher training colleges or university. Now that my older child has reached the age at which I left school, I feel a little foolish explaining my school failures while at the same time urging him to work harder.

David was wiser – but only just. He had managed three 'O' levels the first time around. He had a better excuse than

I, in that he had spent a great deal of time off school, with various illnesses and no fewer than fourteen broken bones in fourteen years – many of them broken on the rugby field. He was an enthusiastic player until his brittle bones forced him to give it up. Table tennis was less hazardous and as a boy he won his way to London to represent the south-west. That too he was eventually to give up, when it became apparent that he might have the chance of going to London as a representative of another kind – if he worked instead on the game of politics.

David took his 'O' levels at Truro School, a boys' public school which specialized in sending their brighter pupils to Oxford or Cambridge. David, however, did not want to go to university. He wanted to become a chartered engineer. The school did not teach the course he wanted; so he left. He decided to take the hard road to get the qualifications he wanted and entered the local engineering firm of Holman Brothers as an apprentice, on the understanding that they would give him time off to get first an OND and then an HND at Camborne Technical College. This kind of training scheme was comparatively new at the time and Holman's were so unused to it that they gave it an original twist that David was to relish and refer to for the rest of his life. Because Holman's then had no established apprenticeship scheme for technicians, they gave David a craftsman's training instead. As a result he was able to boast in later years not just that he was a chartered engineer, but also that he had his indentures as a fitter and turner. The whole training would take five years but would give him an exceptional grasp of both the practice and theory of mechanical engineering.

David's method of work was nerve-wracking for his

family. He liked engineering but could never get down to what was required in the exams till the last few weeks. This was none too easy as the family bungalow was always buzzing with activity. His father not only ran the garage and the caravan site but was also chairman of the Motor Agents Association. His mother helped with the caravans; Margaret, his older sister, was taken up with dogs and dog shows; his brother John (now a fellow Liberal Democrat councillor with me on Carrick Council) was three years younger than David and still at school. David would come in from work, eat and go straight to bed. When the rest of the family went to bed, his mother would wake him and he would then get down to studying. As often as not, she would find him still at work next morning. He was to be a night-owl for the rest of his life.

David certainly had a natural bent for engineering. He had after all been brought up in a garage. 'Why have you got your shoes jacked up?' was his reaction at the age of four to seeing his mother in high heels. Perhaps it was the first sign of an obsessive interest in engineering but I don't think so. It sounds to me like the first of those Penhaligon quips. Certainly he always had the gift of the gab. His mother remembers prophesying when he was only three that he would go into the church, or politics, or be a comedian. 'I wasn't far wrong, was I?'

As a teenager, however, David never thought of any career beyond engineering. 'I was always the one amongst my contemporaries,' he once said, 'who could make things work. I was the one that could put the bicycle wheel on. It was not because of any inherent ability but because I was brought up with it and I learnt how to do it.

'Also I always wanted to know *why*. I remember that

when I was young, the sort of newspapers that were normally in our household would just tell you that the Hindus were knocking the socks out of the other half and I was always wanting to know *why* they were doing it. That sort of curiosity is essential in engineering, as it is in politics.'

As a boy, David had satisfied that curiosity by taking on the job of delivering the Sunday papers around the caravan site – and reading them on the way. It gave him a far wider grasp of what was happening in the world than most of his contemporaries. It also increased his knowledge of what life was like on the site. I was taken to a party there on Guy Fawkes Night, when the Penhaligons and residents alike enjoyed one of the largest bonfires I had ever seen. David's father was obviously well respected by the tenants but he was very much the 'boss' and they doffed their caps to him. With David, however, it was very different. He had grown up with many of the families and had a very easy relationship with them. After all it was in the recreation hut on the site that he and John practised their table tennis and that David would often act as bingo caller.

I vividly recall David's concern when one of the young girls on the site badly damaged her new cardigan. Not only was it new, it was not yet paid for, as her mother had only recently received it from one of the many club books used on the caravan site as a convenient form of shopping. The agony for the family, as David knew, was that the payments would have to continue even though the garment was now unusable.

Over the first few months our own relationship was one of take it or leave it. Sometimes we would make arrangements for a date; at other times we would not bother. Then there would be a phone call or a note through my front door and we would see each other again. We had in fact decided to finish altogether in the summer of 1964 when David went on holiday to Scotland with three friends from the Tech. However, things turned out rather differently. Instead, while David was on holiday, I received a number of letters. They were the nearest that David ever came to writing love letters. He was no romantic, and we were never good at keeping such souvenirs, but these I did keep and now I treasure them.

As always, most of his news concerned how the cars were going – 'the exhaust has fallen off twice and I have had two punctures already'. There were also descriptions of how the four of them were sharing out the camping chores – surprisingly well, it seemed, though obviously none of them could cook. Typically too there are comments on the people he saw – 'The young lads up here have long hair to the last man and give the Cornish lads an air of respectability that I had not credited them with . . . The Scottish men all seem very small compared to us. Perhaps we have only seen the short ones.'

There is also in the letters a real sense of adventure. 'The Lake District is really marvellous, nothing like what I expected. Last night we went to Wastwater (a lake) but to complicate matters we went off the main road and charged across the mountains. The roads were only approximately one foot wider than the car, the hills as steep as 1 in 3 and the bends beyond description. But the views were beyond compare; it really looked as if it had come from a picture book. The vegetation was arid and sparse, the rocks had that marvellous appearance that comes with severe weathering and age. The sheep, who were apparently the only occupants of this desolate valley, were very different from our sheep at home: they are a lot smaller and stronger looking. I estimate that twenty per cent are black.' Who but David would end such a vivid description with so precise an estimate!

That letter ended: 'The present arrangements seem to suggest that I will arrive home late Friday night or Saturday morning, so we will be able to go out somewhere on Saturday evening. xxxxx David.'

So much for our plans to 'finish altogether'! We went out.

That autumn there was a General Election. It proved to be a milestone in British political history: it marked the end of thirteen years of Tory rule. It was also a milestone in David's life – and in my own.

Party politics had never been of very special importance to our families. Indeed they were not of any very special importance to anyone in Truro except during General Elections and even then, our two families, although they might discuss the issues, did not get involved. The Penhaligons were, if anything, Conservatives. They owned a business; David's mother had even been a member of the Young Conservatives in her youth, her branch only failing to win a cup for public speaking, she claimed, because their chairman lost vital marks by forgetting to ask for the National Anthem to be played! My own family, on the other hand, was traditionally radical. Such differences, however, mattered very little in Truro. They were academic. The Tories always won.

David and I certainly did not discuss politics in the first year of our courtship. I was therefore quite unprepared when one Saturday morning early in the General Election he suddenly announced that he wanted to help in the campaign. 'Which party?' I asked. 'The Liberals,' he replied. 'That's fine,' I said. 'So long as it's anti-Tory.'

I was not the only one to be unprepared for David's decision. I think he was too. He had not realized until then how much he cared about the way the world was run and certainly did not realize at the time where this first step would lead us.

Over the following years, in the odd moment of calm between those bouts of elation and exhaustion that seem to make up so much of political life, we would sometimes reminisce about that day. Why did David make that first move, and why did I go along with it so cheerfully? It was easier to account for my reaction. I thought it was just one of David's bright ideas. His ideas were always fun but would soon be dropped when something more entertaining came along. David's motives, however, were more serious than I thought and considerably more complex than he himself realized at the time.

The trial at Bodmin had disturbed him deeply. He had been asked to give evidence, and had grasped how vital it was, only to see how little weight that evidence carried. That was disturbing enough but he was just as shocked that the court showed no understanding of what it was to live, as Whitty lived, on the fringes of society. David used to say that had his father run any other business, he would have been brought up at the prosperous end of the town and things would have been very different. As it was, he had lived beside what was probably the poorest community in Truro. 'They were my friends and they made me very aware of a whole series of problems that such people face, problems that cannot be solved by the typical middle-class response of "they should pull themselves together".'

David himself, of course, had been brought up in comfort but he had seen injustice and thought it should be fought. In other circumstances – and perhaps another constituency – he might have been inspired much earlier to join a political party and work for change. But this was Truro, where politics slumbered between elections. It was not until there was a General Election that there were manifestos to be read, speeches on television and even political debate. Now there was an election and he felt that he ought to do something.

But why help the Liberals? Why not Labour? After all in Truro, despite its Methodist tradition, the Liberals always came third. That choice, David always claimed, was easy. The answer sprang from his work at Holman's. At the time Holman's was a successful, if rather old-fashioned, company and one of the largest employers of labour in the county. David's socialist friends had been saying for some time that it should be nationalized. 'Garn,' David would say, in his broadest Cornish accent, 'if it's run by London, it won't make fourpence.' David had no time for state-controlled monopolies and was fiercely against Labour's policy of taking over successful companies. 'I see nothing wrong with Holman's making a profit, so long as they give some of it to David Penhaligon!' It sounded like a joke but he was deadly serious. Profit-sharing was the key to his own attitude to economics then and for the rest of his life.

It was not that David personally cared very much about money. As long as he had enough to satisfy his fairly modest tastes and keep him in cigarettes he was happy. In later life he mixed with people considerably better off than himself –

in a different world, in fact – but it never bothered him a bit that he would never be able to afford their lifestyle. David did, however, care very much about workers sharing in the profits of their work and he had now discovered from his voracious reading of the newspapers that profit-sharing was an essential part of the Liberal creed.

The Liberal manifesto of 1964 thumped this message home. It also called for a 'classless dynamic society'. It wanted greater promotion opportunities for young technologists and executives. Jo Grimond had launched this theme back in June with his 'Charter for New Men'. David was typical of the new men it was aimed at, and he now responded. Liberals, he felt, held the right balance between concern for the disadvantaged and the encouragement of initiative among the young.

The problem was that in Truro the Liberals never seemed to win and we quickly saw why this was so. The local party headquarters were in River Street, housed in the top-floor office of a solicitor who was at that time chairman of the Truro branch. When David marched up the stairs and offered to help, he naively imagined that the offer might well be rejected: they might not need any more help. Far from it! He was met with open arms – and 3,000 envelopes that needed addressing by the day before. It was nice to be welcomed but unnerving to discover how frail the organization was. He took the envelopes and promised to return with more help. The extra help initially turned out to be myself and my sister.

The Liberal organization may have struck us as distinctly ramshackle but, as we were soon to discover, it was not unusually so for Liberals in the 1960s. Although there were a few glorious exceptions in the south-west, such as North

Cornwall, North Devon and Bodmin, what you generally found in any constituency was a handful of devoted workers who had spent their years of service to the Liberal cause on a treadmill that had taken them from one association office to another, from secretary to chairman to treasurer, and then back again, all for lack of others to take on the burden. It produced a reassuring atmosphere of continuity and stability but it was not a recipe for progress.

The couple who had greeted David when he first walked into the office were fine examples of such a system. Norah and Cecil Trewin had joined the party back in the thirties. In those days there had been a Liberal Club in Truro, very much like those that are still active in many West Country towns. The club was a place where one could go for company and a cup of tea, and play a game of billiards. You did not have to be an active Liberal to be a member. Your Liberalism was taken for granted. A few members, however, would become involved in helping with elections. The Trewins got involved.

The problem in Truro was that the Liberals only leased the club premises, they did not own the building. After the war the building was sold and the club closed down. The meeting rooms and billiard table were gone but the Trewins and their friends in Truro soldiered on, as branch and association officers and as party workers. Now they had to hire halls or meet in each other's houses. Year after year they would organize coffee mornings, fêtes and jumble sales. They would see the other constituency branches in the neighbouring towns and villages wax and wane. They would discuss their successes and problems together at the proper meetings of the association executive, and the finance and general purposes committee, and report once a year to an ill-attended annual general meeting.

The high points of the association's life were provided by elections. In those days no one stood under party labels in local elections, so serious political campaigning was restricted to the three or four weeks of the General Election campaign. Then the members would go out to battle for their Liberal candidate, but since the Liberal always came in third, there was not much competition for the job of standard bearer. Under these circumstances, it was hardly surprising that the organization was ramshackle. It was remarkable that it existed at all.

In one way, however, the Truro association was exceptional. It boasted its own paid agent, though under an arrangement that typically had its peculiar element of Liberal eccentricity. For years Truro had had as one of its vice-presidents someone who could best be described as its patron. This was the Lady Aurea Macleod. The wealthy widow of a local landowner, she was a Liberal of the old school. Where most of her rich neighbours were Church and Tory, she was Chapel and Liberal. She was also fiercely teetotal. At any fête or garden party where alcohol was on sale, she was quite likely to buy up the lot and tip it down the nearest toilet bowl.

Lady Aurea employed, variously as her man of affairs and her chauffeur, a remarkable person of considerable presence, Gerald Webster. Gerald too was a committed Liberal – were he not, indeed, I suspect he would not have been considered for his job – though he did not entirely share her commitment to teetotalism. I distinctly remember that he was rather partial to a particular brand of whisky! It was understood that, at Lady Aurea's expense, Gerald could devote to the Liberal Party any time that could be spared from her ladyship's service. Truro Liberals, therefore, had in him an experienced agent for whom they did not have to pay themselves. The only hazard was that his schedule was at the determination of his employer, which may have contributed to the bizarre style of organization he pursued.

Gerald's style was instinctive, rather than based on any recognized business practice. Details, he decided, could be left until he had the time to deal with them. What was important was to 'know what was going on'. (His strength was that he knew everybody – throughout the West Country.) In the middle of an election campaign he was quite likely to walk out of the office to get the 'feel' of the electorate. The candidate and workers then had to manage for themselves, until he reappeared, refreshed by rumour and inspired by inside information. The legend was that in the 1950s Gerald was agent concurrently for three constituencies, between which (at that time he had no car) he would commute by hitching lifts.

Although he was generally a genial figure, Gerald could also be fiercely partisan. I well remember him taking us off with him to a Labour Party meeting because he was incensed by the choice of guest speaker – a renegade Liberal. When this wretched man got up to speak, Gerald leapt to his feet and start to chant 'Traitor, traitor!' at the top of his very considerable voice. So determined was he, and so effectively did he drown the speaker's own voice, that the meeting was brought to a premature close. (Gerald was a very large man and no one would even try to throw him out.) I found myself both admiring Gerald's commitment and at the same time burning with embarrassment. David in contrast came running down the stairs laughing his head off at the experience.

Gerald made politics fun and it was Gerald as much as anyone who taught David to look at all sides of a political argument because you could always find a comic aspect. He taught us too never to get involved in any of the dirtier sides of politics, though he did turn a blind eye to what was then accepted practice in Cornish campaigning: the battle of the posters. One night in that election, David, I, Gerald's son and one or two others went out armed with torches, posters and paste, and made a few changes to the election posters adorning local fields. When car lights approached we would quickly hide down behind the hedges, our delight all the greater for the illicitness of the act.

That tradition has very properly, I suppose, now died out. Certainly David never ever admitted to our Young Liberals what he got up to in his youth, and he and his agents firmly discouraged any such behaviour in his own elections. In 1979, however, a gang of youngsters not involved in politics travelled from St Austell to Truro swapping all the posters in gardens and on hedges. As a result irate Conservatives woke up next morning to find Liberal posters in their gardens, while Liberals were incensed to discover their property decorated with Tory posters. I bet it was fun for the youngsters.

The Liberal candidate in 1964 was William Hosking, a farmer, an excellent speaker and a hard worker. William boasted that before the 1964 election he had met over 10,000 of the voters. Very probably he had done so but it was largely in vain, as no record was kept of who they were, nor of what he learnt; nor was there any system to take advantage of his efforts. The literature we delivered with so much enthusiasm was also worthy rather than inspiring. It was mostly supplied from Liberal headquarters in London, overprinted with William's name. It was not geared to appeal to Cornish tastes, nor directed specifically to Cornish problems. Later we would discover how great a disadvantage that was. At the time no one knew any better. Still, all the Liberals made up in enthusiasm for what they lacked in expertise and David immediately established himself as the most enthusiastic and most effective campaigner of them all. He was also the best at bringing others in to help.

Throughout his life David had an extraordinary gift for friendship. He always had a great crowd of friends and a natural knack for persuading them to join in whatever he was doing, largely because he made it so much fun. He recruited a whole band of teenage helpers and we addressed, it seemed to me, tens of thousands of envelopes, amazed and secretly amused to find we could do it three times as fast as our very much more experienced seniors. We did not canvass – after all none of us then had the right to vote ourselves – but we delivered leaflets, tramping miles round village after village few of which we had ever seen before.

Sadly, we achieved no miracle. Although 1964 gave the country the first of the Wilson governments, the Tories retained Truro, with the Liberals coming third yet again. However, they did do better that year than they had ever done before. William got 12,575 votes, less than 2,000 votes behind Labour and less than 6,000 behind the Tories. With the recent great Liberal capture of Orpington still fresh in our memories, that gap did not look too broad for us to bridge. At the count all the talk was of what we should achieve next time. After all, to be a Liberal you have to be an optimist.

3

YOUNG LIBERAL

'In one sense I don't think David changed over the years. At executive meetings of the Young Liberals he would always, but in a very constructive way, say "Yes, that may be true, but how do all these issues affect where I come from?"' – Simon Hebditch

Looking back today I can see that it was really at the 1964 General Election that my relationship with David changed. The boy–girl affair had taken on another dimension: we were now best pals united in a new interest that was to ensure that from then on we were never without a topic of conversation or something to do. This, I am sure, sustained our relationship for the next twenty-two years.

At first this change was not very obvious. Certainly, we were now spending all our spare time together but it was not all given over to the Liberals – I don't think my enthusiasm for David and politics could have endured that. We met friends in coffee bars. With their steaming hot expresso and their juke boxes, coffee bars were very popular at the time and David enjoyed the pop music. His heroes were Elvis, Eddie Cochrane, Buddy Holly, Little Richard and Jerry Lee Lewis. In fact they remained his heroes and only Tina

Turner and Johnny Cash were added later on, as his interest in music waned as politics took over.

It was about this time too that David's father decided to educate us in the art of ballroom dancing. We had been separately taught the basic steps at school, which enabled us to 'get around the floor', but David's father enjoyed taking his family to dinner dances, where it was important that we could all dance fairly well. He booked a course of lessons for us both. Neither of us took this very seriously. Whilst we followed the steps with the instructors, as partners we invariably came unstuck. Both of us were left-handed and this clearly extended to our feet. Certainly, David's approach to dancing was very mechanical and I used to swear he never ever listened to the beat.

By now we were regular visitors to each other's homes and David got on very well with my parents. The time we spent at his parents' home was generally combined with his great passion for doing up old cars. Many was the time I helped him rub down newly sprayed cars and I can vividly picture him now with his head in the engine, his hair falling over his face, a cigarette in his mouth and a coffee cup balanced on the wing. His great enjoyment lay in making something work.

At this time, too, David was also likely to decide, quite unpredictably, to join some marathon walk. Dr Barbara Moore's famous walk from John O'Groats to Land's End had set a fashion in the 1960s, especially in Cornwall, for massively attended endurance walks of some twenty-five miles. These would often start at midnight when the roads were quieter. One of the garage mechanics at the Penhaligons' garage was a walking enthusiast and David would set off to watch the walk, only to join it in ordinary shoes,

22

without any training or preparation. He would still be walking many hours later when the people to whom he had been giving moral support had left him far behind. Once he had started something he would have to see it through, even if it was fairly pointless and even though he was pushing himself well beyond what he was physically capable of doing.

Life was never dull with David and I would never know what idea he would be coming up with next. That was why neither I nor his family really believed that he would stick at politics. How wrong we were. He might sit around in coffee bars, still have his madcap ideas and stagger back from walks that he should never have attempted but his mind remained preoccupied with politics and what we ought to do to further the cause.

For all of us the General Election campaign had been fun but for David it had been far more. It was a watershed in his life. Not only had he found a cause in which he passionately believed, he had also found that he had skills he had never been asked to display at school or work or college. He had suddenly discovered in himself a flair for organization and for leadership. Above all he had fallen passionately in love with politics and it was a passion that would never fade.

Throughout his political life, first in Truro but eventually countrywide through television, people would say of David, 'He is a lovely man, but then he is not your typical politician, is he?' Maybe he was not typical but he was devoted to politics in a way few viewers probably realized. His sense of humour and blunt commonsense concealed not a distaste for the political world and his fellow politicians but the very opposite – a deep and abiding love for politics and an absolute conviction that politics alone could achieve the changes he wanted to see. If he was to be seen as the acceptable face of politics, that was all to the good in David's eyes, so long as that encouraged others to get involved.

From the very first David was hugely influenced by someone who was to become our closest friend and ally for the rest of David's life, Malcolm Brown. By an extraordinary stroke of luck, Malcolm had arrived in Truro only just before the 1964 election. Shy and serious-minded, he was then only sixteen and was attending Truro School. He had been a Young Liberal in Maidenhead, where the post-Orpington revival had revolutionized political and social life for his age group, and he was now eager to get a Young Liberal group going in Truro, if only he could find like-minded teenagers. We were a little older but we soon struck up a friendship and together established the first such group in Truro – to the delight of the older members, who were much cheered by the prospect of a new generation of eager workers.

Over the next few years the Young Liberal movement both in Truro and the county became very strong. We combined political discussions, generally led by David and Malcolm, with energetic social activity. At that time folk singing evenings were very popular throughout Cornwall and we knew we were on to a winner when the chairman of the Truro branch kindly offered us his barn – the real thing with bales of hay to sit on. There was no shortage of folk singers, and booking acts was both easy and cheap. However, getting them to the venue was not so easy and on more than one occasion we found we had a large, patient audience and no acts. David would then have to drive the two or three miles to Truro and scour the pubs looking for our acts. He always came back with some. No one was certain if they were the ones we had advertised but no one minded.

David generally provided the transport in those days, as most of our friends were too young to drive. His vehicles were never very reliable. On one occasion he borrowed a landrover from his father. This was full of youngsters when David changed gear in the middle of a ford, the gearstick came away in his hand and we were marooned in the middle of the river. We all got wet feet on that occasion and the landrover had to be towed back to the garage. David never turned a hair at these antics – but why should he? They happened so often they were normal.

Not all our social events were successful. Once, for instance, we decided that we could do wonders for our funds by organizing dances with live groups. We booked the annexe to the City Hall right in the middle of Truro and set about getting a group. The group was fine but the audience was minimal. Undaunted, we decided to try again and to advertise more efficiently. It worked. On the night, the teenagers poured into the hall and my sister sat at the door happily collecting the half-crowns while the rest of us sat at the back worrying. This time it was the band that was invisible. Discreetly, all of us, including David, crept out of the back door, leaving my poor sister to give back the money to the disappointed audience.

We even organized a jumble sale. David had the good idea – original at the time – of putting leaflets through doors and calling back later for the jumble. It worked well. Unfortunately, on the day all the female members were busy at work. That meant all male staff at the jumble sale, for which it so happened that we had collected sufficient bras and corsets for a complete stall. The men drew lots and one of them sat red-faced all afternoon helping ladies with their undergarments.

We were also very active members of the Cornwall Young Liberals, which gave us a chance to meet other enthusiasts from St Ives, North Cornwall and Bodmin. We met regularly and again organized both political and social events. For David this wider involvement was especially useful as he was elected to represent the county on the National Executive of the Young Liberals. He found himself travelling all over the country to their meetings and encountering a totally different breed of politician from those he had met so far in the west. The Cornish Young Liberals held opinions that were distinctly radical in Cornwall but they were themselves essentially conventional, even staid, in their behaviour and the way in which they expressed those opinions. The same could not be said for most Young Liberals elsewhere in the country in the 1960s.

This was the time of the YL 'Red Guard'. Over the next few years, to the fury of their seniors, many of them would be campaigning for Britain's withdrawal from NATO, for support for the Palestinians and an extension of the EEC to include the Communist bloc. The party establishment accused them of being Marxist, though it was their style rather than their views that caused so much concern. David, himself an internationalist and pro-NATO, had little interest in most of the causes of the others on the YL National Executive. They in turn could make little of his rural radicalism, which was fired mostly by his concern for regionalism within the UK. Yet for him it was an education to meet other enthusiastic campaigners, whether or not he shared their particular enthusiasms.

Few of his contemporaries in the YLs were to become MPs, as David would, but they did show extraordinary political stamina. They did not give up. Tony Greaves was to mastermind the Association of Liberal Councillors. Michael Steed became president of the Party. Two of the most active, Peter Hain and Simon Hebditch, would pursue their ideals within the Labour Party, though Simon was later to return to the fold. He was working in the Whip's Office in Westminster when David arrived in the House and became one of his biggest supporters there.

In the sixties, however, many of the Red Guard must have found David and the Cornish YLs as strange as he found them. The highlight of the our Cornish YL year, for instance, was an annual dinner and dance held at a very respectable Newquay Hotel. At this event older Liberal members were invited to join us and the YLs' parents and relatives came along for a nice meal followed by a political speech and ending up with a dance. I cringe with embarrassment now at the memory of the competitions we ran then for 'Miss County Young Liberal' – a Bodmin and North Cornwall tradition, not from Truro, I hasten to add. The male YLs were neat in suits and ties, and the women smart in short party frocks.

One such event, shortly after John Pardoe was elected in 1966, coincided with a weekend conference held by the National League of YLs near Bodmin. Naturally they were all invited. Their dress alone made the rest of us look like Young Conservatives! Worse was to come. After the speeches we, conventionally, rose for the loyal toast, whereupon most of the London visitors remained seated. John Pardoe was furious, and with good reason. The press was there and he would not be allowed to forget it.

We were of course equally embarrassed, especially as we were somewhat overawed to be mixing with Members of Parliament, whom we had otherwise seen only on television. However, both John and Peter Bessell always gave us tremendous support and gave David special encouragement as he was then just beginning to discover the excitement and hazards of public speaking. He and Malcolm had even accepted the challenge of a public debate with the Young Conservatives and found themselves addressing a meeting packed with opposition. David and Malcolm did not win the debate but the Conservatives did a lot that evening to help David hone his debating skills. It would not be long before they would pay dearly for their victory.

While we were building up the Young Liberal group, and generally enjoying ourselves, the Truro association continued in its customary way to hold its meetings, raise its funds and prepare for the next election. Although the YLs in the West County were politically well to the left of most association members, we were generally seen as an asset in our constituencies. In Truro, we were even encouraged to take on responsibilities within the association. Had we done so with real enthusiasm in 1965, we might have seized the chance to transform it there and then. As it was, with one exception, we were happy to leave our elders to what we saw as their tedious meetings and concentrate our energies on our own group. The exception was David.

Within a year, and before he had the vote himself, he was elected vice-chairman of the association with responsibility for the western half of the constituency. This, as we were rapidly coming to appreciate, was a very considerable area. The name of the parliamentary division has always been misleading. It should really be called 'Mid-Cornwall'. 'Truro' suggests that Truro is in the middle of the constituency and the sole major centre of population. It is not.

The constituency stretches some twenty-five miles from east to west, and twenty from the English Channel in the south to the Atlantic in the north. The cathedral city of Truro is almost at its western end. Balancing it at the eastern end is the major industrial town of St Austell. David was to concentrate his efforts at this time on the area he knew best: Truro and all the little villages and not so little seaside towns at the western end. It was only later that he was to get to know the eastern half of the constituency as well.

He soon found himself proposing the re-adoption of William Hosking as parliamentary candidate, this time for the 1966 General Election. In his reply William went in for prophecy – and got it almost right. 'In due course,' he said, 'I am sure that David Penhaligon will himself be a parliamentary candidate, and not only a candidate, but a Liberal MP . . . though, mind you, not in this particular constituency.'

It was a generous tribute, despite the blunt warning to keep off William's patch, and it was followed up by a request for David to join the candidate on a loud-speaker tour. David was to make the 'warm-up speech' at a series of places. The first was at the village of Feock. This was an unusually important challenge. David prepared his speech carefully, especially as the village of Feock was well known to be a Tory stronghold. How could he cope with the hecklers, we wondered. No problem. Not a heckle was heard. In fact, nothing was heard. The prearranged stop was close by the church and not a person was in sight. David delivered his first campaign speech to an entirely silent graveyard!

Sadly, that turned out to be all too clear an indicator of how the Liberal campaign was going. Despite increased enthusiasm, the local organization was no improvement on the previous election and the national campaign was distinctly less effective. Truro was no exception to what was generally a poor Liberal performance throughout the country. The Liberal vote went down, the Labour vote went up. The only good news was that Bessell had held on to Bodmin and John Pardoe had taken North Cornwall. Truro now had two Liberal constituencies on its borders.

At least we now had time to take a holiday. It was a chance to celebrate David's completion of his HND, which he duly passed comfortably that summer. We set off with four friends in two cars, David's towing a caravan and carrying a very ancient round tent borrowed from his father. We went to the Lake District and Scotland, as far as John O'Groats – well, with David there was no point in going if you didn't see the lot.

The mountain scenery was tremendous. It was also useful. At one stage we had to find the highest point we could – not for the view, but because we had to hear the finals of the World Cup football. All the boys decided the game was brilliant. Well, we won, didn't we? Years later when we had one of our rare holidays abroad, much the same occurred. On that occasion we booked a holiday flat at the very top of a hotel in Normandy. I did not think when I booked the room that we would be able to receive Radio Three. David found he could. Every afternoon there he would stay, glued to the Test Match commentary!

On the Scottish holiday, David visited one of his father's

friends in Edinburgh, who owned a garage. There David spotted a Mini that was a good buy. He bought it, put me behind the wheel and we set off home. It went well till it died on me when I had the impertinence to try to overtake the caravan. After that I struggled home more modestly in convoy, with a stocking in place of the fanbelt.

It was soon after this that we got engaged. We had been going out together for nearly three years and we wanted to show our commitment. There was, however, no chance of an early wedding because David had only just started earning and there was no way we could afford anywhere to live – unless of course we considered moving from Cornwall.

The only chance Cornishmen have of earning a substantial salary is to move elsewhere. That was something that sadly was to remain a major problem throughout David's political career. It was true for him too in 1966. When we were in Scotland, David and his friends had visited the Marconi factory in Edinburgh and discovered just what attractive jobs and salaries were available there. He thought about a move, then decided against it. I would have been prepared to go. He was not.

He did not make very much of the decision at the time, nor would he a year later when his great friend at Holman's, Des Honey, urged him to join him at Cranfield Institute of Technology and get a degree. The reason not to move was the same on both occasions. David might love his engineering but he loved his Liberalism more. He thought he could achieve something in politics but only so long as he remained in Cornwall.

Still, David's enthusiasm for politics was only slightly greater than that for engineering, and Des could see, better than most, why David enjoyed them both so much. 'He seemed to have a special knack for getting to the bones of a problem, whether it was political or a matter of engineering research and development.'

David was working then as a development engineer specializing in rock-drilling equipment in Holman's research and development department. He entered a competition run by the Junior Chamber of Commerce to find the Junior Technician of the Year. He won through the local heats and went on to the regional heats in Bridgwater. (He came back from there full of talk about one very friendly member of the interviewing panel who turned out to be a Liberal candidate. He was the yachtsman, Donald Crowhurst, whose entry for the race around the world was to end in so bizarre and tragic a way.) On the day I celebrated my twenty-first birthday, David won a prize as runner-up in the national finals in Birmingham. The prize was a visit to various engineering works in Scandinavia.

David continued to divide his time between Holman's, the YLs, the association and, to a minor degree – or so I protested – myself. He now persuaded several of us to get more involved in the meetings of the executive. William had indicated that he would not stand again. The selection of the next candidate would be crucial, David said, and we might be able to influence that choice. It was by then clear to everyone that it was only a matter of time before David stood for parliament. Yet it was not for himself that he had decided to campaign. Michael Steed, whom he knew well as a fellow YL from Yorkshire, had put his name forward and David was convinced that Michael could transform Truro. When David was convinced of anything he had no difficulty in convincing others. Michael Steed was chosen.

It may now seem extraordinary that David, and indeed his friends, looked outside the constituency when he himself was so obviously suitable. It was not so obvious then. In fact, David was well aware that for him the time had not yet come, not in Truro anyway. He was still only twenty-two and, by then, it was not only William that had warned him off. The Devon and Cornwall region, which had to give its approval before anyone could be a parliamentary candidate, told David in 1967 that he was too inexperienced. Even the Truro chairman, Dr Clyne, had failed to back him.

This was his first major setback in politics. David was always so optimistic, so positive in all he did, that it was a shock for me to see how deeply hurt he was by this. His response, however, was positive. Despite their decision he decided to apply to the neighbouring constituency of Falmouth/Camborne, which was still looking for a candidate. They immediately shortlisted him. They would not make their decision until February 1968. That gave him ample time to persuade Liberal headquarters in London to overrule the regional decision and to sort out a little domestic matter: our wedding.

4

ACTIVIST

'I have never known anyone with such commitment as David had. Once he had decided to do something, that was it.' – John Penhaligon

When David passed his HND he was earning about £17 a week at Holman's. It was not enough to marry on, but we reckoned that we might just manage when he reached £20 a week, so long as there was some other way in which I could supplement his income fairly substantially. Coming from the background he did, it was not surprising he looked for some small business that we might run.

It was through my father that we found the answer. A friend of his was selling the sub post office at Chacewater, which she had run for a very long time. The premises alone were a huge commitment. They were on the market for £6,000 and we had to borrow every penny of it. Also, as David's father was standing guarantor and he did not trust women in business, David had both to be owner and formally the sub post master. Our own few savings went to pay for certain changes to the property on which the Post Office insisted.

We eventually took over the post office in October 1967 and I was to run it, though for much of the time not in my own name, for the next twelve years. The hours were long and tiring and to begin with we could not afford assistance. Our reward, however, was that it enabled us to pursue our increasingly expensive hobby of politics and stay in the county we loved.

Until we married I was living at home and I had to travel the five miles each morning in time to open up the post office for our postmen by 7 a.m. This had to be done six days a week and for the Christmas period we had to open up an hour earlier because of the amount of extra mail.

With the purchase of the post office there had been no time to arrange a wedding, so we decided not to mix a wedding with a busy Christmas period but to get married on the first Saturday of the new year – 6 January 1968. As I was too busy learning the ropes at the post office, I had to leave all arrangements for the wedding to my parents. My one contribution was on the bridesmaids' dresses, made by my mother-in-law and myself. The two older bridesmaids wore emerald green, my favourite colour at that time – I don't know why. The three smaller ones wore white. They all carried violets, which went nicely with the colours, which was just as well as flowers were not easy to get at that time of year.

I felt that it would all look more finished if David, his best man and his ushers wore morning dress, but without tails, which would have been considered pretentious. David went along with this idea but only reluctantly. However, as always, he had the last laugh. He hitched his trousers so high that they were at half-mast. I swear he did it just to send me up. I did not complain. Although it rained, it was a lovely day and, incredibly, David actually turned up at the church on time, even though – of course – his car broke down on the way.

My husband proved no more of a romantic than my fiancé. Our first stop after the reception was at Dr Clyne's house, for tea and a political gossip. Dr Clyne might have voted against his acceptance as a parliamentary candidate but David was never one to bear a grudge, and anyway he had left the car there, secure from the attentions of our friends, ready for our journey to London. I had thought London ideal for our honeymoon. David agreed. He could go to Liberal headquarters and make them change their minds over approving his candidacy.

Neither of us was familiar with London. I had been only once before and so I considered David the expert. He had been there with his father as a boy and more recently had attended meetings of the Young Liberals. What I was not to know was that places did not interest him, and as he was hopeless at walking around, he was hopeless at finding his way. Perhaps that was why we never even found our way to the Houses of Parliament.

We did, however, find Liberal headquarters, where David was due to discuss his appeal to be allowed to stand for Parliament. That went very well but in some ways a more important meeting was with Evelyn Hill, who was in charge of the publications department there. Over the next few years, Evelyn was to advise David on what he ought to read, and she would be there when he got to Parliament to introduce him to other interest groups and campaigners. For the first time, we were made to feel that we were not on our own. We had friends watching out for us, even up in London.

When we got back to Cornwall, however, everything was

new. It was a new home, a new job and a new marriage, all at once. There was not much we could do about our home since all our money had gone on getting it. We managed on borrowed and second-hand furniture and it would take years before we could complete the decoration of the rooms. Our living accommodation was very limited. Upstairs was not too bad: we had three bedrooms, a bathroom and a separate toilet. However, downstairs we were confined to a small kitchen cum everything else, as the only other room previously used for living accommodation had been needed by the post office for extra mail sorting. We decorated the bedroom and furnished it with the new bedroom suite my parents had given us for a wedding present.

The kitchen had a new cooker, a present from David's parents, a second-hand fridge and second-hand table and chairs. The cooker and fridge fitted neatly into an alcove, which we could then curtain off to make the rest of the room look less like a kitchen. The alcove was previously a cupboard, in the floor of which was a large hole with an earth base. We filled it in. We puzzled for some time over what the hole might have been used for. Perhaps it was for salting pigs in the war. It never occurred to us that the hole actually had a use until it rained heavily. We were flooded out. David had been getting hints from people in the village but he had not understood them. 'How's the spring?' they would say or 'Have you found that spring yet?' When he asked what they meant, he had received evasive replies. Clearly no one wanted to tell us that the house was built on a spring and the hole in the cupboard was a soakaway. That was our first experience of old houses. Plenty was to follow.

The radio had pride of place in the kitchen and it was permanently tuned into the Home Service. We had no time or money for television, although we did weaken later in the year and hire one in time for the Mexico Olympics. David always enjoyed following competitive athletic sporting events and the Olympics were a highlight. They made a break from politics. The Olympics of 1968 were not without their own politics, of course, with the Black Power protests of the US runners and Mexico itself disrupted by student and teacher demonstrations. They seemed to us to reflect the political unrest throughout the world of that decade: the cultural revolution of China, Soviet troops in Czechoslovakia, student demonstrations in France.

If I remember rightly, the television coverage of those games did not start until after 10 p.m., which enabled David to do a full day's work and attend to any Liberal business before settling down to watch the big events of the night. The highlight for us was Bob Beamon's record-breaking long jump and I particularly remember the medal-winning activities of our own David Hemery and Lilian Board. David would have remembered the statistical detail of those games and indeed all the games that followed. He was superb at remembering results, whether they were election or sporting events, a skill he shared with Malcolm Brown, whose recall was even better, and between them they could remember all sorts of what I considered totally useless facts.

The new job, running the post office, may have been officially in David's name but in practice it was entirely my responsibility. David was now a fully qualified chartered engineer, running his own research and development team at Holman's. We needed every penny of his salary. It was up to me to make a success of the post office. We dealt only with postal business and our income depended entirely on how many letters, postal orders and pensions went across our counter or out through our sorting office at the back of the shop. This 'sorting office' was in fact no more than a little room four yards square but every morning at break of dawn I and the six postmen who covered the Chacewater area would sort out the letters there.

Most of our postmen used bicycles and worked part-time but we did have one full-timer with a van, Gerald Spear, who delivered to a very wide area indeed, including delivering to three other smaller sub post offices. From time to time we received telegrams which needed to be delivered quickly. These were usually delivered by our postmen as they finished their duties. However, inevitably we got some at the end of the day when there was no postman there to deliver them. David would often come home late and exhausted only to be sent out with some urgent telegram to one of the remote hamlets surrounding Chacewater. Before long he knew every road in the area and – because he could never resist a chat – almost every person.

In the first few months we went through a crash-course in getting to know our customers and how to serve their needs. Chacewater had originally been a mining community but the tin mines had nearly all closed and there was a fair amount of unemployment in the village. Unemployment benefit was paid from our office, as were all social security payments. This was a real eye-opener and I have always felt very irritated by better-off people talking, as if with inside knowledge, of the hundreds of pounds paid to people on the dole or of the payments available for televisions. I saw just how little they got, and David and I always wondered how the hell they managed.

By happy chance, after we had been at Chacewater for only a few years, we were to see a minor miracle occur. One of the local tin mines, Wheal Jane, was reopened and modernized. Quite suddenly, the community boomed. Accommodation was required for the contractors. The local men were offered work. Suddenly we were paying less in unemployment benefit and the village enjoyed a mini-boom. Some of the postal business of the mine came our way, which was good news for us, and also we got to know many of the new people working on the construction of the mine. At the time Wheal Jane seemed like a fairy godmother to that part of Cornwall, and indeed a second mine, Mount Wellington, was opened later. Ten years afterwards David would find himself in a position where he could repay the debt our community owed to Wheal Jane.

The first few months of our marriage saw most of our energies absorbed by our house and our work. Each morning David would dash out of the house, invariably behind schedule, with his cup of tea still in his hand (the car was cluttered with cups), while I struggled with sorting out the house and post office. It was a hard, but interesting, start to married life, rigorously controlled by post office schedules and procedure.

We had a lot of support from my parents at this time. For the first two years we could not afford a washing machine and so we used my mother's. Well, actually she did the washing and miraculously it came back ironed as well! My father helped with the weekly balancing of accounts which had to take place at the end of trading on each Friday. Any silly mistake I had made during the week would ensure a late night whilst the error was detected. David was not much help on these occasions. He was far less interested in identifying my mistake than in coming up with some quicker method of tackling the problem, only to discover that it did not comply with Post Office procedure. Methods and procedures that I took for granted, David always queried and questioned. He needed to know why it was needed and why the method needed to be so bureaucratic.

One method turned out to be beyond us. We had to number the postal orders by hand and we always numbered them in the wrong place. The problem was that David and I worked the wrong way round to most people since we were both left-handed. It caused complications for anyone else helping in the Post Office and irritation for anyone in the house, as we automatically organized everything on the 'wrong' side. Coincidentally, Malcolm Brown is also left-handed, which often caused people to do a double-take when they saw all three of us writing or using a spoon in the 'wrong' hand.

Among my memories of this time is the shock I received at the realization of having to cook a meal *every* day. I had enjoyed cooking previously, the odd meal to impress David, a cake for tea, but someone else always cleared up, and suddenly I had to do it all. My grandmother, who died just six weeks after my marriage, had given me a beautiful set of Le Creuset cast-iron saucepans. Looked after properly they should still be in use. They are not. In an effort to have supper ready by the time the post office closed so that we could be off by 6.30 or 7 to campaign for the Liberals, I would cut corners. Sometimes it worked but generally I would put the vegetables on to cook in a quiet period, only to be suddenly inundated with customers and unable to keep an eye on the cooking. I would end up scraping the burnt carrots into the bin just as David returned from work.

With so much to learn and organize both at home and at work, David was not too despondent when Falmouth did not in the end invite him to be their parliamentary candidate. He had at least impressed them, as there were only three votes between himself and the local candidate. We thought he should now wait and try again after the next election. Meanwhile we could help Michael Steed win Truro. Certainly we could also do with a bit more time to ourselves. But it was not to be.

In 1968, Peter Bessell unexpectedly decided that he would not contest the next General Election, and Paul Tyler was invited to succeed him as Liberal candidate in Bodmin. Paul, whom we knew well, had been planning to stand in the South Devon constituency of Totnes but even in Totnes his friends felt he should seize this far more promising opportunity of getting into parliament. Certainly he was not likely to win Totnes. Paul therefore shifted house and ambitions to Bodmin and Totnes started to look for a new candidate.

It was not an easy task. The new parliament was already over two years old, most associations had chosen their candidates and the constituency of Totnes was a difficult one for Liberals to fight. It covered a vast area, stretching along the coast of South Devon from Totnes to Newton Abbot and way up into Dartmoor. It was a Conservative stronghold and was becoming more conservative by the year as retired people moved in and bought up its attractive houses.

By now David, though every inch a Cornishman, was very well known to Liberals in Devon as well as Cornwall. He had served on the regional executive. He had just been elected on to Party Council, the body that met some four times a year to oversee the running of the Party and to take policy decisions between the annual assemblies. He had been a popular guest speaker at associations from Land's End to Exeter. The talk was that Totnes would do well to attract him, and David was tempted by the talk.

We knew that it was quite impractical. Truro was 100 miles from Newton Abbot, along some of the twistiest roads in Britain. David could not take time off work. Anyway, he was unmistakably Cornish and the Anglo-Saxon Devonians are as suspicious of the Cornish Celts as the Cornish are of them. It was not just impractical; it was impossible. Yet that was part of its attraction. David throughout his life was fascinated by the challenge of the impossible and when it came to the point of decision I was just as incorrigible. I hate to be beaten. Anyway, both of us wanted to show how wrong the Liberal establishment had been to suggest that David was not yet ready to be a candidate. So David wrote to Totnes.

That was for both of us the start of a hideously exhausting yet exhilarating eighteen months. Not only did Totnes Liberals accept David, they welcomed him with open arms. They laid on an elaborate adoption meeting in November 1968 to introduce him to the members and the press. This was held at their own club premises in Newton Abbot, which at that time was both their headquarters and a very valuable source of income. Peter Bessell came to speak and, as always with Bessell, it was done with considerable panache.

Despite his chapel background, Peter Bessell favoured a style more appropriate to a nineteenth-century Whig. A parking space had to be held for him outside the club, regardless of no-parking regulations, then up he swept in a white Bentley, and strode into the hall. The contrast with

David – young, radical, down to earth – could not be more marked, yet Peter genuinely appreciated the strength of the West Country YLs and had frequently forecast that David and his generation would in time sweep Liberals into power all over Devon and Cornwall.

Several friends from Truro also came across to that meeting to wish us well. They helped our campaign financially, but we knew that there was little else that they would be able to do for David after that. They had their responsibility to Truro and to Michael Steed. What David was going to miss most was Malcolm's companionship and advice, but Malcolm was not even going to be in Truro for much of the time. He had won a place at LSE, rather to Truro School's dismay. They saw him as a defector from their Oxbridge tradition. David would have to make his mark in Totnes without his help, and mostly without mine too. He did so – in style.

From that first meeting David's energy and enthusiasm were infectious. His months as candidate are still remembered by the Liberal activists as one of most enjoyable campaigning periods of their experience. Though time was far too short for David to make himself known right the way across that huge constituency, they found they had a candidate whose friendliness made an immediate impact on all who met him. 'David's great strength,' Paul Wilkinson, the Totnes secretary, discovered 'was that he could talk high-power politics, or discuss everyday affairs with equal ease, and he had a seemingly endless fund of appropriate stories or parables to illustrate his point of view.' This was never more important than when there were industrial problems in Newton Abbot. On the strength of his experience at Holman's, David spoke with real authority in a way few Liberal candidates could, and when there was a march against low wages David was welcomed by the workers as a natural ally.

David could generally get over to the constituency only at weekends. Sundays were sacrosanct in Totnes, so he would set out every Saturday in his aged second-hand car, be briefed over lunch by Paul Wilkinson, then get to work. If there were no major issue to be pursued, he would lead a canvassing team in search of new members. Potential converts might be thin on the ground but David never grew discouraged.

The General Election was called for June 1970, in the middle of a heatwave. By then David had been there for only eighteen months. Totnes Liberals knew, and David knew, that they were onto a hiding to nothing. Yet, amazingly, morale was high. 'With David you would always have a good laugh,' Paul Wilkinson recalls. 'It was the most *enjoyable* campaign we ever fought.'

It is one of the wonders of politics that even when there is no real hope of victory, those who care deeply for their cause – whatever the cause – will still come out undaunted and battle for that cause, so long as they believe in their candidate. Clearly Totnes Liberals believed in David. They saw him as someone who had won the respect of those who had met him and someone well able to put across the Liberal message with vigour and a sense of humour. In those three sweltering weeks that sense of humour would be a blessing.

When they discussed election costs, he would solemnly tell them how lucky they were that his mother had not won her way over his name. He had been born on D Day and the family story, which she hotly denied, was that she had been all for calling him Montgomery rather than David. 'It's bad enough trying to fit Penhaligon on a window sticker,' David would say, 'but think what Montgomery Penhaligon would cost!'

For the campaign itself, to the amazement of the electorate, the Liberal candidate based himself not in some smart hotel but on a Totnes caravan site in one of his father's caravans. From there he would sally forth in an open-topped car to proclaim the Liberal message by loud-hailer from village to village.

Happy though they were with this energetic young radical, Totnes Liberals could offer few workers on the ground. It was vital that I get across to Totnes and give all the support I could. I could not have done this without my parents' help. They now stepped in and ran the post office while I helped David – the first of many times over the next sixteen years when they unselfishly came to our support when we most needed it. David also cajoled Des Honey, his closest friend at Holman's, into acting as driver for much of the campaign. I acted as relief driver when he was not there.

The car was a green Hillman Avenger which David had built himself from two scrapped cars. It was not a huge success and frankly David was the only one who really knew how to drive it. It had an overdrive stuck on the steering wheel and I would try to indicate with this stick and go into fifth gear with the indicator. So confused did I become that I was quite incapable of managing the slow steady speed required for David's loud-hailing and I would sweep through villages at such a pace that the voters were left with scarcely a single complete sentence from their Liberal candidate. As an alternative David had to interrupt his message to bend down and assist with the driving. It did not do much for our relationship, and I still remember the pretty village of Aveton Gifford not so much for its charms as for David's embarrassment when I broke down there in floods of tears and refused to drive another yard.

After that I was spared from the job of driving the candidate but even greater embarrassment was in store – this time for me. We still had the Mini we had purchased in Scotland but it was beginning to look a little tatty and David's brother volunteered to respray it. To my horror it came back two-toned, and hideously two-toned too – in purple and yellow. I suppose I should have guessed the enthusiastic John was up to something when he checked on the campaign colours of the Liberals in Totnes. (Local Liberals did not campaign then in the distinctive orange and black but in a variety of colours. Truro once used blue and yellow.) To our intense embarrassment I and Des's wife had to drive this vividly painted little car with a three-foot-high campaign poster attached to the roof all the way from Truro to Newton Abbot on a busy June Saturday. We wore dark glasses.

It was all new to us then – the press briefings morning after morning, the motorcades, the canvassing (not much of it, and with all too few experienced campaigners), the meetings where I had to sit trying to look attentive, the visits to schools and hospitals, the post-mortem last thing at night and after that the piles of letters to be answered before we went to bed. The heat was dreadful. Food would go off in hours in that oven of a caravan. We would consume pints and pints of water. It was too hot even for David to survive on cups of tea. Yet the excitement was infectious and it gave David a taste for electioneering that he would never lose.

The political language of those 1970 leaflets now seems extraordinarily dated, with references to the 'crawling peg' on exchange rates and a minimum farmworker's wage of £13. 2s. 6d., yet the principles behind the Liberal proposals then were the same as they are today. Unemployment and low wages were David's major concern in 1970 and sadly they are still major problems in the west country. He proclaimed, as he was always to proclaim, the virtues of profit-sharing, works councils and workers on the board. He stressed the value of the EEC but maintained that we could not join without a referendum. His concern for local power over local matters was to be another continuing theme. In particular he argued that tourism should be controlled, not from Whitehall, but by a regional board.

What was of course new for David were the problems of Devon's farmers. At one public meeting David was asked by one of them if he did not think the price local farmers were getting for barley was a disgrace. David had no idea what the price of barley was. Rather than try to talk himself out of it, he admitted his ignorance. To his amazement, the farmer replied, 'I'll vote for you, boy. I asked the Tory and Labour the same question and they both agreed it was a disgrace. Barley isn't farmed for fifty miles around here.'

Sadly, too few followed that farmer's lead when it came to voting but at least election day gave David one of his favourite stories. 'On polling day the candidates were expected to drive from polling station to polling station and thank the staff for their work. I never understood why, as they got paid for their work and I didn't, but I did my best to visit as many as I could. At Totnes I entered behind a well-dressed lady in blue. Being a gentleman, I let her collect her ballot slip before introducing myself to the presiding officer. She looked down at the candidates' names and pointed to mine. "I wouldn't vote for him. Would you?" she asked him. Looking at the result later, I don't think he did but he was too polite to say so and in any case he had seen me. "Why not?" he said. "Well," said the lady, "he sounds Pakistani to me."' David always claimed that it was then that he knew he had to get back over the Tamar to a county that could recognize a Cornish name.

The 1970 election results were a grave disappointment for the Liberals nationally. They had only recently chosen as their new leader one of our West Country heroes, Jeremy Thorpe, but the new look had done them no good. As the Tories swept back to power, only six of our MPs survived and Bodmin was one of the seven that we lost. Indeed, Jeremy very nearly lost his own seat and the national vote fell from 8.5 to 7.5 per cent.

David was later to joke that his own result proved how dangerous it was to send any Cornishman out to fight on the other side of the Tamar and how he nearly lost his deposit. In fact, he did nothing of the sort. The Totnes vote moved with the swing. It fell from 11,000 to 9,500 – not a good result but depressingly similar to those elsewhere.

David's successor in Totnes, Tony Rogers, was to do very well four years on, in the 1974 elections. Many years later when the Totnes seat was split into two, David was able to say to Tony, 'We two now both hold records that can never be beaten – you got our highest ever vote in Totnes, and I got the lowest.' It was indeed the lowest but at least it had been fun.

5

CANDIDATE

'There was a very serious side to David that the public never saw. He used to get angry about things: housing conditions especially, low pay, and the fact that we had a system in this country that made that sort of thing possible.' – Malcolm Brown

We returned to Truro to find that Michael Steed had done no better than we had. Truro, like Totnes, had lost votes, not gained them. For the next few weeks we kept well out of Truro politics while we licked our own wounds. We were depressed not so much by our own result or Truro's but by the disappointing national result. This was our first experience of fighting an election when the national swing was from Labour to Tory, always a difficult situation for Liberals, especially in the West Country. Added to this was the sorrow everyone felt at the appalling personal blow that befell Jeremy Thorpe at the end of June when his wife, Caroline, was killed in a car crash. I remember we were both totally stunned when we heard the news on the television and could not believe life could be so cruel.

So far as I can recall, those few weeks on our return from Truro were the only complete respite that we ever had from politics, and they were few indeed. The Liberal Assembly was due to meet at Eastbourne in September. David and Malcolm never, and I hardly ever, missed an Assembly. It was not that we found Assembly debates inspiring. They were not. They were generally monopolized by establishment figures who appeared to us to have no real interest in spreading Liberalism, only in debating Liberal philosophy. We went because it was the one time each year when we could meet friends of our own age from all over the country. Several of these had been colleagues of David on the YL executive but there were others too from a variety of backgrounds, such as Andy Ellis from the Union of Liberal Students, whom we would get to know even better over the years to come. We would, it seemed, sit up all night in those days, exchanging ideas on how activists like us ought to change the world – or at least as a first step change the Liberal Party. It so happened that that is exactly what we did that September in Eastbourne.

Up to this point, David's Liberalism and mine had been deeply felt and energetically proclaimed but we accepted the general assumption that we would get very little chance to put our ideals into practice. As David put it, 'If you want to get into power, you don't join the Liberal Party.' He said it as a joke but when we were young there was all too much truth in it. Torringtons and Orpingtons might come and go – and they had gone indeed – but they did not really change things. For years David had therefore contented himself with the thought that we ought simply to spread the Liberal gospel as best we could because 'the stronger the strand of Liberalism the better it is for Britain'. Yet now things were changing. Liberals might not be taking parliamentary seats – indeed they were losing them – but they were certainly taking council seats.

They were also pioneering a new approach to local politics.

Some five years before that Assembly a new political idea had begun to take root, apparently quite spontaneously, in a number of Liberal associations. It was that the role of politicians was not simply to set out political philosophy and proffer solutions but it was also to encourage constituents to campaign themselves for what they wanted, to advise them on how to go about it and to act as their leaders. This idea was to be given the name of community politics.

Community politics was at least partly inspired by the direct action common in the sixties throughout the Western world, from the student protests to the marches of the CND and black activists. What made community politics distinctive, however, was that it did not appeal only to the underprivileged. It appealed just as much to those in the middle-class suburbs who had seen their rights eroded by the centralization of power by local and national government, and who welcomed the chance to re-establish something of the sense of community that had been destroyed by urban sprawl.

Although it had obvious attractions for Liberals, this concept had at this stage no official standing in the Party. Certainly it was being practised widely, from leafy Richmond to the slums of Liverpool, sometimes being seen as an end in itself and at others simply as a strategy to increase the power and influence of Liberals. At Eastbourne it was bluntly proposed that it be accepted as part of Liberal strategy.

The proposer was the new chairman of the Young Liberals, Tony Greaves. To many of the Liberal establishment in 1970, Tony and his obsession with this community politics was a welcome relief from his predecessors and their obsession with the Palestinians. They saw no reason to make an issue of it and the proposal was accepted. At the time it looked as if the Liberals had taken this step in a fit of absence of mind – or perhaps because they were still shell-shocked over the General Election results. 'The Party leadership do not understand what community politics is all about,' said Peter Hain, 'and if they did they would not like it.' That may have been so in 1970 but they were to learn to like it over the next decade, if only because it was to transform their fortunes.

David and I supported the proposal as a matter of course but without any sense of its historic importance. The philosophy of community politics was old hat to us. What interested us more was the practice. At Eastbourne we were concentrating our attention on discussing the practicalities with those who had achieved major council successes in this way in Liverpool, Leeds and, most especially, Birmingham.

In Ladywood, a very depressed corner of Birmingham, Wallace Lawler had gone one better than the others. Using just the same techniques, he had not only built up a formidable Liberal group of councillors in the heart of what was believed to be a rock-solid Labour constituency; he had gone on to win the parliamentary seat itself in a by-election. Sadly, he had lost his seat in the General Election but he had shown that proponents of community politics could win not just council seats but parliamentary seats as well.

For David, Lawler was an inspiration. Lawler was convinced that it was only through community politics that his fellow citizens, most of them appallingly ill-housed, could regain their pride and self-respect. David felt as strongly about this as Lawler did. Bad housing was one of the very few subjects to which he could find no funny side. He also found that he could identify with Lawler far more easily than with the other MPs he had met. I well remember the impact Lawler made on all of us when he came to Truro and spoke at a meeting held at my parents' house. David noticed that Lawler sounded like a man of the people, using the same accent as his constituents. If a man could get to Parliament speaking Brum, why could not someone who spoke with a Cornish accent?

Malcolm, David and I returned to Truro full of what we might achieve there if we followed the Lawler route. Truro, we knew, was very different from Ladywood, yet they still had much in common. There was the same problem of unemployment, the same feeling that London neither knew nor cared about local problems, the same history of local councillors who, with a few exceptions, never bothered to tell the voters what they were doing or what their rights might be. Truro, however, presented an extra problem. Councillors there did not stand under party labels. What would happen if long-established 'independent' councillors found themselves challenged by Liberal candidates? What indeed would our fellow Liberals think of the idea?

Not only would we have to convince them, we would also have to find a team of enthusiastic canvassers and able candidates prepared to serve on the council. To our amazement, Malcolm assured us that that would be no great problem. He had returned from LSE in 1969 to a job on the county council, working at Liskeard, and had been able to spend a few days helping Michael Steed in Truro at the election. The campaign there may have lacked impact but he was amazed at the calibre of the canvassers. Truro, he assured us, had both workers and potential candidates simply waiting for the tide to turn, or for someone prepared to turn the tide himself.

The credit for this was due to Michael Steed. Michael may have lost the election but he had attracted a number of highly intelligent, skilful new activists. On election day itself, however, so sparse had been the canvassing and so weak the organization that well before the polls closed a group of these new recruits had found themselves with nothing they could do. They had already ensured that every one of the pitifully small number of known supporters had gone to the polls. Frustrated by the failure of the campaign to make any real impression, they had sat down there and then with Malcolm Brown and committed themselves to reorganize the association. All they needed was a leader. If David wanted to lead them, they would be his team.

Although in the early 1970s community politics became the popular Liberal buzzword, something else was afoot, something that in the long run would be just as significant. This was a countrywide development of a distinctively Liberal approach to the conduct of local government. The Liberals were not simply committed to mobilizing the community to fight for what it wanted, they also realized that such a revolutionary change must be accompanied by a change in the conduct of the local councils themselves. Otherwise there would be no way in which the local authorities could react constructively to the demands of the community. This, of course, could only be achieved by winning power, something that would take time even for those who had made the first breakthroughs, as in Liverpool, but at least they knew what they wanted to do.

They wanted to pioneer a new style of open government. This included measures such as the opening up of committee meetings to the general public, a register of interests for all councillors, reporting back by councillors to their electorate and a consultation of the electorate between elections on matters such as the level of the rates. Ideally this Liberalization of the local council would be matched by the election of a Liberal MP as well but it was recognized that in most constituencies that might be far harder to achieve.

Local government in the Truro constituency was fairly typical of other areas of Cornwall and indeed of the country as a whole in the early 1970s. We had urban and rural councils based on Truro and St Austell. We also elected councillors to the Cornwall County Council. Almost all the councillors stood as 'Independents'. They did not advertise their political allegiance. However, in practice they were conservative by inclination and mostly Conservative members as well. As most meetings were held during the day, few could afford the time or expense of the job and inevitably the majority came from those who owned their own business. They no doubt carried out their duties conscientiously but it was hardly a democratic process, let alone a Liberal one.

David believed that local government in Cornwall was in desperate need of liberalizing but he did not believe that he was the man to do it himself. He felt that he could do more for the cause by helping others to get on to the local authorities. As for his own future, David could perhaps stand for parliament again but there was no need to make any decision now. There was certainly no opportunity in Truro at the moment. Michael Steed had the prior claim and Michael was a close personal friend. David would not consider challenging him. Besides, Dr Clyne was still chairman and had given no indication that he thought David any more suitable now than he was two years ago.

For the moment, if David really thought Liberals could do something for Truro, he must concentrate on getting others elected. We should aim to follow Ladywood, he said.

He decided to begin with our own branch of the association, the Truro branch. It was not only the strongest branch in the constituency then but it was the one that had benefited most from the influx of new members over the election. If David was to get anything going quickly he must begin in the city itself. That autumn the Truro branch met and agreed a programme of work that amazed even those who had moved in from constituencies that were used to campaigning all year round. For many of them it was the first time they had met David and they were carried away by his enthusiasm.

People familiar with the laid-back image adopted by David in later years would find it hard to recognize the style he projected at this time. It was not that he had to work harder then – in fact he was to work probably twice as hard once he was an MP – but in those early days he could only achieve the kind of action needed if he showed everyone personally what was required.

Under his leadership, the Truro branch took off in style. Not only were there weekly campaigns to increase membership but they duly took the historic decision to put up a candidate, for the first time under the Liberal banner, at the very next round of elections for Truro City Council in the spring of 1971. The candidate was John Snell, who worked with David at Holman's, and David agreed to be his agent. Day after day I had to get a meal for them both for six o'clock. Otherwise, if John went home first, David would not be able to get him out on the doorstep in double quick time and set the gruelling pace required. David was a hard taskmaster but it worked. John was elected, at the expense of a former mayor of Truro, and became an outstanding councillor.

This was the first victory for a Liberal, standing as a Liberal, in the constituency within living memory. The city fathers were shocked by our success, especially as the new councillor was only twenty-three years old and his father had been a valued member of the local Conservative Club. They were also shocked by our leaflets. They displayed a crudely drawn but effective sketch of Truro's municipal offices with a lighted stick of dynamite under them.

Our leaflets were even criticized by some of our own members at the next meeting of our association's executive – most especially by a few of the older members who anyway deplored the decision to use Party labels in a local election. Most local council literature in those days merely gave a biography of the candidate: age, marital and family status, war service, membership of organizations and employment history. It never told the electors what the candidate stood for, what they would fight for or what their principles were. Our leaflets had the same effect on some of our members as a quick jump in the Atlantic – they took their breath away.

It was not only our leaflets that shook the establishment. Our candidates over the next few years certainly did not fit the usual image of a Cornish councillor. Doris Ansari, who was appealingly pretty, was married to a Pakistani doctor and would often campaign in colourful saris. She certainly quickly made her mark in local government and I am glad to say still does. Then we had a young twenty-one-year-old, Alastair Holman, who, with long curly locks reaching his shoulders, wore kaftans to council meetings where traditionally the uniform was three-piece suits. It was about the same time as the musical *Jesus Christ – Superstar* was popular and Alastair did look as if he would be more at home as part of that cast! I hope we would be prepared to be just as unorthodox today.

Our style may have been strong stuff for Truro but David was always very clear that you could not have it both ways. We wanted a totally different kind of council, one devoted to the underdog, stripped of nineteenth-century ritual, prepared to open up its committees to the public that paid for them. It was a radical message and it deserved a radical campaign, and that was what David gave it. It might shock some of our fellow Liberals but it clearly appealed to the voters. We were very selective over the seats we chose to contest in those early days – leaving alone those represented by effective councillors and concentrating on Truro until 1973 – and we were to win every local election seat we fought from then till 1975.

For David, however, there was a more immediate battle to be fought and it was the one that he had not thought would have come so soon. In February 1971 Michael Steed announced that he would not stand again in Truro and the executive decided to advertise for applicants to be their next parliamentary candidate. If David was ever going to put his name forward, it was probably now or never. David decided it was now.

It would have been easy in 1986 for anyone to list the reasons why David was the ideal candidate for Truro – many people did so after David's death – but in 1971 it would have been far easier to list reasons why he was quite unsuitable. What is extraordinary is that the two lists would have been identical. In 1971 the typical candidate was expected to exude experience, polish and the kind of gravitas that would impress on other MPs and civil servants that Cornwall had spokesmen as smooth as anyone from the home counties. In contrast, David offered youth, a Cornish accent and a reputation for funny jokes. In 1971 they hardly seemed assets for a prospective parliamentary candidate.

This was largely why, despite the obvious attraction of his down-to-earth commonsense, even his closest friends underestimated David's chances at the time – just as his opponents would do to their cost for many years to come. David, I think, even underestimated himself. He was happy to be the Liberal standard bearer in Totnes or Falmouth, yet he was surprisingly diffident about his ability to represent his own community. Much as he wanted to stand for parliament, it was only now, when fate virtually forced his hand, that he decided to have a go.

The problem was – and it was a problem – he had a clear run. Despite determined efforts to attract other candidates, no one else applied. David therefore had no chance to pit his skills against a challenger. The only question was whether the association executive should wait and re-advertise or decide for or against David without delay.

Dr Clyne advised delay. He was supported by one of the vice-presidents, Stan Broadribb. Was this a sign that all the old guard was going to stand shoulder to shoulder against the new? Not so. It was now that David reaped the benefit of all his hard work and enthusiasm. If doubts were expressed over David's lack of experience, they were swamped by stories of what he had achieved. Without him there would have been no activity at all since the last election. Not only had he led the Truro branch to success with John Snell but he was responsible for running the action group that was reviving derelict branches throughout the association. And it was not simply the new recruits who wanted him to stand. There were those who remembered his first arrival on the scene in 1964 and all the work that he had done for them. Clyne and Broadribb were on their own, and decided to resign office. The others wanted David, and wanted him now. He was asked to address a selection meeting open to all members on 4 December.

He came to that meeting with yet another victory to report. Doris Ansari had just won our second seat on Truro Council. For the first time in their lives the Truro Liberals could see a Liberal bandwagon on the move and, with an optimism they had not enjoyed for years, they endorsed David as their prospective parliamentary candidate, by a majority of thirty-three to four.

It was not only the bandwagon that was on its way. So was our first child. I vividly remember sitting in the committee rooms at Doris Ansari's election, feeling dreadfully sick without any idea of why. Now we did know. 1972 was going to be a doubly exciting year.

6

CAMPAIGNER

'The fact that David had this great mechanical ability and feel for machinery meant that he was well ahead of the rest of us on the production of his leaflets.' – Andy Ellis

The size of the task we had taken on can be gauged by what happened at that selection meeting. First, it was clear that hardly anyone thought Truro Liberals had any chance at all of ever winning the parliamentary seat. It was extraordinary, even embarrassing for the association, that no one else applied for interview. Then the attendance at the meeting itself served only to confirm the impression that this was a lost cause. The total electorate of the Truro constituency in 1971 was 66,000. The total Liberal membership was less than 200 and of these only thirty-seven came out that evening to select their candidate, most of them elderly and no longer able to do much political campaigning. Yet political campaigning was what we were going to need if we were to transform the political face of Truro – and that is what David was determined to achieve.

Luckily for Truro, David had more than determination to spur him on. He had ideals. They were ideals in which he believed passionately. One above all he was convinced was shared by all his fellow Cornishmen. It was that they were fiercely proud to be Cornish and, while they accepted that Cornwall was part of Britain (not necessarily England, mind you), they felt they had the right to decide on those matters that concerned just themselves. They knew the problems and their solutions far better than civil servants did in London. This was the classic Liberal policy of regionalism, geared to Cornwall, articulated by a Cornishman who sounded like a Cornishman. Churchill had once said that Britain had the lion's heart, and that he had the luck to be called upon to give the roar. In the same way David was to earn the nickname of the Voice of Cornwall because he expressed for the Cornish what they all believed.

Everyone in Britain knows that the Cornish see themselves as a race apart but only those who have lived in Cornwall can feel how deep that conviction goes, and David had lived in Cornwall all his life. His father had never allowed him to forget it either. Typically, he was brought up never to put himself down as English in a hotel register, only as British or Cornish. I used to tease him by pointing out that he had only three Cornish grandparents to my four but I was prepared to admit that his name could not be more Cornish – Penhaligon meaning 'Head of the Willow Valley'.

Once it was suggested to David that he came from people that were born outcasts. 'You misunderstand the situation,' he replied. 'We Cornish live in the centre of the civilized world. There are just enough people around to be pleasant. It's when you get to the great urban areas that you get fed up with people. The Cornish have got the balance just right. There are enough people there to make life enjoyable but there is also enough space that you can occasionally wander off and be by yourself.' He laughed but he meant it.

David knew what he wanted to say. He knew what he wanted to achieve for his community. He even had ideas of how he might achieve it. His problem was to get that message to the voters. If he could attract only thirty-seven Liberal members to a meeting, he was not going to attract 66,000 to hear him speak. He must get his message across in some other way.

David already knew what way that must be. He had recognized what Liberals had recognized elsewhere. However original and important your ideas, it is pointless to rely on the local press to give those ideas the publicity they need. The local press, with all the good will in the world, is incapable of it – and in Truro then, as far as the Liberals were concerned, the local papers were even short of good will.

If you are a member of a minority party, and want to make any impact, you have to have to be a good communicator and have your own means of communication. David was an exceptional communicator. His written English might not be all that good but he had a genius for hitting on the right phrase to illustrate his message. He had learned that in the hard school of public speaking. He now had to learn how to translate that on to paper, print it and get it into people's homes. That was what they did in Ladywood. That was what he would do in Truro.

David was to be first of the Liberal campaigners in the 1970s to persuade his association to buy their own offset litho printing press, a supposedly refurbished second-hand machine which he would nurse devotedly and on which he would produce leaflets of remarkably professional appearance. However, the first few leaflets came from an ancient duplicator. Our home was small enough, especially as we were now preparing a room for the baby, due to arrive at the latest estimate in July, but space still had to be found for the duplicator. For hour after unforgettable hour he and I turned its cumbersome handle to produce the first of the leaflets that were to transform politics in our part of Cornwall. The leaflet was called simply *News from the Liberals*.

That first leaflet looks distinctly amateurish to me now but its message has lost none of its power. David learnt fast. He set out very simply the brutal facts about low pay and unemployment in Cornwall in a way that no one had thought to do before – and then followed that with notes on what benefits were available and how they should be claimed. On the front was a picture of himself and a message from the newly elected Doris Ansari. On the back was a report from the councillors on what they were trying to do for their constituents: they were already pressing for opening the council committees to the public and for the rating of empty properties.

We had the leaflets. Now all we needed was a team to put them through the letter-boxes. At election time it is amazing how many people come forward to help with delivery: not always enough of them but always more than you feared would be available. Between elections, however, workers tend to drift away and the party faithful have only time for the occasional fête or jumble sale. It was now that David really benefited from the efforts he had made to keep a team together since the last election. The Truro branch were ready to deliver the leaflet to the whole of the city. That was only about a fifth of the constituency but it was a start and the city was the most influential area.

The effect on the electorate was remarkable. No one had ever done anything like this before. It was the first time any politician had told them what benefits they could claim and explained how underpaid they were. It was the first time councillors had reported back to their constituents in this way and publicized their addresses. It was the first time they had seen political workers delivering leaflets between elections.

For the local Liberals it was an historic event as well, though they were not to realize it till later. It was for them the first of what would be an ever-increasing round of such deliveries over the years to come – deliveries that would in turn give rise to a saying that would become their battle honour. 'You must either be the postman or the Liberals. We don't see anyone else round here.'

I have been looking back at those early leaflets that David, Malcolm and I put together. In a way they were David's personal manifesto. Each centre-spread spelt out what he saw as the most important issues of the day, what the Liberal answer was, what he would fight for if he ever got to parliament. He began with benefits; next there was industrial democracy and also the environment (an unusual concern in the 1970s); inflation and rates were in nos 3 and 4. No. 5 summed up the philosophy entire: the concern for the individual and right of every region to take its own decisions.

This is what David believed and it was by leaflets that he intended to spread the word. It was a principle he was to thump home to colleagues at Assembly after Assembly, for year after year. It was to be his battle cry. 'If you have something to say, stick it on a piece of paper and stuff it through the letter-box. They might not read it in the newspaper and they won't hear you say it, so stick it on a piece of paper and stuff it through the letter-box.'

David certainly had something to say. He also had friends whom he inspired. The leaflets went through those letter-boxes.

In the first few months of David's candidature I was busy preparing for motherhood. We had by this time been married for four years – no one could accuse us of ever rushing into anything. Indeed, it would be another five years before number two arrived. This is probably where we differed considerably. I was always in a hurry to do things and I was disappointed we had not started a family earlier but with David there was always plenty of time for these things. Children, he would say, changed life too much, cost too much and were much overrated.

My pregnancy did not particularly interest David. He came to the ante-natal classes but was clearly embarrassed by them and generally carried on his political life as single-mindedly as ever. His favourite record at that time was Scott Joplin's 'The Entertainer', which he played endlessly. For years afterwards I could not hear that record without feeling sick!

The baby duly arrived a week late (something he has lived up to ever since) on Friday, 21 July. I had taken it for granted that David was not anxious to be present at the birth and much to my embarrassment I remember all too vividly David walking into the labour ward during the last stages and me screaming at him to go away. He did so, quite relieved I think, and went to his mother's and played ball against the wall of the bungalow until he heard that Matthew David had arrived. Matthew was probably only ten minutes old when he was first introduced to his father. From that moment on, David's reticence was gone. He immediately became the proud father and remained so always.

After meeting his son, David left to allow us to have some rest. He came back at visiting time with some beautiful flowers and an embarrassed look on his face – not from carrying the flowers but because he had to leave in a hurry – to open a Liberal fête at Perranporth. I gave my son a little lecture that night on the sort of life he could expect in the future.

That evening at Perranporth David celebrated his son's birth with a speech that linked it with his joy over parliament's long-delayed decision to join the EEC. The Liberals had first proposed this in parliament in 1955, when the entry fee would have been zero and the regulations to which so many people now objected would have been drawn up with Britain as a partner. Much as he deplored this long delay, David's vision was undimmed. What he wanted for his young son was 'a Europe where we have no wars, where barriers of language and tradition are broken down, and the people of the Community work together to build a Europe that is fair and democratic, and will go out and offer that fairness to the world'.

Once we were back at home, David proved a far more interested father than I had expected. He was quite happy to help out in the usual chores, when he was there, but I don't think he ever achieved the art of pinning on nappies that actually stayed on. By now we did have a full-time assistant at the post office but unfortunately this assistance proved none too reliable. Frequently I would be left to look after the post office and baby alone. On these occasions it required a quick phone call to Mum, who then caught the next bus to Chacewater. There were times too when I would be feeding baby on the stairs out of sight of the customers. Poor Matthew was for ever being interrupted as customers came and went. My nightmare, which fortunately never happened, was that I might not adjust my dress properly on these occasions. It was not until Connie Reed came to work for us that life became simpler. Connie was an 'incomer', recently moved from London to make a home for her son, whose firm had relocated to Cornwall. She was a treasure of a find, an invaluable worker, a friend and a beloved spoiler of the children.

Meanwhile, however, we had our political problems to solve. *News from the Liberals* happily was not one of them. It was going beautifully. Indeed for the next fifteen years it was to be David's hotline into every home in the constituency, without which he could never have got his beliefs over to his fellow Cornishmen. However, leaflets on their own would never have won the seat. David had to offer more. It was not enough simply to have the right ideas. He had to show that he was the right man to fight for them at Westminster. This meant that he had somehow to impress his personality on the electorate – and the people he had most especially to impress were those he had hardly met before, the industrial workers of the eastern end of the constituency.

That this was the key area was in a way identified well before David became the candidate, by Michael Steed. The team of workers was not all that Michael left David as his legacy. He also left him a psephological message. Psephology is not a word used every day in Cornwall, or elsewhere I suspect, but it is one that we all got used to when Michael was our candidate. It was Michael's profession: he studied, and wrote books on, the voting patterns of elections.

(Psephology was also to become David's hobby, but that was later.) During the 1960s, Michael had argued that the best opportunities for a Liberal breakthrough occurred not just in those seats where we had come second (the favoured view) but also in those constituencies where the Tories had about forty per cent of the vote and won without trying, the Labour vote was large but 'soft' and the Liberals regularly came a good third. What had led him to Truro was that it had exactly this profile.

The Tories had held Truro with few alarms since the constituency was formed in 1950 and over the last decade we had seen its Tory MPs represent the seat to the best of their ability. Yet they were indistinguishable from their colleagues in any other part of England. No more seemed to be demanded of them. Meanwhile, the Labour Party had benefited from the existence of several important industries in the constituency, although there had been very little trade union activity on behalf of the employees, who voted Labour by default rather than from conviction. The existing Liberal votes came from the active chapel-goers and a few middle-class idealists attracted by the Grimond philosophy of internationalism, regionalism and industrial reform.

Michael had rightly identified the potential of the Truro constituency and the opportunity there to capture the loyalty of the industrial workforce. Indeed, among these workers there remained an instinctive Liberal sympathy, founded on two centuries of Methodism, to which a Liberal candidate might appeal. Michael, however, had neither the time nor the background to realize the opportunity. He was an academic from a far county, or at least that is how he appeared to the Cornish. (Mind you, the Cornish rate Devon a far county!) David had also had the benefit of higher education but he did not sound academic. He sounded down to earth, and he sounded Cornish. He had the chance Michael never had of appealing to Cornish manual workers, and that he now set out to do.

Much of the industrial wealth of the constituency is centered on St Austell. It is in some ways a less privileged community than the city of Truro, which has the cathedral, the council offices and the best of the shops. St Austell, however, benefits from its position as the natural outlet for the china clay pits that dominate this part of Cornwall. It is significant – and to the credit of its directors – that the management of this key industry, English China Clay, is established not in London but in St Austell itself. So influential indeed is this business that it was said that a former Tory MP for Truro called in at those offices every Monday morning before leaving for Westminster, to discuss the management's concerns. What was good for ECC, he said, was good for Cornwall. David would agree with that assessment but viewed it from a different angle. What was good for the *workers* of ECC, he would say, was good for Cornwall. He had now to discover what those workers needed of their MP.

Since the autumn of 1970, our team of activists had been re-establishing – often from scratch – the Liberal branches in the villages. The technique was to deliver to every house an invitation to attend a local meeting at which David would speak. Those who responded would be shown how to set up a branch and how to recruit other workers. The key to this was David's readiness to go out with them on their recruiting campaigns. This built up a tremendous personal loyalty.

David used to say that it was people like these who were

the bedrock of our democracy. They are the people who never have any wish to stand for council or for parliament but believe passionately that democracy cannot survive unless good candidates are persuaded to do so. They devote their energies to backing those candidates, without any wish for the limelight. They can be seen sitting outside polling stations in the freezing cold collecting the voting numbers, knocking on doors canvassing for the candidate, raising money at jumble sales, tramping the streets delivering leaflet after leaflet. David was extraordinarily lucky in those who worked for him in this way, and never more so than over the months in 1972 when he set out to spread the word to St Austell.

To build up the Liberal organization in the St Austell area was a far bigger project than it was in the villages. There was a small number of known Liberals on the spot, including Mildred Curtice who would be our first councillor there in 1973, but too few to cover the whole town on their own. It was here that David benefited from a friendship that he had established some years before. As a Young Liberal he had entered and won a speaking competition at one of the regional weekend conferences and had very much impressed one of the judges, Vera Harvey. She felt then that he had the potential to become the Liberals' most effective voice in Cornwall.

Even among dedicated Liberal workers Vera, who sadly died in 1989, was exceptional. She had worked for years with Peter Bessell in Bodmin and had been persuaded in 1970 to act as regional organizing secretary. One of her jobs was to provide speakers to put the Liberal view at public debates, in schools and at conferences. Whenever possible she would send David, to give him further experience. Now when he needed help in St Austell she used all her influence to gather help from all over the region.

For one Saturday, St Austell was flooded with workers. David and Malcolm had created the leaflet, Vera had supplied the foot-power, and the organization was a miracle of military precision. This organization was in the hands of another exceptionally gifted volunteer, one of our latest recruits, Brian Tucker. Brian had recently moved to Truro from North Devon, where he had worked for Jeremy Thorpe. He had a natural flair for organization, which not merely ensured the success of this first major campaign in St Austell but was also to make such an impression that he was offered the job of paid agent in Bodmin a few months later. It would be a sad loss to us but vital to Bodmin.

The St Austell campaign attracted so many new members that what had been an almost skeletal presence was transformed into one of our best organized branches. More significantly, however, it provided a base for David as he set out to stamp his personality on the villages to the north of the town, where thousands of the clay workers lived.

In the clay villages David took a more tentative line than elsewhere – with good reason. He still had a lot to learn about them. He knew about Truro. It was the community in which he had been brought up. He knew the people there, both rich and poor, from personal experience. He knew too about industrial relations in companies like Holman's. He had also learnt about the concerns of the villagers nearby from his months of work there since 1964. He had even become more expert than he realized on farming problems from the time he spent in Devon. Yet what it was like to be a claypit worker, and to live in the villages that snaked between the claypits above St Austell, was entirely new to him.

There is a temptation for every politician to look at a problem, then tell people what it is they need, start a campaign and demand their support. David began from a different premise. He admitted that he did not know what was needed. He set out to learn. He had one great advantage over most politicians in this area. He could speak on equal terms with both the management and the workers. To the management he was an engineer who understood their technical terms – sometimes all too well. To the workers he was a man who spoke as they did. He was Cornish.

The intense feeling his family had for their origins had not only moulded David's own opinions. It also, very clearly, affected the way he spoke. He had had a privileged schooling, where most of the boys discarded the local accent, if indeed they ever had one. Not so the Penhaligon boys. Their father sounded Cornish and was proud of it. So did they. David's accent was once described as sounding as if he had been marinated in Cornish mead. It was now that he was to discover how great an asset this could be to him politically. As Malcolm put it, 'David never had to say that he was sympathetic to Cornish nationalism, or power for Cornwall. His voice said it for him.'

China clay mining is one of the very few big industries left in Cornwall and the great majority of it lies within the Truro constituency. It is also of special importance because – unlike, for example, mining and fishing – it has expanded rather than contracted over the last few decades.

In the 1970s English China Clay Lovering Pochin, known for short as ECC, was a highly successful and profitable company. It was also well run and had a reputation for good labour relations. Where, however, its record was less impressive was in the attention it was prepared to give to the environment in which its labour force lived and worked. The claypit workers lived in small villages up in the hills where the clay was mined. Those hills were, and still are, an extraordinary sight. As you drive up from St Austell, the claypits crowd in upon you from every side like huge open-cast coalmines seen in photographic negative – a bright white lunar landscape, pitted and scarred where the workings have torn off what turf there was and left the clay exposed. You are not surprised to learn that it has been used as a location for filming *Dr Who*.

At that time the area was dominated by great pyramids of waste which could be seen for many many miles around, known romantically (from a distance) as the white mountains. For the visitors they had a certain bleak magnificence – but it was not a place that visitors would choose to stay, for it was not just the hills that were white. On windy days the china clay dust would get everywhere. The gardens would be covered with a white film that even got inside the houses.

David was amazed that the people living there put up with it uncomplainingly. The workers were not only breathing dust all day long, they came home to it. The families had put up with it for generations. ECC, however, assured David that they had few complaints. He soon discovered why. All those who lived there were almost entirely dependent on the company they served. Many of the houses belonged to ECC, and the workers had no wish to risk their employment by making complaints.

What the clay workers did not realize until David came along was that they were in no danger of being thrown out.

They were too valuable and anyway ECC had no wish to lose their reputation as good employers. So David talked to the workers and found out what changes they would like to see. He then made a few discreet scientific investigations, discovered what could reasonably be asked of ECC, then asked for it.

As far as the workers were concerned, David was a godsend. They were suddenly receiving the sort of support that others got from trade unions. What was more, their jobs were not being put at risk, while the technical arguments were all going in their favour. They had got themselves a one-man trade union negotiating team.

Geoff Aver, a local schoolteacher whom we got to know through Malcolm was fascinated to see the effect David's personality had on the clay villages. 'At that time nearly everyone thought the votes around Truro were the only ones that mattered. What David saw was that there was a huge industrial electorate in the east of the constituency that had never felt involved in the democratic process. It was David who got them involved. His sincerity and obvious commitment made people believe that the impossible could be done. He also had an extraordinary ability to revive flagging spirits. I felt it myself. I was never one of the real workers who kept going from year to year but whenever I got involved, I could feel the warmth and excitement he generated.' He certainly generated it around St Austell.

It so happened that it was while David was so concerned with the houses of the clay workers that the one matter that was worrying me was the state of *our* house. Not only did it lack space but also it lacked any real sense of home. It was merely a set of rooms we used. Even turning one of the bedrooms into a sitting room did not help because it was such a distance from the kitchen that we rarely used it. Before Matthew was born this did not matter much, as we were rarely at home, but since his birth I was getting thoroughly fed up with making do. I wanted a proper home.

One evening when David came back from campaigning I raised the subject for the nth time. David exploded. 'Stop that nagging, woman,' he shouted. 'You should see what the people in the clay villages put up with – you don't know your luck.' It was, though we did not recognize it then, a classic scene in any politician's home. In one way he was right: we were luckier than many in the clay villages. But equally he was entirely wrong. Whilst he was fighting for better living conditions for everyone around us, he had become totally blind to our own. In a rage I dragged him to our bedroom and for the first time he noticed the black plague up the walls and along the ceiling caused by condensation and, even more seriously, the dry rot attacking the window and skirting board. We both calmed down and decided to look at ways of improving our situation.

David was never in a hurry to make decisions affecting the family but when he did, he did it with style. It was not long before we sought the services of an architect and some very imaginative plans were drawn up. They involved the total demolition of the 'extension' which housed the kitchen, bathroom and toilet. This would be replaced with three bedrooms and a bathroom, leaving the entire area above the post office quarters for a large living room with an integrated kitchen off it. The process would be slow as we had to obtain planning permission for the work and we also had to remember that there was little alteration we could make to the front of the property as it was 'listed'. Still, the decision restored the smile to my face and harmony to the home. We even – miracles of miracles – got away for a holiday.

Matthew was a year old now and prospering well. I wanted to take him away on holiday and have an opportunity to get away from the post office for a week, possibly two. David was uneasy about any break from campaigning but accepted a compromise. We borrowed my sister's touring caravan and drove scarcely twenty miles to the south coast fishing village of Mevagissey, where we spent a happy holiday on a nice site a couple of miles inland. Not once did we step outside the constituency and David was able to combine the holiday with campaigning – or should it be the other way around? That holiday would have to last us another three years.

David returned to the clay country to find a major issue awaiting his attention. ECC had plans to open up new pits in an area that would necessitate the removal of a road on which some of their workers depended for access to St Austell. This was the Carslake Road. If it went, the proposed alternative route of the Whitemoor Road would add one and a half miles to the journey. It would also add to the congestion in other villages whose own roads were already grossly overcrowded.

David was invited to lead the local campaign. I well remember the local butcher at St Dennis, Ralph Burnett, coming with his wife to the our post office armed with information which David translated into a leaflet. He did so to remarkable effect. He put most of the blame on the county council for the poor condition of the roads in the area but ECC had to recognize that they were not going to get their new claypits without concessions and expensive months of negotiation. They were faced not just by the indignation of 200 Carslake and Old Pound villagers but by the combined weight of all the villages. This was partly because all of them would see an increase in traffic, but even more because, through years of intermarriage among the clay workers, what one village hated they all hated. What one village liked they all liked. They hated the loss of the road. They liked David.

ECC liked him rather less. They were used to telling politicians what to do, not being told themselves. They looked for allies. The ECC empire was not confined to St Austell. Its tentacles spread into the neighbouring constituencies of North Cornwall and Bodmin. In 1974 John Pardoe and Paul Tyler were asked to lunch in the ECC directors' dining room. The lunch meandered on agreeably with no indication of why John and Paul had been invited, until they were just about to leave. At this moment the chairman cleared his throat a little nervously and said: 'I was wondering, gentlemen, if you would have a word with this young man of yours, Mr Penh—, Penha—, Penhaligon, isn't it? He seems to be causing quite a lot of *reaction* in our clay villages.'

John just laughed. 'If you think,' he said, 'that I have any chance of stopping David doing what he thinks is right, you have no idea of what he is like.' The chairman looked considerably less amused. 'Is there any chance,' he asked, 'that he might get into parliament?' 'If he is not the next MP for Truro,' John replied, 'I shall be very much surprised.'

7

BREAKTHROUGH

'Never in all our time as Liberal activists did we work as hard as we did then.' – Nan Hurst

John Pardoe had every reason at that lunch to be confident that David was on his way to Westminster. That was in 1974, and in 1974 he was not the only one to believe it possible, but it was to John's credit that he had been convinced of it for many months before. He had said as much on many occasions. So too had Vera Harvey and each in their own way had been giving us superb support as we battled to explain to our electorate what David could do for them.

Liberalism had always attracted sympathy in Cornwall and Devon, even if most of the electorate voted for the other parties. The problem, as John and Vera knew all too well, had been in building up sufficient self-confidence among the Liberal workers to believe that they could take that seemingly gigantic step from the comfort of a respectable third place to challenging for victory. In the West Country, personalities could and did inspire such a change of attitude. Jeremy Thorpe had the flamboyance to do it; Peter Bessell's gift was fervour, his non-conformist preaching reminiscent of the style that had swept Isaac Foot to Westminster between the wars; John Pardoe radiated energy. David had something of all of these qualities but he also had something that the others did not have. He had the common touch. Everyone, from clayworker to cathedral clergy, knew him simply as 'David'.

John and Vera recognized his special gifts and did everything they could to back our efforts. In particular they built up a team spirit among the Liberal parliamentary candidates in the years from 1970 to 1974. Previously there had been a tendency for each candidate to propose his own solution for every problem in the south-west. The result was chaos, and a gift to their opponents, who would play one Liberal off against another. Now, at Vera's instigation, the candidates met on a regular basis to exchange views and coordinate policies. This was hugely helpful, not only to new boys like David, but also to Paul Tyler who had the hardest job of all. Paul had lost Bessell's old seat of Bodmin in 1970 and was fighting to win it back. Paul is a man of immense resolution and he was going to need all of it, especially as, despite his Cornish ancestry, he had previously lived and stood in Devon.

Paul and David would sometimes go off together to meet important interest groups, working as a team in a way that they were to recapture twelve years later when Paul was to be Liberal Party chairman and David the president. Each would take the subjects that suited him best. On one occasion they were summoned to meet the officers of the local branch of the National Farmers Union. Paul was by then a battle-hardened candidate and David insisted that he should act as spokesman. Paul remembers it as a fairly sticky occasion. There was never much good will towards the Liberals within the NFU and matters did not improve as the questions turned to the Common Market. The Market was not popular and the Liberals were known to be pro-Europe. Paul recalls that it was at that moment David intervened. 'I don't remember what David said, but I do remember how the atmosphere changed dramatically. All the old farmers recognized a real Cornishman. David was clearly one of them. From then on it was an easy ride. I don't know whether David's answers were Liberal policy or not but they sounded good commonsense. What was important was that there was an immediate rapport.'

Over those first campaigning years David would have to spend some time over such meetings but most of our efforts were expended on more direct contact with the voters, through the leaflets David and Malcolm wrote, and I spent hours typing and putting together. David's friendship with Malcolm was a remarkable case of mix and match. Their views and their aims were identical. Their skills were totally different, yet complementary. Neither could have done without the other.

David was always the practical one. Whether it was a matter of making a speech or making the printing press work, David was in his element. In fact he never really comprehended why some people cannot immediately see how things go together. Some years later at a Liberal Party Conference, we were staying at the same hotel as Jo Grimond and I watched with some amusement David's air of total incomprehension as Jo struggled to open a plastic marmalade container. Here was a man of enormous intelligence baffled by a product of modern technology. David always believed that the day that Jo Grimond first took him seriously as a politician of ability was when they were discussing terrorism and bombs over the House of

Commons dinner table. Jo, according to David, did not see how the terrorists would have the technical knowledge to make anything other than a very crude bomb and was amazed when David explained in some detail how accessible were the materials and skills needed to construct an effective weapon.

Malcolm, like Jo, possesses very few practical skills. However, he is a brilliant theorist and planner, and when it came to organization, whether it was just a leaflet or a whole campaign, Malcolm was vital to the partnership. He is a researcher by training and a gifted organizer by nature. He is also a very knowledgeable and shrewd politician, though he was not to deploy those skills in public for many years – his career as a council officer compelled him to keep a very low profile at that time. In the 1970s he used his skills solely to make sure that David won the seat. For the 1974 election, with Brian Tucker going to Bodmin to act as a professional agent for Paul Tyler, Malcolm agreed to act as David's unpaid agent – so long as David did the printing!

The printing then, and for many years to come, was done up at the caravan park, where David's father housed the litho press in one of his sheds. It was not only not a new machine – we could not afford one – it was not even a very good machine. Yet somehow David kept it going, though often at the cost of spending whole nights and even weekends in that shed. He would often come back covered in ink, to find me beside myself with anger at the time he spent working on the press rather than working on our house. It was one of the ironies of life that David, who had all the necessary engineering skills, could never get down to repairing even the simplest breakage. Yet it was just as ironic that I put up with it. The fact was that, however much

I wished to have a perfectly decorated house, I wanted even more to see him succeed. I shared his ideals and therefore had to accept, despite my protests, his crazy order of priorities.

It was therefore in an atmosphere of domestic chaos and frenetic political activity that we survived that winter of 1973/74 and the great coal strike, well aware that it would probably bring a General Election in its wake. In fact, the election was called for February. The announcement when it came made no great mark on our friends or ourselves. What were a mere three weeks of campaigning to us? We had been campaigning for every week since the autumn of 1970.

On one appallingly wet day Doris Ansari got three coats soaked through while delivering leaflets. At seven o'clock she sank thankfully to rest in a chair with the confession that she had never felt so tired in all her life. 'What do you mean?' said David. 'We have got to complete another delivery tonight.' And they did. 'The difficulty was,' Doris recalls, 'that you knew that even after that delivery David would be back at home slaving over the production of yet another leaflet. You could not let him down.'

It is easy now to forget how unused we all were to campaigning such as that in Cornwall. It was even unusual in other areas of the country where they had a tradition of intense political activity, as we learnt from members such as John and Nan Hurst, who had joined us just before the 1970 election. They thought we were appallingly ill-organized in 1970 but recognized that under David they were inspired to work as they had never worked before. Indeed, we may never again work quite as hard as we did over those four years when we were making our first breakthrough but that kind of activity is now – quite rightly – taken for granted by those who feel that Liberalism matters.

Because it was then unheard of in Cornwall, our opponents were totally unprepared for the impact our campaigning had made until a few weeks before the election. Then it was too late for them to counter it. David anyway projected an image that was exceptionally hard to counter. He even mystified some of his greatest supporters. 'I'm told you're Church of England,' ventured one of them. 'That's right,' said David. 'And I'm told you're teetotal.' 'That's right,' said David. 'What's the point of you being teetotal if you be Church of England?' asked his mystified supporter.

The answer was that David simply did not like alcohol. He liked tea. However, David was positively intolerant of those who drank too much, and in favour of a very tough line on drink and driving. This attitude was reassuring, I suppose, to the Methodists. Here was a candidate they could approve of as well as vote for – because it was inconceivable to Methodists to vote for anyone else. Paul Tyler tells a story of one of his predecessors at Bodmin. In one village he visited the local undertaker, a staunch Methodist, to be told that things looked good for the Party. 'How do you know?' he asked. 'Well, this last year we buried ten of they and only six of us,' was the reply. There are stories too of villages where, in preference to a canvass, the senior Methodist simply goes through the voters' list picking out those with good Methodist credentials.

In Truro, we had always been a little more practical than that but it was under David and Malcolm that we became a great deal more professional. In the 1970s, the days of unquestioning allegiance to one party or another were almost over – and for us that was to the good. We could not win on the Methodist vote alone. People now were deciding to back those who were prepared to work for their votes, and it was David with his campaigns for local amenities and the support he had from our excellent team of councillors who would benefit.

One of our friends reminded me the other day of his experience working with David then. This friend had always been a supporter, was happy to help, but far from happy when he was sent out canvassing. 'David was clearly desperately busy that day but he had spotted my despondent return. He came across and said, "You didn't enjoy that much, did you?" "Not much," I admitted. "I think I will stick to stuffing envelopes." "Oh no," he said, "that would be a waste. Come out with me this afternoon."

'I did and we had a great time. David was in tremendous form and I totally regained my confidence. This was easy after all. David was delighted and gave me an area to do on my own. The second house I went to was palatial, set like some Cornish Taj Mahal beyond a huge pond. I stepped delicately across the bridge and rang the bell. The lady who answered looked down at me. "Ah, Liberals," she said, "they are all either black or queer, and you are clearly not black." Perhaps, it was not so easy after all.'

One more bizarre memory of that election remains for me. It was about a week before polling day and we had returned from an evening of canvassing that had brought home to us for the first time just what all our work had achieved. Voter after voter had told us that we had their votes. In a panic I woke David up that night. What if we did win? Would he get paid? Neither of us knew. David struggled out of bed and found the *Whitaker's Almanack*.

Yes, he would get paid – about the same as he got at Holman's. We could afford to win.

I was not the only member of the family to panic at the thought of success. The printing for our campaign was being done at Kenwyn Hill Garage. One day whilst David was up to his armpits in printer's ink, his Dad came rushing in. He had been down town talking to some of his Tory friends. 'Here, boy,' he said. 'They think you are going to win! What are you going to do?' For the first time it occurred to my father-in-law that David could be on the road to parliament and all his engineering career would be set aside. Like me, he was somewhat reassured that David would at least be paid, even though he rightly thought it a dangerously insecure career.

In fact, a few more nights canvassing in areas where we had done less work convinced us that David would not have to leave Holman's – at least not yet. We were not about to achieve a miracle. We would do well but we were not about to win.

Nor did we win – not then. However, we did achieve a miracle of a kind. In 1970 the Liberals had come a humiliating third, 8,000 behind the Labour candidate and 16,000 behind the Tory winner, Piers Dixon. In February 1974 we came second, only 2,500 behind Dixon. We had gained 12,000 further votes. For the first time since it was established in 1950 the Truro seat was a Tory/Liberal marginal. We were almost too tired to cheer. Our reward was the shock we saw on the faces of our opponents. We had come up on the blind side, as we always said we could.

For myself, I vividly remember, at the count, a guilty wave of relief sweep over me. I was glad we had not won. I knew that David and I were not ready for it yet – and anyway what were MPs' wives supposed to do? I needed time to find out. Now, thank heaven, I was to have the time. I little knew it was to be only seven months.

After that election of February 1974, every Liberal I knew wanted only one thing – to take a rest. That was not just in Truro but in other constituencies too. They realized that another election must soon be on the way (Harold Wilson had the slimmest of majorities) but everyone needed a rest to recharge their batteries – everyone that is except for D. Penhaligon. David decided that now was the time to double his work rate.

Later, when talking to other Liberal candidates who had come within easy distance of winning their seats in February but who had all failed in October, we could see why Truro was the only Liberal gain that autumn. David was the only one who took no respite at all and I was too naive and realistic to ask him to give up any of his time to us. He was not being selfish – I was as determined as he was that we should succeed – but it was only after the election that it occurred to me that I had been working extraordinarily hard to change my whole life in a way I was not, at first at least, going to enjoy.

David was gifted with a remarkable instinct for timing, whether he was telling a story or organizing a political campaign. His instinct now told him that the election would come very soon indeed and that he only had a few months in which to win the votes we needed to snatch the seat. He also knew that the Tories must now make the effort that they should have made before. They would not let the seat go for lack of effort. He must not only match their effort, he must exceed it.

Fortunately, fate – and the Tories – played into his hands. Not only was the Whitemoor Road becoming throughout that year a more important issue day by day, with the Tories quite unable to come up with any solution of their own, but another issue dear to David's heart was getting special attention from the BBC. This was tourism. At that time, tourism was for Cornwall both one of its major industries and a real threat to its way of life. It accounted for twelve per cent of the employment but facilities, especially road space and the social services, had not kept pace with the numbers of people who wanted to visit the Duchy. Three million came every year and there were suggestions that even more should be attracted in future.

At the end of 1973 David and Malcolm had put together a questionnaire on the subject under the title of 'Tourism – Menace or Salvation?' It took up the centre-spread of *News from the Liberals*. Both the preamble and the questions it asked were distinctly provocative, as they suggested that any further growth in the tourist trade might be disastrous unless major changes were made to accommodate it. It was so provocative that some of our branches that were economically dependent on tourism refused to distribute it. The replies, however, confirmed the line taken by David. It was clear that the majority of the constituency was very worried that the quality of Cornish life could be destroyed by too many emmets. ('Emmets' is the Cornish word for ants and is often used derogatively, though not by David, about the armies of summer tourists.)

The commonsense solution had to be that any increase in the tourist trade which brought employment (good) must be matched by an immediate investment in the facilities (inadequate). It was not a sensational answer but it was an interesting one, in that until then no political party had even thought of putting the question to the public. David's concern with the subject must have won him votes in the February election but it was not a major issue then. However, when the BBC picked up the subject in the summer, it was acutely topical and the Liberal initiative was inescapably part of the story.

Brass Tacks on BBC2 decided to film interviews in Cornwall, and David was invited to give his views. For balance, they also asked Piers Dixon to appear. They were the only two politicians involved. The programme came out that summer and it attracted a huge audience. It is not often that Cornwall's problems are discussed on television and this problem concerned everyone there.

For most of them, even in Truro, it was the first time they had seen David or Piers Dixon. It was also the first time David had been on television. He had no training for this but he had got something to say and he put it across with his usual flair for illustrating the problems and solutions in a way that everyone could understand and with which not even the landladies of Mevagissey and Perranporth would disagree. What was more, he found that he enjoyed his first encounter with television and, as we were to discover later, a sense of enjoyment comes across on the screen. He was completely at his ease. In contrast, Piers Dixon, despite his experience of public affairs, appeared inarticulate, totally out of touch with public feeling and even cold and academic. One could not help but feel sorry for him, as he was clearly a very nice man, though totally unsuited to a Cornish seat.

In its own way, this little programme acted on the Cornish public as the gladiatorial contests between presidential candidates are sometimes supposed to do in the USA. The

Truro electorate had the chance to see their candidates effectively face to face for the first time. The less well-known contender had the chance to make his mark. He seized it and won the bout. We can now see that that programme was the key to the next election, though at the time David greeted its showing merely with a sense of relief that it had gone as well as it did. There was no time to gloat. There was too much still to do.

The Tories were making tremendous efforts, as David knew they would, to rouse their supporters and to convince backsliders that a Liberal victory would achieve nothing except a continuance of Wilson's 'dangerously left-wing government'. The nature of the challenge they faced was illustrated by the confession of one of their own committee members that in the privacy of the ballot box in February he had found himself voting for Penhaligon! He promised he would never repeat the crime but they knew now that no one was safe from seduction.

In response, David had his own secret weapon: a full-time agent. Jeremy Thorpe, who had found a little money for us in February from his special seats fund, now promised even more. It was suggested that Brian Tucker, our organizational genius of 1972, might return to work in Truro. In February, Brian had masterminded Paul Tyler's campaign in Bodmin and Paul had won back the seat, one of our very few gains in an election that had seen our vote go up to an unprecedented six million votes, yet with a pitiful reward of only fourteen seats. It was a hard decision for Brian, who had great admiration for Paul and would have been happy to go on working for him. On the other hand, he loved a challenge and Truro was obviously winnable if it had a full-time agent. Paul, generous as always, urged him to go.

He had someone in Bodmin who could act as his agent, he said. Brian should move back to Truro.

The difference Brian made was tremendous. David and Malcolm were freed to concentrate on the political and tactical decisions. Brian worked on the organization. Every young voter about to vote for the first time received a special message from David (such 'targeting' is commonplace now, but was then unheard of) and David himself was given a schedule that made it certain that he wasted not a minute of his time. Brian knew that the more people David met personally the better his chances were. David would be packed into a minibus with half a dozen helpers, who had instructions on exactly how long David was allowed to stay in each village or street. David needed minders. He enjoyed chatting far too much.

When Harold Wilson called the election for 10 October, the odds were still officially in Dixon's favour but we now knew that it would be desperately close. This time we could just win. In addition to Piers Dixon, we faced a new Labour candidate but he had been chosen too late to offset the lead David had established in the clay villages. There was also Dr James Whetter from the Cornish nationalist party, Mebyon Kernow. He had polled 850 votes in February. His performance could make the difference between defeat and victory for David. Would David's Cornish credentials be enough this time to attract sufficient of those votes?

By now the fight for Truro was attracting interest not only in Cornwall. The *Guardian* and *Financial Times* both sent reporters to study the form and found the odds at evens; but, for Piers Dixon, the hardest blow was to find the *Daily Telegraph*, of all papers, writing admiringly that 'this powerfully built articulate young man could charm the pastry off a Cornish Pasty and has built up an organization – complete with its own newspaper – which is devastatingly efficient'.

However, there were unexpected problems. One of these was a prejudice against David's background that we certainly would not have found if he had been a teacher or lawyer. Time and time again, mechanical engineering qualifications were mistaken for the qualifications of a car mechanic. Personally I am all for car mechanics in politics but a surprisingly large number of the Truro electorate then thought they did not want one as their representative in parliament.

The fact that a qualification in engineering was rarely recognized by the public at large irked David not just then but throughout his parliamentary career. He frequently complained that youngsters looking forward to a university education were never encouraged to train to 'make something' as opposed to getting a degree in say 'Egyptology' – David's example, not mine. This was clearly David's view of a pretty useless subject and perhaps an example of an engineer having no understanding of the science of history. *Touché*.

During this campaign, as was usual then, we canvassed all day around the constituency and met up in the evening in time for one and more often two public meetings. At these events it was customary for the candidate's wife to sit on the platform looking suitably decorous, attentive (laughing at the same joke time and time again) and faithful – about as useful as a lap dog. However, for me (not David, of course) it was virtually the only time of the day I could sit down and relax, provided I did not actually go to sleep. One evening David was speaking at Fowey and we had got to the stage where the chairman was asking the audience for questions. David was quite good at handling questions and this in some way was the more interesting part of the evening for me, as I had heard the actual speech many times before. On this occasion, however, I heard the lady questioner say she wanted to direct her question at me, not David. Good heavens, I thought, what do I do now? I started to panic and no doubt looked very uncomfortable.

The question was, as it turned out, quite easy. 'Would you,' the questioner enquired, 'expect your husband to sit demurely beside you, if you were the candidate?' I decided I had to give an honest answer. 'No,' I admitted, 'and I think it very unlikely that he would do it.' There and then I made a mental note never to sit on platforms at public meetings just because I was married to David, unless it upset the organizer or unless David definitely wanted my support, which quite frankly he generally did at election times in the constituency.

During the campaign we moved in with my parents, who took over looking after Matthew, making sure David had plenty of clean shirts and having a meal ready for us at the end of each day. It enabled me to be totally single-minded in helping with the campaign and in any case I do not think I could have coped without such help. I was not blessed with David's placid nature and became a nervous wreck at each and every General Election – even when the prognosis was good, I was always convinced of disaster. I was probably cushioning myself and him against defeat – a bit of a mother hen.

Later, during other General Election campaigns, Malcolm would send me off in a different direction from David. This made practical sense, as between us we were able to meet many more people. However, I was also aware that it was done to keep me away from him, as my forebodings of doom and gloom were very infectious. My concern, which could only be revealed to David and a few people close to us, was, I believe, a natural reaction and would be shared by many other women if they had been in my position. Here you were with your husband's job totally on the line and your future very much depending on the whim of the electorate. You had to suffer at least three weeks of uncertainty, not knowing in which direction your life would be heading after polling day.

Some people can be philosophical about changes in their lives and merely believe 'what will be, will be' – not me! I was ambitious for David, and I desperately wanted him to succeed, but at election times we could never be totally in control: so much depended on the performance and appeal of the national parties – and in October 1974 the national appeal of the Liberal Party was clearly slightly less than it had been in February. It would be harder than ever for us to win.

In the Truro consistituency after the polling stations close on polling day, all the boxes are transferred to the council chamber but there are so many polling stations to cover all the villages that there is no time to complete the count overnight. However, the votes still have to be tipped out of their boxes to verify the number of votes cast. This entails the votes being put in bundles of twenty ready for the next day. Each political party may have a number of witnesses there to ensure that the counting of the votes is being conducted in a proper manner. These hand-picked and privileged workers are generally able to get a good idea of how the vote has gone by mentally keeping a tally of how many votes their candidate has out of each bundle of twenty.

In October 1974 I joined David for a while whilst this process was going on but left some time before him, going back to my parents' home to watch the national results. David returned very late and very unsure of his position. He and Malcom had stayed until the very last box had been checked. Then they had looked at the top vote on each bundle of unsorted bundles. Thirty-five were for Dixon; thirty-six were for Penhaligon. It was a rough sample – desperately close, too close to predict victory either way. My reaction was equally desperate. 'Don't ever put us through this again,' I shouted. 'I cannot bear it.' A sympathetic wry smile came across David's face. He knew he would and he also knew that I would bear it too.

We had to go to the crowded council chamber for our count on the following day, knowing that the Party had not done well elsewhere. Even worse, the piles of votes on the table in front of us were none too comforting either. Penhaligon and Dixon seemed neck and neck but realistically we had to admit, when we could bear to look at the piles, that Dixon's seemed just a little higher than Penhaligon's. I was standing with Nan Hurst, now chairman of the Truro branch. David came over to us and said sadly, 'I think I am going to have to be a good loser.' Nan nodded wretchedly. 'It looks so,' she said.

There was now only one box of votes to go. It came, though we did not know it at the time, from one of the clay villages. The votes spilt out and we watched transfixed as eighty per cent of those votes went on to the Penhaligon pile. Calmly Malcolm asked if the postal votes had been included. (If they had not we knew must have lost, as at that stage in our organization we could not compete with the

Tories in sweeping up the postal votes.) They had been included, he was told. We had won.

The margin was 464. I was standing with Nan and Doris when three blue-rinsed ladies politely enquired as to the majority. 'Four hundred and sixty-four,' Doris told them. 'Oh,' one replied. 'You must be disappointed. You worked so hard.' 'But it is we who have won,' explained the jubilant Doris. The Tory ladies could not believe it. It was a moment to savour.

The Tory, Labour and Mebyon Kernow votes had all gone down, Mebyon Kernow crucially by just 466. We had needed those. Piers Dixon, gentlemanly to the last, did not request a recount. David's agony was not to be prolonged.

He gave his victory speech and we took him out into a street alive with a laughing, crying, cheering crowd. David's was the only Liberal gain throughout the country but we were not cheering that. We were simply cheering him – a Cornishman, one of us, who had shown that a Cornishman born and bred could win his way to Westminster and fight our battles there.

8
NEW BOY

'David was in absolutely the right job and enormously happy in it. He was a natural politician. You never thought that there was anything else he wanted to do.' – John Pardoe

The next few days were a series of celebrations and interviews. The celebrations were wonderful and the interviews no problem: asked what he wanted to do when he got to parliament, David was never short of an answer. However, after a day or two he became uncomfortably aware of the fact that no one had told him when he had to go there. In fact he had no idea of what he was supposed to do next.

Eventually, on Brian Tucker's advice, he rang the Liberal Whip's Office. After announcing who he was, he had to cut short a flood of well meant congratulations by saying: 'Hang on, hang on! I've had plenty of that, but tell me what on earth do I do *now*?' There was a bemused silence on the other end of the line – not for the last time there, I suspect. Then he was told that the new session of parliament started on 22 October.

He decided to go up to London for a couple of days in the week before the opening, to visit the Whip's Office and 'get a feel of things'. On this occasion I was able to accompany him. This was to be our very first visit to parliament. I do not know why we had not bothered to go before but I suspect it was because David had less interest in the mechanics of parliament than in getting things done down in Cornwall. We arrived there hand in hand – naive, countrified and raw. I was embarrassed by this but David was proud. We made our first mistake right away – one that David never repeated, I might add! – in that we arrived at 9 a.m. No one had told us that as parliament does not sit until 2.30 p.m., most of the MPs and many of the staff do not get there before 10 am.

The Pardoes had very kindly invited us to stay with them in London and during those two days we were able to talk things over with John and Joy. John had been a tremendous help to us over the years and a great supporter of David. His responsibilities as one of the major spokesman in parliament would give him very little time to coach David in what to do once parliament opened but he gave us invaluable advice at this stage. We certainly needed it. Although we had lived with the prospect of victory for the last six months, its achievement had inevitably left us somewhat shocked and quite unprepared for what had to be a radical change in our lifestyle.

Some things, however, we had discussed and agreed on already, at least in principle. First, David would have to leave Holman's. There was no way that he could run a research and development department in Camborne while working in Westminster. Many other MPs – though few of the Liberals – were better placed. Barristers could still spend mornings in their chambers giving legal opinions. Company directors could attend board meetings. Most MPs, like David, had to live on their salaries.

One problem was that David would have his home in Truro, while working and living in London, all on a salary no larger than he got at Holman's. Fortunately he would be reimbursed up to £1,050 for expenses incurred on accommodation in London and his travel costs between London, and the constituency would be paid in full, along with a petrol allowance for all travel on constituency business. However, secretarial costs would eat into the salary. He would receive £1,750 towards these but that would clearly be too little.

We would have to retain the post office to maintain anything like our previous income. This, of course, would also allow us a little security in the event of David failing to retain his seat at the next election. (In view of his very small majority, this had to be a possibility.) As before, I would run the post office – but now in my own name. David could not be both an employee of the Crown and an MP. Fortunately David's father no longer seemed so worried over the post office being in my name.

Parliamentary salaries increased the following summer, making life a little easier. Indeed the Review Body under Lord Boyle's chairmanship had recommended that MPs' salaries should be increased to £8,000. However, as parliament had just approved anti-inflation measures it was hardly appropriate to recommend an increase for itself of seventy-eight per cent! A more modest increase was eventually agreed but it was none the less welcome – an extra £1,250, making the new salary £5,750. At the same time secretarial allowances increased to £3,200 and the London living allowance went up by £300. Whilst this was certainly more than most of David's constituents earned, it was still a fairly modest sum, as we soon found our expenditure was now markedly higher than we were previously used to.

This worried David hardly at all. He was never much concerned over money and I have always suspected that most of the rich people we met were more envious of David than he of them – with good reason. He was perfectly content – even smug! – about the fact that he had achieved something that money cannot buy. He was, as he would say, paid for pursuing his favourite hobby. 'If I had a maiden aunt leave me a million pounds, I would still want to do exactly what I am doing now, being Truro's Member of Parliament.'

David was, like many politicians, totally absorbed in his career and would enjoy talking politics with anyone regardless of their background or what car they drove home in. Indeed, the older the car the better. In this we were very different. I have always liked being surrounded with nice things and I remember my father warning David that 'Annette was born with Rolls-Royce tastes into a Ford family'. I of course denied it but it was close enough to the truth for David to enjoy the joke. Anyway, despite those Rolls-Royce tastes of mine, we managed perfectly happily on his salary throughout his career in parliament.

The job, of course, was the unknown quantity. Although David had met several of the Liberal MPs on Party Council and at Assemblies, he knew none of them very well. Paul Tyler, who would have been the one to whom he would first have turned, had lost Bodmin. The twelve Liberal MPs who had survived were delighted by David's victory but they were mostly so busy with their own responsibilities that they would clearly have little time to advise the newcomer.

Luckily David now took exactly the right decision over

where he should stay. He chose a room in the National Liberal Club. There was nothing very glamorous about the Club. It might sound like a smart address but the accommodation was distinctly shabby at that time. However, it was inexpensive and – most significantly – Cyril Smith also used it as his base.

Life in London is notoriously lonely for those who do not know their way around and that is just as true for new MPs as it is for any young person at the start of his career. The only difference is that the MP has to start his career not in private but under the sceptical gaze of the country's press, which is as ready to advertise his incompetence or peccadilloes as it is to praise his eloquence. At this key period of David's life, Cyril was to prove a godsend. He had a room close by David's at the Club and, as a privileged resident there, he had been allowed a kettle. Cyril shared David's passion for tea and on either side of that kettle a friendship was formed that was to make David's first few years at Westminster not just bearable but a launching pad for his parliamentary career.

When asked about his first impressions of the House of Commons David typically would describe what he first thought of those around him rather than the splendour of the chamber itself. Although he was to grow immensely fond and proud of the building, he knew it would be fatal if he allowed himself to be overawed by the history it represented. 'As I sat down,' David recalled some years later, 'I looked around at all those national political figures and found myself wondering what on earth David Penhaligon was doing here. "Hang on, boy," I had to say to myself. "I got elected as well they did. Let's get stuck in."'

David got stuck in with a vengeance. Most new MPs tend to wait until they can speak in some debate that covers their favourite subject. After all, they have plenty of time to make their mark. Liberal MPs have no such dispensation. They cannot afford to wait. David, for instance, found himself appointed the Party's spokesman on social services at twenty-four hours' notice. Jeremy Thorpe chose him for this role, he said, 'because I recognized that he had a very strong social conscience'. It would now be David's job to put the Party's point of view forward whenever the social services were debated and to ask questions of the relevant ministers if the Liberals wished to raise issues that were not on the agenda.

Cyril was the ideal adviser. Although he had himself been in the Commons for only a few years longer than David, he had spent a lifetime in Rochdale's municipal government, much of that time as a Labour councillor. He knew how government worked and for some months he had himself been Liberal spokesman on social services in parliament. He could advise David on what was important and what could be left alone.

David did not wait for a debate on social services. He made his maiden speech at the first opportunity, during the debate on the Queen's Speech – on only his tenth day in the House. In accordance with tradition, he chose a non-controversial subject – concentrating on the problems of his own constituency. Though his audience were not to know it, his choice of subject was less of a formality than it seemed. They were to hear an awful lot about the problems of Truro over the years to come and much of it was to be anything but non-controversial.

The content of that speech may have been unremarkable

but its delivery was not. "He immediately arrested the attention of the House," Jeremy Thorpe recalls, "because of his rich burr – an enormous advantage in the House of Commons." His fellow MPs listened intrigued. Here apparently was yet another of those characters in which the Liberals seemed to specialize. Was this one going to be just a 'character', or was there something else there to watch out for?

The Liberals have, of course, always been known for the colourful personalities they have sent to Westminster. This is largely because their MPs have to be colourful to attract the attention of their electorates when most of the country's attention is focussed on the larger parties. Few at the time were more colourful than their leader. Jeremy Thorpe was an Old Etonian, *bon viveur*, brilliant raconteur and wit. It was largely thanks to his flamboyant style that he was able to command the attention of the press – to a degree quite out of proportion to the representation of his Party within parliament. In his constituency of North Devon, Jeremy had built up a fanatically loyal following, partly on the strength of his personality, but also thanks to his phenomenal ability to remember the names – and often the family history – of the hundreds of people who worked on his behalf. In politics this was an invaluable gift and one that every other member envied.

Despite his affability, however, as a leader Jeremy was somewhat remote from the other Liberal MPs, and especially so from David, whose style and tastes could not have been more different. The Commons cafeteria was hardly Jeremy's favourite stamping ground, nor tea his favourite tipple. On the other hand, over the next few years on those occasions when Jeremy did join the rest of the

Liberal MPs at the round table reserved for them in the dining room, it would immediately become the centre of attention because of the roars of laughter set off by Jeremy's and David's stories. In their very different ways they could both find humour in even the direst circumstances — excepting, of course, those that were to bring the end to Jeremy's glittering career. That drama, however, was not to break until 1976.

Of more immediate influence on David were the two MPs from the Border country: David Steel and Alan Beith. Although only a few years older than my David, David S. had already established a reputation as a parliamentary tactician, gained from his historic private member's bill on abortion. As Chief Whip, David S. was responsible for explaining to David what he could and could not do in debate. He could also, and he did, make a point of congratulating him when things went well. Alan Beith could do even more. He could sympathize when things went wrong. He too was a newcomer.

Alan had entered parliament only a year before, in a by-election. His constituency of Berwick, like Truro, was non-conformist by tradition. Unlike David, however, Alan was himself from that tradition, being a Methodist preacher as well as a university lecturer. Their backgrounds were different, their styles were different (Alan was known as a political academic, David as speaker), yet they were to become each other's closest friends and confidants. At that time Alan also was based at the National Liberal Club, and it was on Cyril's advice and Alan's sympathy that David was to depend as he began what had to be for any Liberal spokesman a solitary battle to get across Liberal beliefs and policies.

Making speeches was no great problem for David. He had already acquired the most necessary skill: he spoke from notes. He had never in fact resorted to writing out his speeches. He was quite happy, he said, if he had 'a few notes on the back of an old fag packet', and these notes were enough to make sure that he covered the points he had to. The words he used, however, and the time he devoted to each point, depended on the mood of his audience and on what had gone before. For the Commons this approach was ideal. The members are there to listen to argument. It is fatal simply to repeat what has been covered in a preceding speech.

What could have proved more difficult was the size of the chamber. The House of Commons is surprisingly intimate in scale and the members never like to be subjected to the kind of emotional oratory suited to public halls. As most of those who become MPs have won their way there in part at least through their skill in such public speaking, each has to learn how to adapt his style to the requirements of the chamber. Over the years David had developed his own platform manner, which he now modified rather than changed for use in the chamber. The press dubbed it 'rustic radical'.

'His handwaving, airsawing, crouching style, is reminiscent of other West Country radicals of the Isaac Foot pedigree,' pointed out one commentator, 'but his down-to-earth Cornish approach is unusually refreshing in a Commons dominated by Oxbridge lawyers.' 'At the age of thirty-two, he is still the archetypal backwoodsman,' wrote another in 1976, 'treating the sophisticated Westminster scene with the shrewd cynicism of the died-in-the-wool rustic.'

Bill Rodgers vividly remembers his first impression of David, 'walking up and down between the benches as he made his speech. It was late in the evening, and it was a fairly empty house, but it was most peculiar. Normally you stand still. Yet it seemed with him a perfectly natural thing to do.'

If the initial impression was one of unsophisticated innocence, that suited David very well. He built on it, putting his points in what was a disarmingly conversational manner, often modestly deferring to what he described as the great experience of the ministers. For the ministers, however, the problem was that the content of David's speeches was anything but unsophisticated. David was a trained scientist with a brain that worked at the speed of a computer. One by one ministers found themselves acutely embarrassed by the 'innocence' of the points he made.

Genuinely aghast at the government's inability to see how illogical many of their proposals were, he would politely ask the minister for explanations. 'I never cease to be amazed by how frequently I speak in debates of this nature when, to be candid, I do not understand what we are doing. I suspect that I am in the majority in the House, but I am one of the few with the courage to admit it.

'I will set out the position as I see it and, if I am wrong, I hope that the minister will correct me. I instance a family which gets interim benefit and family income supplement and pays income tax. The £1 allowance for the first child could in some circumstances be lost in the following way: 50p off the family income supplement, 35p in tax, and another 35p in clawback. That means a net *loss* of 20p a week ... I do not understand it, but I look forward to hearing the minister's reply. Perhaps the minister will tell us how much the government will save by this 120 per cent tax rate on families which claim family income supplement.'

David had always been concerned over the loss in real value of pensions and also over the lack of incentive for the elderly to earn any more. 'The person who works after retirement,' he pointed out in one of his early speeches, 'is in effect taxed at sixty per cent on £13 a week. Therefore, work after the age of sixty-five is not really voluntary but probably comes into the classification of masochism . . . If we look back through the copies of *Hansard* we will find there has been virtually a unanimous vote on the opposition benches for the reform of the earnings rule. It appears that members go through some sort of conversion when they escape from opposition to government.'

Later he was to condemn the removal of the Christmas bonus for pensioners in 1975, on the basis of our own experience. 'Until I was elected, it was my job to serve in the post office on Saturday mornings but I am now banned from doing so. I met many pensioners and it was a great education. The government underestimate how much the Christmas bonus was appreciated. It meant that there was at least one time in the year when many of our pensioners were not desperately short of money . . . What pensioners need is an election every six months,' he observed, comparing this decision with the two increases granted earlier in 1974.

At first most of the points he made were in speeches but in time he began to use 'oral questions' too. Oral questions can be an agonizingly difficult experience for newcomers. If you are to have any chance of getting a question answered orally by the minister, you generally have to serve notice of it some two weeks before, then be prepared to leap to your feet when called and put the question. That requires planning but is not in itself too difficult. The problem is that the answer is likely to be bland or evasive and the art is to follow it up with a 'supplementary question' that forces the minister to admit more than he or his department might wish to reveal. You can also spring up and ask a supplementary question after some other MP has raised the subject – or a subject related to it.

Although David never had any difficulty over thinking on his feet, he was for ever falling foul of parliamentary procedure over this. He would be pulled up by the Speaker for failing to cast his supplementaries in the correct form, or taking too long over them, or straying too far from the subject. All this would take place against a background of barracking and raucous laughter from every corner of the House.

This is, of course, the kind of reception any new MP must expect. It is in the interest of the other parties to shake his nerve if they can, and it is especially an ordeal for new MPs from minority parties, who have only a handful to cheer them on. In later years, when he was recognized as a witty speaker worth listening to whatever his opinions, David had only to rise to his feet for there to be an expectant hush. It was very different when he first arrived.

In frustration David would resort increasingly to the use of 'written questions'. These are responded to in writing by the ministers' departments and are invaluable to any MP who is intent on gathering facts, either to help himself understand an issue or to help a constituent. However, they do little to get across his own point of view or to embarrass the government into changing theirs.

Once, in despair at yet another failure to pose his oral question in the proper parliamentary form, he turned to

Geraint Howells and said: 'That's it. I'm never going through that again.' Geraint, a fellow Celt who had found the procedure just as daunting himself in the early days, was sympathetic but answered bluntly. 'Oh yes, David bach, you will. You will have to.'

Geraint was right, as David would acknowledge some years later. 'I think, oddly enough, one of the advantages I had in early days,' he said, 'was that I was a member of a small parliamentary party. If one had something go wrong – and on one or two occasions I have to confess I did – there was great pressure from one's associates and colleagues next week to go in and say something else, because if you didn't there was nobody else to say it, while if you were one of 392 Tory MPs it was quite possible to just slink away and do nothing.'

David was not in the habit of slinking away and he could not afford the luxury of doing nothing. It was to take him many months, and much encouragement from his colleagues, before he mastered what he considered a ridiculously archaic ritual. When he did, it transformed his performance. In his first year in the House he asked just two oral questions. In his second he asked five, fifteen in his third, sixteen in his fourth, and so on. By the 1980s he had become a lethal master of the art.

It was not only over oral questions that David would be in trouble with the Speaker. The House has another tradition that at first flummoxed David. Being a gregarious person, he soon got to know a great number of the MPs in the other parties. Consequently, when in a debate he agreed with a point that one of them had made, David would find himself saying, 'I quite agree with my honourable Friend.' There would then be an outcry from every corner of the House; it would be pointed out to the honourable Member for Truro that he must not refer to members of other parties as 'Friends', however much he might agree with them. Officially he had only twelve Friends in the House.

Life at Westminster, he was discovering, despite the friendship of those twelve, could at times like these be peculiarly difficult and depressing. As he said sadly to Evelyn Hill, the one member of Liberal headquarters whom he knew well from the past, 'This is the most illogical place I have ever been in. Nothing happens in the way you think it should.'

While David was feeling lonely and irritated in London, I was feeling exactly the same back at home. In fact, the next twelve months were without doubt the worst period of our lives together – a period, in fact, when we were not so much together as apart. That was the trouble. David might be finding things difficult at Westminster but at least he was totally absorbed in his new role. I, for the first time since we had met, felt completely isolated. This was alien to me and I did not like it. Until now we had always worked together as a team, both as a family and for the Liberal Party. Now I seemed only to be involved in the social aspects of an MP's life. Indeed it felt as if the only time we were ever together was at some function or other.

David's week in Westminster would start from Monday morning, when he would usually catch the 9.10 train from Truro. Exceptionally, if he had to be at some urgent meeting, he would fly to and from Newquay. This was not always reliable and often delayed flights led to missed appointments and total frustration. On one occasion David set off from Newquay only to find the plane could not land at Heathrow because of weather conditions and it was redirected to Nottingham. That was bad enough but worse followed. As the coach bringing David back to Heathrow reached London, David asked to be let off as it was only a little distance to go to Westminster. This, he was told, was impossible, as the contract was to take all passengers to their airborne destination.

His Westminster week would usually end on Thursday, when he would hope to catch the night sleeper down to Cornwall. Once home, David would begin on the other end of his business responsibilities – dealing with local problems. That would take up Fridays and Saturdays. Fridays were the only days when he could visit the council offices, factories, schools and local businesses. These visits not only kept him in touch with how his constituents worked and lived but also gave him the chance to deal with the problems they raised in their letters. Friday evenings and Saturday mornings were crowded out with his 'surgeries', held both in Truro and St Austell. Then too on Saturdays there were the inevitable invitations to attend fairs and coffee mornings. Only Sundays were real family days.

Functions dominated our weekends. They always would, though we learnt to handle them more easily as we gained experience. It was not so easy for the children. A year or two later, when Matthew was being slow to finish his lunch, David said to him, 'Hurry up, son, we're going to a fête.' 'Ah,' was the resigned reply from a four-year-old Matthew. 'It must be Saturday.' It was nice to see David's dry humour coming out in Matthew.

To be an effective MP you have, of course, not only to be an affable opener of fêtes. You must also be exceptionally well organized. It is like running a business based on two different offices. A flood of letters would come in day after day, both to Westminster and home. At first David's secretarial work was undertaken in London but not for long. Mistakes were being made. David soon decided that on balance it would be more efficient if it were based in Cornwall, in our house, despite his absence all the week in Westminster. He also felt strongly that it would be more appropriate. He was MP for Truro and he was determined that his centre of gravity should remain in Cornwall. In this he was almost unique among MPs, nearly all of whom have secretaries at the House.

We appointed our first local secretary, Sheila Post, a member of the Party, and the pattern was set for the next twelve years. For most of this time Janet Bawden did the work. Janet, who was to become a close family friend as well as an excellent secretary, would in time see our equipment develop from simple typewriters to the computers and photocopiers that are now such a boon to MPs.

Inevitably, I soon became once more involved myself, as I took over some of the jobs for David, typing letters when necessary, keeping the diary and – probably most important of all – being the contact between David and his constituents as well as between him and the local Liberals.

Giving me the diary to keep was a very clever move on David's part. I had control of what events he attended and because I was often in personal contact with the organizations requesting David's attendance, the diary was always hectically busy. However, I then could not complain that he had little time left for us, as David would make a joke about it being my fault. David was of course a very funny man to live with. If I ever wanted a serious conversation it never lasted for long. He always got me laughing, however irritated I might be.

For the first time I was to learn that when it came to business, far from being a bit disorganized and untidy, which was the impression he tended to give – and certainly he never made any attempt to be organized around the house – David was meticulous. I suppose that as an engineer he had to be methodical and it was natural that he ran his office in the same style. David wanted a system which enabled anyone in the office to find a file at almost a moment's notice, so that if he rang us from London with a query on a constituent's casework we could produce it without keeping him waiting. It was Brian Tucker who came up with a fairly foolproof system which we operated without too many hiccups. The system we set up then, with only minor changes, survived the strains of what was to be a rapidly increasing workload over the next twelve years.

Even in his first year David soon found himself writing some forty-five letters a day to cope with his constituents' problems. He lived by dictaphone. He would send large envelopes of letters to us every day with the replies on tapes. We would send back the typed replies. Fortunately, there was only one occasion that I can remember when the system broke down. The tape fell out of an envelope *en route* and he had to start all over again. Once there was a lucky escape when I chased after the postman going down the road to find that a missing tape had fallen into his bag!

David's system might be meticulous but he himself kept highly eccentric hours in London. He had an office in what is called the Norman Shaw building, on the other side of Bridge Street from the Houses of Parliament. This he shared with Stephen Ross, who had won his seat in the Isle of Wight in May 1974. David usually arrived at his desk in the middle of the morning but that was hardly surprising as debates often went on into the early hours and he seldom got to bed before 1 am, and occasionally much later. He and Cyril would generally 'brew up' and discuss the day's events well into the early hours. When he reached the House, he would either go to work on one of the committees to put the Liberal view on the bill under discussion, or spend the rest of the morning personally sorting out his mail, dictating answers and signing those letters we had typed and sent up to him from Truro.

He lived on an endless supply of black sugarless coffee all morning and combined breakfast with lunch, which he generally ate in the members' dining room. Then it was time for him to take his seat in the chamber and see if he could catch the Speaker's eye and make a point on behalf of his Party or his constituency.

The hours of work at Westminster are of course quite crazy. Important debates would go on deep into the night. Those with their own flats in London would sometimes spend the evenings at home, emerging only for important votes. Many lived within a minute or two of the building and had their homes connected to the House of Commons division bell. Those who live close by can therefore reach the House in time to dash into the division lobbies in time to have their votes recorded.

Few of the Liberals lived that kind of life. Generally, they were not able to afford it and if if they were, they felt it their duty to cover every debate they could, not simply turn up for the vote. This was, of course, especially important for the Party spokesman on any subject. Tory or Labour members could always find experienced colleagues to cover a debate. The Liberals had only one spokesman on each subject and that spokesman had to be there. Anyway, it was often only late at night, when the numbers dwindled even further than usual, that backbenchers would have the chance to make the points they wanted.

As a result, the Liberals in general established phenomenal voting records and David was one of the best attenders. At the end of his first year in parliament, despite his inexperience, David had voted in 317 divisions, by far the most of any West Country MP. Only John Pardoe had asked more written questions. Even in oral questions David was ahead of most of the others.

David was proud of his voting record and he was amazed at how few of the other MPs seemed to take their duties as seriously. It was not simply that they did not stay up as late as he did – that was at least understandable – but they made very little effort to attend the House at any time unless dragooned into voting by their Whips. When asked for his first impressions by the local press, who had now begun to be very interested in their new MP, he put it bluntly: 'Out of a total of 635 MPs, except during Prime Minister's question time, there are rarely more than eleven members in the House.' He elaborated on this in his first report back in *News from the Liberals*. 'It appears that fewer than 250 members take an active part in the proceedings. I am still trying to discover what the other 385 do apart from turning up like toy soldiers to vote at the end of each debate.'

Despite their conscientious devotion to duty, the Liberals kept their sense of humour. They would have been lost without it. David would recall with relish one such occasion. John Pardoe rushed into the chamber in the early hours during the debate on the Scotland Bill. 'When's the amendment?' he asked. 'Which one?' asked David. 'You know, Number ZZ ZZZZ.' 'In about fifteen minutes, I think.' 'Right,' said John, 'I'll hang on and vote for that.' 'Ah, yes,' David said, 'It's desperately important. There won't be a person in Cornwall tomorrow morning that won't turn their radio on at eight o'clock to find out how you and I voted.' They didn't stay!

'I think there is a danger once you are Member of Parliament,' David explained, 'that you get desperately involved in these detailed debates about some piece of legislation that are interesting to you, perhaps in an intellectual way. Yet at home here in Cornwall who is interested in amendment ZZ ZZZZ to the Scotland Bill? You have got to be very careful not to get too sucked into it.'

One effect of the extraordinary hours of work at Westminster was that David ended each week so tired that he seemed always in danger of sleeping throughout the weekend. Sleep was important to David. He needed plenty of it and he was pretty good at it too! He could fall asleep anywhere, any time, on anything – and he did. If David had a spare hour or two between engagements on a busy day he would lie down on the settee in the sitting room and go to sleep.

It was a fantastic gift to be so relaxed and an hour's rest often made all the difference as the day went on. It was, however, probably one of the least endearing of his habits from my point of view. I found it most irritating that when my part-time husband was actually at home I still could not tell him what the children were up to or nag him to cut the grass – perhaps that is why he slept! But even more annoying was David's total unconcern for the shirt and suit he was sleeping in, or the fact that he often did not bother to remove his shoes!

Whilst David was going to and from London, my own life, over a considerably shorter distance, was proving equally nomadic. We had received planning permission for the extension , work had begun, our home was in store and I was living with my parents. The result was that all David's office work at this stage was being conducted from my long-suffering mother's dining room. Meanwhile I was travelling back and forth from Truro to Chacewater once and more often twice a day.

Although Connie Reed was totally reliable, she was still working only part-time, so my time was divided between doing my stint in the post office and helping David with his casework. One of the advantages of living with my parents at this time was that we had built-in baby sitters, both at weekends when I could accompany David to local events and during the week when I worked closely with Malcolm Brown and the rest of the constituency.

As the months went by, David and I found ourselves beginning to work together again. It would take over a year before we would be working as closely as we had always done in the past but my feelings of isolation were beginning to subside. Then the late spring of 1975 saw us all, office included, moving back to a greatly improved home.

Matthew was by this time a lively three-year-old and he and David were very close. Whenever possible David would take Matthew with him, always saying, 'Come on, boy,' as they went through the door. One of David's favourite places to visit when time allowed was still Kenwyn Hill Garage, although sadly by this time his father had died.

Charles Penhaligon had been a very proud father indeed

when his son won the Truro seat. However, even though two hip operations had been successful and he was soon getting around as well as he had for some time, he was taken ill with a kidney complaint from which he never recovered. David was always grateful that his father did at least manage to get to London to see his son in parliament.

It was the day after my father-in-law's death that I realized how demanding some constituents can be. I remember receiving a telephone call from someone who wanted David to call to discuss a problem. I explained that he was not in as his father had died just the day before. 'Oh, I know that,' said the constituent. 'I read it in the paper and that's how I knew he must be at home.' We really were public property!

9
RADICAL SPOKESMAN

'David would be so funny about things, yet strangely it is very difficult to recall any particular jokes. Perhaps it was because he always used a joke to make a much more serious point, and what you recall is the point and not the joke. He was of course a deeply serious politician.' – Evelyn Hill

'When I arrived at Westminster,' David was to say, 'I didn't know anything of how the procedure went but I had a lot things I wanted to say.' He had indeed. He had all those points that he had explored in the first numbers of *News from the Liberals*. Now he began to pursue them, one by one, in parliament itself.

With uncanny premonition, his first subject back in 1971 had been the problems that should be, and so seldom were, dealt with by the Department of Health and Social Services. He might not have the power to solve all those problems but now that he was Liberal spokesman on the subject he could at least do what he could by making sure that they would be aired. However, although David soon began to make his mark as an authority on social services, he was determined to follow up on the other subjects that he had raised in *News from the Liberals*: the environment, the economy and regionalism. He soon found it would be peculiarly difficult to pursue the first of these. He had raised it in Truro as early as the summer of 1972, under the title 'We have only one world; let's look after it'. Now it seems so familiar a concept that no one would do other than nod agreement. Not so then.

Nearly all major debates in parliament are instigated by the government of the day or the official opposition. Neither the Labour nor the Tory Party was much concerned with the environment. David had to make his points as and when he could. There was a discussion on lead in petrol in 1976, in which he infuriated his Tory opponents by refusing to accept that a drop from 98 to 90 octane would produce anything more disastrous than a small reduction in the efficiency of their cars. He then went on to suggest that MPs should not be paid so much per mile for using them. They should use the railway.

'A great deal of driving is done just to make a profit out of mileage expenses. Every honourable Member knows that — although it is obvious that no one will have the courage to admit it. If my honourable Friend the Member for Orkney and Shetland [Jo Grimond] had a bridge at the end of his journey from London he could solve the Liberal Party's financial problems in two or three trips.' (Jo, whose inspirational leadership of the Party had first attracted us in 1964, had now become more than a guru to David. He was a friend as well and was happy to give David support in debates such as this.)

The only major parliamentary debate in the 1970s that involved substantial environmental issues concerned nuclear power and there the debate was not so much on environmental questions as on whether the government should assume that nuclear power would supply fifty per cent of our power by the 1980s, or possibly a little less. David intervened, poured scorn on such a forecast and then suggested that there might be reasons for concern over relying on nuclear power at all.

David and Alan Beith were nicknamed the 'brown bread and sandals brigade' because of their criticisms of nuclear power – somewhat inappropriately. In fact, then, as so often later, David concentrated on scientific facts. He was one of only a handful of engineers in the House and he repeatedly made a point of deploring the shortage of engineers in parliament and in the country as a whole. Although his expertise gained him a grudging respect for some of his opponents, others accused him bitterly of spreading unnecessary alarm. His warnings and their comments are worth recalling in our post-Chernobyl world.

'In the next ten or fifteen years,' he said in 1975, 'without doubt there will be an accident involving nuclear power'.

'The honourable gentleman carries a tremendous responsibility in creating anxieties of this sort,' he was told. 'What he should now be doing is placing his confidence in the industry and giving some reassurance to the people who are living near nuclear installations so that they do not have the sort of fears that he has expressed.'

'Unfortunately,' he retorted, 'dangers do not disappear by not talking about them.'

As the Liberal Party had far too little money to employ researchers to brief their spokesmen on the finer points of issues such as this, the MPs were very dependent on their own expertise and that of any other interested parties. It was here that Evelyn Hill was to be of the greatest help to David. Ever since the days when she had first kept him supplied with the books and pamphlets he had needed as a young activist, she had followed his career with interest. Although her job in the Liberal Publications Department did not involve supplying the MPs with briefing papers, she did know what publications could be of value and what people and organizations could be useful too. She now introduced David to Friends of the Earth and other pressure groups who were happy to supply him with ammunition.

'He then went quietly into the subject – from both points of view,' Evelyn recalls. 'I know he also talked at great length to the CEGB as well. He then decided for himself. That was the way he always worked.'

He was selective over what he used – his scientific training helped him sort out the really useful material – and he then presented it in his own personal way. 'I am by training an engineer. Experience of running a research department, dealing with something very different from nuclear power, has convinced me that one is always tripped up by the unknown . . . Fifty per cent of Europe's power by 1985 is a quite ludicrous target – one which we shall not achieve and to achieve which we may take real risks with the community in which we live, risks that are not acceptable.'

'If the honourable gentleman walks across the road he takes a greater risk than if he stands outside a nuclear power station,' he was told.

The prospect of taking fifty per cent of our power from nuclear power stations was duly abandoned by 1977 but by then there was a new vision for the government to pursue – that Britain in general, and Windscale in particular, should become the reprocessing centre of Western world. David thought it crazy, coined the image of the UK becoming the nuclear rubbish dump of Europe and, Cassandra-like, he once again stressed the risks. Desperately he resorted to the use of the 'adjournment debate' procedure, under which a backbencher can raise a matter and force a reply out of the minister, often in an empty house at the very end of another debate. David rose at 6.27 a.m. He set on record all his own and his supporters' arguments. Then he concluded: 'I still think that in fifty years from now our main source of energy will be the sun and not nuclear energy.'

Then in March 1977 he moved an amendment that the government should not commit public money to build a reprocessing plant at Windscale before the results of the public enquiry on the project were reported. The minister and parliament were not to be moved. The amendment was lost.

Later that summer the minister responded to David's further warnings with this: 'The chances of a nuclear accident involving 100 deaths in a country with 100 nuclear power stations is about once in 100,000 years, according to a Massachusetts Institute of Technology report.'

The following April David was invited along with Leo Abse to address a demonstration in Trafalgar Square – the first time he was to speak on a major public issue on a joint platform in London. There were 10,000 there to hear him put across in public the points he had been driving home in parliament.

The last of this long series of debates in which David had mounted a formidable challenge almost single-handed against both the Labour and the Tory opposition culminated in an unsuccessful Liberal motion that the Windscale development order should be withdrawn until more information had been secured on safety procedures. David Steel moved it but it had been David Penhaligon who had persuaded his colleagues that this must be their cause.

It was good to see at the first Social and Liberal Democrats Conference, just a decade after those debates, that David's friends and colleagues chose as one of their major concerns the cause he championed and pursued in parliament over his first years there in the face of such real hostility and prejudice.

In the spring of 1975 David was very much involved in the 'Say Yes to Europe' campaign prior to the June referendum. It was during this campaign that David got stopped by a man who asked: "ere, are you Penhaligon?' 'That's me,' said David. 'Well,' said the man, 'I vote for you.' 'Thanks,' replied David. The man continued, 'Nice to meet you. I've meaning to find out for some time, are 'ee Labour, Conservative or Liberal?' I am not sure if David took that as a compliment or not.

Another story that he loved to tell of that campaign was of an encounter he had with an elderly gentleman in one of the little hamlets in the constituency. The conversation went something like this. "ere David. You want me to vote Yes to go into this 'ere Europe?' 'That's right,' said David. 'All right, boy,' replied the old man, 'but can you answer me this. Where is this 'ere Europe?'

David had recently made two trips himself to 'this 'ere Europe' to study working conditions in the EEC, one to Germany before he left Holman's and the other to Brussels on a parliamentary mission. Once the country had said 'Yes', David was on his feet in parliament singing the praises of the works councils he had seen. It was to involve him for the first time in the whole range of parliamentary industrial and financial debates, on matters which would eventually become his main preoccupation in the House.

In the third of the major themes he had pursued in *News from the Liberals* David had linked the Liberals' call for price and wage regulation with the need for profit-sharing and works councils. As he once said on radio, 'People who work in enterprises give their skills, whatever they are, whether they be a PhD, whether they be an ability to sweep a floor, yet it is generally considered irrational in this nation if you suggest that they have a right to some of the profits of their labour. It is thought to be in some way a revolutionary concept. Perhaps it is revolutionary, but I think it is the one we have got to move towards.' It was not surprising then that he soon found himself very much involved in the relevant parliamentary debates.

In an effort to introduce a 'genuine development of democracy in the workplace', he proposed an amendment to the Industries Bill which would require the setting up of 'works councils properly constituted and elected by all employees', such as those in West Germany, Scandinavia and Holland.

Ian Mikardo said that he had been in Germany and seen how ineffective the *mitbestimmungsrechts* were there. David promptly replied that he too had been to Germany to study them. He contradicted Mikardo bluntly on the picture he had given, though he graciously conceded that Mikardo's pronunciation was far better than he could manage: 'I have substantial difficulty with the language,' he said, 'but then I have substantial difficulties with the English language too.'

His parliamentary colleagues appreciated such self-deprecating humour considerably more that they did some of his more scathing attacks, especially those on the anomalies of taxation, where he showed no difficulties with language at all. He took up the cause of the self-employed.

'Like other honourable Members, I have regular surgeries in my constituency. Occasionally I am asked not "Did you support this?" but "Can you explain why the government did it?" I feel that I ought to rally round my colleagues in parliament and at least try to explain the logic of the government's decisions, even though I may have voted against them.

'For instance, a self-employed man with the enormous income of £31 a week pays thirty-five percent income tax on his marginal pay and an additional eight per cent in national insurance contributions. If he succeeds in increasing his profit by £1 per week – not exactly a large sum – the government require 43p of that for their coffers. I have no wish to defend that situation and I find it difficult to explain to my constituents.

'If the same man increases his income to £90 per week, which is at least a reasonable income, his level of taxation *drops*. In explaining the reasoning behind this to my constituents, I do not defend my parliamentary colleagues with the enthusiasm that an honourable Member perhaps should. I describe it as one of the idiocies of the legislation we pass.'

The 1974/79 Parliament was dogged by the problems of inflation and it was eventually to bring the government, as its majority wasted away, to look to the Liberals for support. The Liberals had for long been appalled by the effects of inflation and had fought the previous election on an unpopular prices and income policy. 'The only way to stop inflation,' David now told the Commons, 'is to reduce living standards. My Party was foolish enough to tell this to people in October 1974 – and perhaps that is why there are only thirteen Liberal members.'

On inflation, David made his point with humour – and his calculator. 'I once tried to work out what the national average wage would be on the day that I retired if the then current rate of inflation – about twenty-three per cent – was maintained . . . It would be just over £2 million a year. But before anyone gets excited by the idea, I should point out that, according to my calculations, a loaf of bread would be £150.'

Mockery was his usual weapon in such cases but occasionally the anger would show through. One of the myths about David was that he was always happy to see the funny side of things. He could see it – far better than most – but the anger and desperate indignation could not always be disguised. Parliament saw it – the more effective for being so often disguised on other occasions beneath the mockery and jokes. It would be especially marked in his defence of his own constituency, as on the appalling effects on Cornwall in the 1970s of the grant of tax relief on mortgages for second homes.

'The economy of my county has been wrecked by the tax relief on mortgage interest. How can a Cornishman earning £40 a week who wishes to buy a house in Mevagissey, Pentewan, Porthtowan, Perranporth, St Mawes or anywhere in my constituency compete with a man who already owns one house and, when he comes down from Birmingham to buy property in Cornwall, gets a government subsidy of up to eighty-five per cent on the interest on his mortgage for the Cornish property? Of course, good Cornishmen cannot compete. A flood of good housing in my constituency has gone to people who have no need of it, and this is one of the scandals of our age.'

It was a scandal that David was to return to again and

again, as he saw more and more of his constituents forced to leave their own county. Cornwall has had for years problems over the purchase of its houses by incomers. Prices have risen so sharply over the last fifteen years that young Cornishmen have no chance of finding houses that they can afford, especially as the Cornish wage levels are far below those elsewhere in Britain. This inevitably breeds resentment.

This resentment is directed not so much at those who choose to move home to Cornwall – after all we can understand why they want to come here – but against those who buy up houses that have traditionally been let all year round to local families, then use them only as holiday homes or, worse, let them at huge profits on short summer lets and leave them empty for the rest of the year. David had stressed this problem in his maiden speech and would doggedly return to it time after time.

He argued that at the very least these people should not receive domestic relief on their rates, as they were running a business. He was told it would be too difficult to administer. The loss of rates went on and so – far more importantly – did the loss of houses that the Cornish could afford.

David's early speeches on industry and economics were significant as much for their style as their content, in that he had deliberately made his general point by stressing what was happening in his own constituency. In those early days in parliament David found that he had, and would always have, two peculiarly difficult roles to play. He was, partly as spokesman for his Party and partly because of his own interests, committed to pursuing matters of essential importance to the country as a whole. At the same time he was

MP for Truro. Of the two, he knew that the latter was the more important, because if he did not look after Truro's interests no one else would. Yet he was determined to find time for all his responsibilities.

The solution he would adopt was, wherever possible, to merge the issues into one. When pursuing points of national concern he would illustrate them with problems that were of concern in Cornwall. When there was some particular Cornish issue that he must pursue, he would draw attention to the national implications. When he first took up the cudgels against the government's plan to expand the nuclear power industry, there was no specific threat to Cornwall – that would come later. However, on the other issues that most concerned him during his first years in parliament there was the closest connection between the plight of Cornwall and the plight of the rest of the country. The UK was just Cornwall writ large.

Nowhere was this more apparent than in the case of the government's attitude to the fourth of the themes from *News from the Liberals* – that of regionalism. David was always most careful over how he expressed his commitment to this cause in Cornwall. He did not want an independent state of Cornwall – that was 'cloud-cuckoo land'. All that was needed – and it was urgently needed, he believed – was that Cornwall should control those matters about which Cornish people knew more than the civil servants in Whitehall. The rest should be left to parliament, and quite rightly so.

What angered him especially was a bastardized form of regionalism that had that been forced on the south-west. This was rule by unelected boards. These boards had responsibility for so large an area that they were even less well-informed than the Whitehall mandarins. The government had lumped Gloucester, Wiltshire, Somerset, Devon and Cornwall all into one area, the top end of which, David pointed out, was closer to the Scottish border than to Land's End. What was more, the headquarters of most of the regional bodies were established in Bristol, which, much to the irritation of Bristolians, he described as 'that well-known Midlands suburb'.

He instanced the effect of amalgamating all the water boards. 'Once there were eighty-five water boards and they all employed people in their own patches. They went to local solicitors because they did not employ any. They also went to local plumbers and so on. Those jobs have now been taken from Cornwall.'

Another of these authorities was called the South-West Economic Planning Council. David was all for economic planning and was for ever trying to push his local county council into doing more to attract business to Cornwall, pointing out that its £3,000 advertising budget was a pathetic response to the problems of an area where the unemployment figures were among the worst in the country. He was told that they had not the funds to do what they would like.

The SWEPC was even worse, however, as it was not an elected body and no one seemed to have any power over it, or could get it to do anything. Certainly David could not. 'I regard this as one of the most ludicrous bodies ever to be set up,' he told the Commons. 'One of the two reports that the Council has produced recently said that in the Council's opinion second homes and what are locally known as "summer lets" have no bad effect in Cornwall. I wish that one or two of the people who wrote the report would come to my "surgeries" to see whether they had any effect.'

It was not only the SWEPC's attitude to summer lets that angered David. A theme to which he was to return again and again was that it encouraged a national tendency which he described as the concentration of brain and decentralization of brawn. He protested at the removal of all teaching training from Cornwall. He checked on the number of day-release students in the south-west. 'The figure in Gloucester was 60, in Cheltenham 69, in Bath 149 – an extraordinary figure – in Plymouth 69, and in Bristol 58. In Cornwall the figure was only 6.'

'There is only one hope,' he said, 'for regions such as mine – namely quick and powerful decentralization of government.'

10
CONSTITUENCY MP

'*Each Liberal constituency was a personal fiefdom, so to speak, and every Liberal MP depended on his ability to do an enormous amount of constituency work, much more than the average MP. Success in politics depends to a degree on the capacity to do a lot of work, and the capacity to grow in the job, learning not to take the immediate view but the long-term view. David had both. He never appeared over-extended in any way by the various burdens that were shoved on him.*' – Emlyn Hooson

As MP, David had, of course, to cope with the problems of every one of his constituents, regardless of their politics. In fact, he had made a particular point of stressing this responsibility when, directly after his election, he addressed the crowds below from a window in the municipal buildings. That commitment he carried out to the letter for the rest of his life.

Still, he was not likely to forget that among those crowds below were the friends who had worked their hearts and shoe leather out to get him elected. He had a commitment to them too, but a different one. It was to get straight back to work with them to make sure that other Liberal candidates, both in and out of the constituency, got elected too.

The Truro Constituency Liberal Association itself now had a new status. It had to adapt to supporting its own MP and all the responsibilities that went with it. In this they did us proud. The enthusiasm remained intact, although there was considerable work to be done in maintaining and building up new branches to ensure that the constituency remained Liberal. I suppose having a majority of just 464 helped, in that members could see only too clearly the need to build on it. Any inactivity would see the seat slip through our fingers.

The association's branches were to be the lifeline between David and many of his constituents, and they immediately set about organizing events to which the public were invited. This had a twofold advantage. First, it introduced David to more and more people, showing them how 'ordinary' and down-to-earth their new MP really was. This built up a relationship between David and the communities which was to continue for the rest of his career. Secondly, these events raised money to run the Liberal organization.

This was absolutely vital, as despite all the enthusiasm at the end of the election campaign, there was pathetically little organization, no premises and no cash. That was hardly new, of course. There had never been any organizational infrastructure in Truro, only energy. Seats, David knew, can be won on such surges of enthusiasm but they can seldom be held. Constituents expect efficient action not only from the MP but also from the members of his Party. At the very least, they expect their MP to have some base and supporting staff for his weekly surgeries.

To the immense credit of our exhausted members, space was found for David's surgeries, both in Truro and St Austell. For our headquarters, we rented two rooms above a shop in Duke Street in Truro, which also held our printing press. In addition we rented rooms in St Austell as and when David and the councillors required it for surgeries.

Staffing was a bigger problem. Brian Tucker, to whom much of the credit for victory was due, was far less happy as a 'peacetime' agent. He was to leave us within eighteen months but we would often meet again at by-elections all round the country. Brian could never resist the smell of battle.

We never really mastered the art of employing an agent. The chief problem was that the agent had to spend nearly all his time earning his salary through fund-raising, as the association could never pay it otherwise. This was a self-defeating situation. It exhausted the agent, who could not attend to his real job of building up the association, and irritated the volunteers, who felt they were working just as hard for no pay. After Brian left, we made one more effort and employed Philip Lotan as agent for a time but, gallantly though he tried, it did not work. In the end, we decided to depend entirely on volunteers, with Malcolm acting as agent for General Elections. It has worked but it does demand exceptional commitment from a large number of people.

In 1975, we had the unnerving experience of failing for the first time to win a council by-election. We had begun our assault on the local councils in 1971 cautiously, fighting only those seats where we would not be threatening to displace some well-respected 'independent' councillor. Now, however, the old town councils had lost most of their powers to the two new, much larger councils of Carrick and Restormel, where there needed to be no such reservations. If we were really going to introduce these councils to the kind of open government we believed in, we had to get more seats quickly and risk a defeat or two. We risked defeat, and we suffered it. It hurt when we failed but it was something we had to get used to now and then. We could not afford to wait and see.

As always, there were leaflets to deliver, above all the *News from the Liberals*, which by now was going out to every corner of the constituency. There were even separate editions for those in the Carrick Council area (the western half) and those in the Restormel area (the eastern half around St Austell). Now that David was MP, he and Malcolm soon found they needed to use nearly all the space available for him to report back from parliament, so the councillors had their own letters which went out at the same time.

Just as the first issue back in 1972 had been on the rights of pensioners, so within a year of David's election he was stressing once again the needs of pensioners. David by then had already made his protest over the loss of the Christmas bonus and was trying to persuade the government to increase pensions over the winter months because those months were invariably more expensive and more dangerous for the elderly. As the government was refusing to recognize the need, he and Cyril Smith were running a nationwide campaign to alert everyone to the dangers of hypothermia and the need to keep an eye on themselves and their neighbours. That Christmas David devoted almost all his space in *News from the Liberals* to the campaign.

There were of course other campaigns for the association to run as well. We might have David as MP but that did not mean that we would no longer have petitions, surveys and marches when things went wrong. In fact, the need was all the greater. David needed evidence if he was to present the constituency's case effectively in parliament and often the evidence could only be gathered by our members – evidence of what was wrong, evidence of how people felt. David, for instance, despite his commitment to the European ideal, was appalled at the mismanagement of the Common Agricultural Policy. Within a month of his visit to Brussels he was handing in to parliament a petition we had launched demanding reforms of the CAP.

Decisions on road improvements – and the lack of them – also caused trouble. A constant source of irritation was the formula used to decide whether or not a village could have a pedestrian crossing. 'It is not Carrick or Restormel Council, nor the county council,' he had to explain to his constituents, 'that stipulated that the number of cars per hour multiplied by the square of the number of people crossing per hour must exceed 100 million, and that a road should be straight for at least 110 yards in each direction before a pedestrian crossing can be provided; it's Whitehall. And, mind you, they don't count those who chicken out half way across, nor those that never make it. And where in Cornwall can you find roads that are straight for a whole 220 yards?'

The idiocy of this formula may have been a source of irritation for David but it was also the source of one of his funniest speeches – John Pardoe says that it was without doubt the funniest speech he ever heard from a public platform. I can so easily picture David delivering it. David was a very visual speaker and he needed considerable room in which to deliver a speech. He would walk so many feet in one direction, turn and walk in the opposite direction, arms pointing and articulating all at the same time.

At after-dinner speeches people who knew him moved

to allow David a larger stage on which to perform. Unfortunately at one luncheon out of the county, where understandably the lady mayor was unaware of David's idiosyncrasy, she came within a hair's-breadth of losing her hat. I am not sure if she noticed or not but the audience certainly did.

On one occasion the dangers caused by traffic got to such a pitch that David brought the problem himself to parliament to illustrate how appallingly inefficient the present system of making vital decisions was. Here his mood moved from mockery to real anger. 'Road improvements have been carried out at a village in my constituency called Mitchell, which nobody here has ever heard of. To the south we have a very wide road . . . There are the inevitable lights – wherever a road is improved, the government's good work has to be illuminated. But I have been unable to have one street light provided for Mitchell itself, that the villagers may dodge the inevitable flow of traffic. I have written to the responsible body in Exeter, which keeps telling me that Mitchell's accident record is not bad enough. It is saying the death of one person was not a big enough sacrifice. If only I could find another volunteer we should probably get street lights.'

David was also very conscious of how many of his constituents were acutely affected by the cost of petrol. Because many of the villages have no public transport, cars are a necessity rather than a luxury in Cornwall. He quoted a case of one constituent who had decided to go on the dole because the cost of travelling to his job now exceeded the difference between his pay and what he would receive from the dole. He proposed, without success, that where there was no public transport the cost of travel should be tax deductible.

Public transport has, of course, always been a matter of special concern in Cornwall, where both buses and railways are inevitably essential to the lives of people, many of whom will never be able to afford a car. Sadly, and equally inevitably, they are unprofitable except in the summer. David discovered that the local bus services were losing money on eighty-six out of the eighty-nine routes. What was worse, the system was already quite inadequate. The policy of closing schools, which meant concentrating education in fewer and fewer places, had already exposed this inadequacy. The county was spending £1 million a year on school transport.

The county council told David that government would not allow them to divert money from their roads budget to help the buses, essential though they obviously were. David then pressed the government to subsidize the cost of bus passes to OAPs, as the local councils could not afford them.

With all these suggestions, so many of which were rejected at the time only to be adopted later, David's chief aim was to highlight what was essential and try to alter the government's order of priorities. He found that central government was happy to spend money lavishly on projects where alternative cheap solutions would do. That money, he pointed out, could have been better used elsewhere.

To illustrate the point, David explained to his fellow MPs that a new unit of currency was now current in Cornwall – yards-of-the-Camborne-bypass. This had been invented by Dr Terry Thorneycroft, who became a close friend and mentor to David, and one of the few people David relied on for advice on economic matters, especially where they related to Cornwall. It appealed to David very much as he quickly saw it as a way of expressing vast sums of money so that everyone could understand its significance.

The Camborne bypass, built to solve what were certainly

irritating traffic jams in Camborne, was made to the highest standards, with the usual display of brilliant lights. It was magnificent but as Camborne is scarcely twenty-five miles from Land's End, no one could see where all the cars were going to go. It cost £5 million. Something much more modest would have done.

'In 1973/74,' said David, 'we managed to spend on building hospitals in Cornwall – which was probably one of the worst health facility records in the country – 1,400 yards-of-the-Camborne-bypass. There is talk of abolishing the whole railway structure in Cornwall, which admittedly loses £500,000 a year. For the cost of the Camborne bypass we could keep the railway line for ten years, and if we were allowed to invest the £5 million, we could keep it going for ever.' It was simply a matter of priorities, he said, and of allowing the Cornish to use such money where they knew it was needed.

At the same time he found himself leading a campaign in the constituency against what promised to be an appalling rate increase in 1975. He was out to persuade the government to restore the special rate relief previously given to Cornwall, in view of its peculiar problems – exceptionally low wages, combined with a fluctuation in the population from 400,000 in winter to three million in the summer. David organized a petition in support, but without effect on the government. (David had even then, well before the Layfield report, reached the same conclusion as Layfield would. He was pressing for a change from rates to local income tax – the solution now favoured by the Social and Liberal Democrats.)

On this campaign David combined forces with the Tory MP for Bodmin, Robert Hicks. David's willingness to work with other Cornish MPs, regardless of their political persuasion, was typical of his view of politics. He was a Liberal, could never be anything else, but he recognized that on some matters members of the other parties either agreed with him or had good ideas that were worth backing. David was always especially happy to work with Robert on any issue that might benefit Cornwall. They used to travel up and down together on the train each week and in time they became good friends – except of course at General Elections, when David would do everything he could to help Paul regain Bodmin.

He and John Pardoe joined with other West country MPs to protest at the removal of the fuel subsidy for horticultural glasshouses and David fought side by side with the Cornish Tory MPs, John Nott and David Mudd, to help the self-employed. Another major issue, on which all the Cornish MPs saw eye to eye, was the threat to the mackerel fishermen in Cornwall.

David summed up that threat in *News from the Liberals*, early in 1976. 'Mackerel, I've always loved 'em,' was his memorable opening. 'The trouble is that the English don't, and so very little is sold in Britain. However, the local fishermen have built up a substantial European market by hard work and by exploiting the Roscoff ferry. But the problems off Iceland have meant that fewer British boats go there, and in another traditional fishing area suicidal exploitation has virtually finished off the herring stocks. So these boats have come to Cornwall and flooded the carefully nurtured European market. Bankruptcy for the Cornish fishermen is inevitable within a few years unless something is done. We must ban seining nets and create a twelve-mile limit for locally based fishermen.'

This problem began with Scottish fishermen taking the Cornish mackerel, and taking them in nets rather than by line, but it soon escalated when Russian factory ships, expert in reducing fish into petfood and the like, anchored off the coast and bought whatever fishermen could catch. The Cornish fishing grounds were not simply being over-fished. They were being totally cleared of any marine life whatsoever.

David and the other local MPs did what they could. As early as December 1975 David was reporting to the Commons that 'a local fisherman in my constituency said only recently that "the only place left for me to fish is up the High Street"'. In March 1977, he asked in one of a series of oral questions he put to the government, 'Is it not time the House recognized that man's ability to catch fish now outstrips the fishes' technical ability to reproduce themselves? Will anything short of banning some of the modern methods save our fishing industries?' The minister was sympathetic but took no action.

In January 1978 he aroused the fury of Scottish MPs by asking if the minister was aware that 'Scottish purse seiners and fishing boats are supplying twelve Soviet bloc factory ships in the Port of Falmouth with 600 tons of mackerel a day.' The minister said he was aware but could only recommend self-denial. By the end of 1978, David was asking the Prime Minister to intervene, and followed that up with explaining the whole problem in an adjournment debate. Though his persistence would eventually reap its reward, at that time David was disappointed at the lack of action. 'The British never seem to get worried over fish conservation,' he would say, 'until there only two left – and one of those is generally in a museum.'

However, despite David's willingness to work with the neighbouring Tory MPs, it would be foolish to pretend that the 'greatly loved by all' image portrayed at his death was true of the first few years as an MP. He was not easily forgiven for taking the seat from the Tories – something most Tory activists had thought impossible. (I felt sorry for the poor Conservative agent for the constituency at the time, John Farndon, who has sadly since then died. He was a really nice man and I always enjoyed his company. However, the poor fellow had been agent in Orpington when Eric Lubbock won the by-election for the Liberals; then he suffered a similar humiliation in Truro.)

It was some time before David was invited to many of the functions we took for granted much later on. He was clearly seen by many of the establishment as a bumptious upstart with a common accent. More than once I was telephoned just days prior to a royal visit to the constituency to say that Buckingham Palace had said the Member of Parliament for Truro should be invited to such and such an event. Clearly the invitations had gone out to everyone else some time before and Buckingham Palace had noticed the omission.

I have to admit to getting some perverse enjoyment out of such occasions, and certainly none of this worried David in the least. All that he was concerned with was getting his job done well. That is what would get him re-elected, not invitations to cocktail parties.

Invitations at that time were coming in from further afield, however – not to cocktail parties but to Liberal functions. David was then of course an unknown quantity to most associations. He was the man who had produced our only gain of the last election, to most people's surprise, and they were intrigued to hear how it had been done.

An invitation to the Welsh Liberal Conference was typical. Emlyn Hooson, who was leader of the Welsh Liberal Party at that time, had liked what he had seen of David in parliament and asked him to speak at Llandudno. As Emlyn had expected, the Welsh were obviously delighted to find that a fellow Celt had won against the trend and that he sounded Celtic too. What he had not expected was that his brand of speaking would prove such a hit. At the annual dinner, the other guest, Michael Winstanley, one of the wittiest and most experienced of Liberal speakers, kindly suggested that the younger speaker might like to speak first. 'Michael was in my view the best after-dinner speaker in England and Wales,' said Emlyn, 'but in the end for the only time in my life I saw him struggling. The audience were completely unused to David and Michael had a devil of a job to follow him. David was totally different from anything they had heard before.'

11

LIB/LAB

'David was an instinctive Liberal of the old school.' – David
Steel

At the time, David's first year in parliament had seemed to
both of us not just the most extraordinary year we had ever
spent but surely the most extraordinary year we should ever
spend. We had to cope with so many changes all at once. We
had suddenly found ourselves living apart from each other
for most of the time. David had become a celebrity
overnight – 'the country boy with the funny accent' sent by
his own people to speak for them in the supreme court of the
land, the only Liberal new boy in parliament, a party
spokesman from his first day there. I had been left behind to
manage the post office and Matthew entirely on my own.
There would obviously be other changes to cope with in the
future but surely not so many all at once. How wrong we
were.

There is an old Irish proverb: 'May you not live in
interesting times.' Over the next three years we lived in very
interesting times – and, to be honest, on the whole we
enjoyed the challenge they brought. We were to see, and be
deeply involved in, dramas that could have totally destroyed

the Liberal Party but were in the end to leave it in some ways even stronger than it had been for the last fifty years.

The Liberals were first to struggle through a year in which they had three different leaders, one of them destroyed by scandal, the second brought back from retirement and the third chosen by the first public election among the members of his party of any political leader in the history of the country. The Liberals were then to find themselves participating in government for the first time in my lifetime, with David at the age of thirty-three, and after just two years in parliament, responsible for arguing the Liberal case not just with one but four different cabinet ministers. Then we had to return to our electorate and seek their approval for all this, with a majority of only 464 to defend.

For most Liberals, 1976 will always be remembered as the year of the Thorpe revelations. Once the press had released the story on which they had sat for so long, it seemed it would never go away. In a sense it never did. Certainly it returned with a vengeance in 1978 with the rumours of a murder plot, and in 1979 when the court case itself hogged the headlines for weeks. Yet it was in 1976 that the Thorpe affair had its greatest effect, as it then enforced a change in the Liberal leadership and set in train the ultimately far more significant drama of the Lib/Lab pact.

What was quite extraordinary, however, was how little the Thorpe story affected political life in Truro. All the Liberals were of course both amazed and deeply concerned as they watched the national press lavish more column inches on Jeremy in the next three years than they had given the whole Liberal Party in the previous three decades. Yet, as for the rest of Truro, the Liberals and David were praised or criticized exactly as before, on the strength of what they did or did not do for the constituency.

Truro was not alone in this. John Pardoe, whose North Cornwall constituency bordered Jeremy's North Devon, was to lose his seat, as did Jeremy, in 1979. Some pundits claimed that he was then a victim of an anti-Thorpe swing in the south-west. John has never agreed. Over the years he hardly ever found the Thorpe scandal mentioned on the doorstep and is convinced that he was simply a victim of a pro-Tory swing at the end of the Lib/Lab pact.

The public as ever were far more intelligent than the pundits allowed. They had what they saw as political grounds for voting as they did. The scandal surrounding a single MP, however prominent he may have been, was not a major factor in how they cast their votes. As John pointed out, Methodists may be against drink on principle but are liberal by instinct and more broad-minded than most on matters of private behaviour.

David was to come to share John's assessment of the situation, though fortunately not his electoral fate in 1979. (There were, as we shall see, factors that made the two seats very different at that election.) At the time, however, he was most concerned over the appalling effect it had on Liberal publicity. It was not that every Liberal candidate and MP was suddenly assumed to be involved in homosexual practices; no one thought that. It was simply that the Thorpe story swamped every message that the Party tried to put out nationally. All the press wanted to know from Liberals was what they thought of the Thorpe affair. David deeply resented this and, however much he sympathized with Jeremy and his family personally, he was never to forgive Jeremy for harming the Party in this way.

Although the senior members of the parliamentary party had known of rumours about Norman Scott back in 1971 – and indeed had looked at the evidence and found it wanting – David knew nothing of the stories until they first appeared in the press in January 1976. For all of us the very suggestion that Jeremy had had a homosexual affair with Scott seemed ridiculous. We assumed that a sharp denial would kill the story stone dead. However, the story refused to die.

From then on, David was to be kept in day-by-day touch with events as they unfolded – not as others did around the bars of the capital but, as so often was to be the case in other crises, over Cyril Smith's teapot in the National Liberal Club; for Cyril was now Chief Whip. David Steel had been appointed Liberal spokesman on foreign affairs in the summer of 1975 and was also Liberal representative on the all-party campaign for Europe. The MPs had indicated to Jeremy that they wanted Cyril to take over the Whip's job from David Steel but Jeremy had delayed making the appointment until he was virtually blackmailed with the threat that they would appoint him themselves.

It was not that Jeremy and Cyril did not like each other. They did. However, they had totally opposite views on how to campaign for Liberalism. Cyril, for instance, was all for the MPs going to the opening of parliament in T-shirts marked with 'Electoral Reform Now'. Jeremy most emphatically was not. Still, they worked together happily enough, except that Jeremy never told Cyril what he was going to do next. This turned out to be a fatal flaw when the Norman Scott affair first broke.

Cyril, as Chief Whip, was expected to brief the press. For the next few weeks, until he himself had to resign on health grounds, Cyril spent his days fielding questions to which he often did not know the answers and spent the early hours of the morning discussing with David what he could say next to the news-hungry journalists. Cyril and David reacted in the same way. They were less shocked by what was being alleged than by the harm the allegations were doing to the Party.

At the height of the crisis, Cyril fell ill and had to hand over the Whip's job to Alan Beith but he nevertheless insisted on fulfilling a long-standing promise to speak in Truro. Once there, Cyril typically managed to make a joke out of his own illness. Announcing that he was embarking on a slimming diet, he fascinated the local press by managing to negotiate his twenty-seven stone through Truro's narrowest alleyway, named 'Squeezeguts Alley'. He then made one of his usual ebullient speeches, waving his arms about in his most histrionic style and only slightly spoiling the effect by sweeping his glass of water all over David.

In Truro David had been careful never to raise the Thorpe issue himself and he would dismiss any questions on it as either irrelevant or unfair to Jeremy. Cyril was sensitive to David's reaction. 'He was deeply shocked by the Thorpe revelations and very cautious in the way he handled the issue. He was a very much more cautious politician than he is ever given credit for.'

Cyril took the same line whenever it was raised, but he did more. He managed unselfishly to raise our spirits at a time when he himself was a very disappointed man. The Chief Whip's job was, he knew, the most challenging job he was ever likely to have in parliament. He would never have another such opportunity to make his mark on Liberal strategy.

Then, in May, Jeremy resigned, on the basis that it was impossible to continue as leader when 'the greater part of his time has to be spent in answering allegations'. David called the whole affair a tragedy. 'Even so,' he went on, 'my view is that he took the right decision.' That comment was for David a very considerable understatement. The question now was who was going to pick up the pieces.

Politics has always been as much about personalities as about policies. This is especially so with leaders. The Liberals have been exceptionally lucky in that in nearly every General Election for the last thirty years their leader has been identified as more attractive and respected than his Labour and Conservative opponents. Had this not been so, we would presumably have done even worse than we did.

The loss of Jeremy in May 1976 was, therefore, naturally seen as a very grave blow to the Party. His ebullience and showmanship had always commanded attention. However, he had been far from the perfect leader, certainly from David's point of view. David thought that Jeremy did not consult his colleagues as he should and that on the rare occasions they did get together formally, Jeremy was more interested in being entertaining than in discussing important issues. David being David, he did not hesitate to tell him so – very bluntly too.

Jeremy no doubt found criticism from the newest recruit irritating. He responded with banter. I noticed that whenever we were together in London and came across Jeremy, Jeremy would affect a Cornish accent and enquire after 'Lord and Lady Penhaligon's health'. I am sure that it was well-intentioned but it was none the less patronizing.

Still, whatever David thought personally of Jeremy as a leader, he knew he would be a hard act for anyone to follow.

What was needed now was someone who could step in and switch everyone's attention away from the past towards the future. Sadly, that was just what the Liberals could not provide – at least not immediately. By an extraordinary coincidence, in May 1976 the Party was right in the middle of preparing an exciting constitutional innovation: a procedure for enabling the whole Party, rather than simply the MPs, to choose any new leader. The idea was great. The timing was disastrous.

In this crisis, Jo Grimond was persuaded to take over as caretaker until the procedure was agreed and an election held. There were many who would have liked Jo to return as more than caretaker but their number did not include Jo himself. He had done the job for ten years and that was enough for him. Still, at least for the time being, we had someone in charge who was highly respected both by parliament and the media.

A special assembly now agreed a formula that laid down that candidates for the leadership must be MPs and must be nominated by two fellow MPs. John Pardoe and David Steel were obvious candidates, Russell Johnston an outsider. In the event only David S. and John were nominated, and the battle began.

David Steel was seen then as the cooler, more calculating of the two. He was recognized both within and without the Party as a supreme parliamentary tactician. He had not only had the courage to promote the abortion law but had gathered together an all-party group to push it through. He had gained even further experience of all-party campaigning during the 'Say Yes to Europe' campaign. With his crossbencher expertise, it was hardly surprising that he had been the Party's major proponent in 1974 of our campaign for a national government. That campaign had not helped us much then but there were many in the Party who sympathized with David Steel's belief that we should take the earliest opportunity to get our ideas put into action even if it meant soiling our hands with pacts and compromises.

John, by nature a much more ebullient character, was all for taking the battle to the enemy, for campaigning outside parliament, for backing and using the expertise we were rapidly building up in local government. He was very much the candidate of the more radical element in the Party and, insofar as there could be said to have been a split among the MPs into left and right, John was on the left.

John's supporters always described themselves as the 'activists'. This was, unsurprisingly, resented by the Steel camp but could be excused in that the 'activists' certainly included the majority of those who had pioneered community politics. Although he had not himself depended on community politics to win or to hold North Cornwall, John had been identified as one of their supporters among the MPs over the last four years.

As always with an election in the air, David's spirits soared. He had no doubts over whom to support. Although David was too much of an individualist – too much of a Cornishman perhaps – ever to be identified as an ally of any particular grouping in the Party, his heart had always been with those who wanted more community politics. Anyway, John had been for years a close friend and ally. Not only did David nominate John, he also spoke for him, both at the launch of his campaign and at rallies around the country. David's comment on John's election address explained his point of view.

'"What? David supporting John Pardoe! Bound to, ain't

he?" That in a Cornish way just about sums up most people's reaction to the announcement of my support for John. It's deeper than that, and I would support him even if he came from Devon! My constituency is next door to John's. In 1970 we were third, 16,000 behind the winner. I know how much his effectiveness next door helped.'

John had indeed been a tower of strength to us in 1974 and had become a close friend at Westminster too. He had also been as interested an observer of David's progress as David had been of his. John had first met us in our Young Liberal days. There had been that occasion when he had been so angry when the visiting YLs had refused to stand for the loyal toast. Ironically most of those anti-establishment figures were now probably going to vote for him!

John heard David speaking at a meeting soon after that YL function, and remembers being 'incredibly embarrassed, because, as he always admitted later on, David could not actually string two thoughts together when he first started. It was as bad as anything I remembered myself doing in my early days as a candidate. Yet, by the time he got to 1974, he had improved to an astonishing extent. He was a very competent speaker. By that time he was probably not yet thought of as the funniest politician on two legs. That came a little later. He had, however, already developed a marvellous raconteur's ability on his feet. He later perfected that, to become without a doubt the funniest public speaker I have heard in the whole of my career.'

It was hardly surprising that John was delighted to have David speak for him all round the country – and David loved it. In a campaign that often degenerated into a rather undignified exchange of trivia between the candidates,

David was often able to restore a sense of humour and perspective.

The ultimate irony was that when the result was announced, the person most depressed by John's defeat was not John but David. John had accepted that he was losing the battle well before the count. The result, however, was conclusive and David was quick to acknowledge its implications. That summer he included in *News from the Liberals* this commitment, all the more important because of his well-publicised support for John: 'David Steel is the new Liberal Party leader. In what was in many ways a significant breakthrough for democracy he was elected by Liberal Party members throughout the country. Well over 100,000 voted. Truro constituency supported John Pardoe by 640 to 405 but now the election is over it welcomes David Steel's victory and will give him full backing. The Liberal Party should now get down to the job of building a Liberal society.'

David Steel had warned the party that the path towards achieving a Liberal society would be a bumpy one. However, the path he chose turned out to be far more bumpy than most of us had expected. John Pardoe had been seen as the one more likely to stir up controversy. David S. was expected to give the Party a period of quiet in which to recover from the Thorpe affair. Again, the popular assumption was to be proved quite wrong. Within a year David S. had led the Party into a quite unprecedented parliamentary pact with Labour and by 1981 had engineered an electoral pact with the Social Democratic Party.

Although David was not always in agreement with his new leader's strategy, he had always enjoyed a bit of drama in his politics and there was to be plenty of that over the next few years. He was also to discover that they had a lot more in common personally than he had realized until now.

David S. is reserved, even shy, by nature and his interests have always been mostly in the field of foreign affairs rather than the domestic issues that at first absorbed our time and enthusiasm. His circle of acquaintances also extended far beyond the Liberal members of the House. This would prove a great advantage when he became leader, though it meant that he spent so little time with his colleagues that he knew less of their strengths and weaknesses than he should.

From 1974 David S. had played a vital role in advising David on how the Commons worked but they had never become close friends. However, they did get to know a little more of each other in 1976 – in the least likely circumstances. It was their mutual interest in cars that brought them together. 'It was,' as David S. recalls, 'during the leadership election. We both turned up at a crowded seaside town meeting, David to speak for John Pardoe and I for myself. Afterwards he offered to drive me back to London in his beloved two-seater TR6. We talked families and cars. Of course, when it came to cars I was a mere amateur. David was a professional. From then on I used to take a lot of tips from him.'

His love of cars was one of the few hobbies David S. then allowed himself and he was fascinated to talk with someone like David who would think nothing of taking a car entirely to bits and reassembling it in a weekend – as I knew only too well! Even after he had moved on to TRs and Rovers, David's greatest joy was working on his old Cortina, which he kept on the road for twenty years. David's first Rover was in fact bought from David S. As the leading teetotaller of the

Liberal group, David had driven his leader home in it from so many functions that he called himself the Deputy Chauffeur and even introduced himself as such at Ronnie Scott's Club one evening.

He used to joke that all David S. ever wanted of him was his engineering skills and that he would drop everything on getting an urgent summons to the leader's office, only to find that the coffee machine had broken down and needed mending. In fact, David S. demanded rather more of his most junior colleague. He began by promoting him to be employment spokesman. This for David seemed his great opportunity. He had been intensely frustrated that so far in parliament there had been virtually no opportunity to raise the employment problems that plagued the south-west – and which he knew were almost as acute in similar areas of the country – high unemployment, low wages, lack of incentive, lack of training.

Ironically, at first that frustration was increased. David found that, however often he raised problems with oral questions, or brought them into the few debates on the subject, nothing ever happened. At least in the social services debates there had been the occasional amendment accepted by the government, or even forced upon them. On employment he got nowhere.

By March 1977, however, everything had changed. Indeed, since 1975 parliament itself had changed. Then Margaret Thatcher had been very much the new girl among the parliamentary leaders. Now both the Liberals and Labour had new leaders too. Soon after the Thorpe resignation, Harold Wilson had also stepped down, leaving his successor, Jim Callaghan, with a paper-thin majority. Within a year, that majority had virtually disappeared and the government was facing a censure motion, with the Tories sixteen points up in the polls.

The Liberals had little love for the government but at that moment negotiations with the trades unions were at last showing signs of progress on some of the prices and incomes measures the Liberals had been urging on the government. If the Tories won control, we would be back to a free-for-all in which the poor would be the greatest losers. Steel and Callaghan now came up with arrangements that would guarantee our support for the government if they would take on board certain Liberal policies and abandon some of their socialist measures. The bargain was a good one but for some of the Liberals it was not good enough. The two that liked it least at that time were the most senior and most junior members of the group – Jo and David.

Over the next few years David would gain the reputation of being distinctly difficult over pacts and alliances with Labour and ex-Labour politicians. This was because he could see very little advantage in an agreement if it threatened the growth of the Liberal Party itself. He was absolutely convinced that the greater the influence of Liberal ideals, the better it would be for the country. However, once he was happy that an agreement was worthwhile, he would work his heart out to make it work.

Any reservations he had over the Lib/Lab pact were never over personalities. In fact David, being naturally gregarious, knew the members of the other parties better than most of the Liberal MPs and, with the notable exception of Tony Benn, would get on extremely well with his opposite numbers in the Labour government. Jim Callaghan himself had a great respect for his judgement. 'He had an acute mind,' he said. 'He always mastered his subject, and had a wide range of knowledge.'

That March the major sticking point for Jo and David was over elections to the next European parliament. Callaghan could not or would not guarantee to deliver what the Liberals had been campaigning for, that there should be direct elections and that they should be held under a system of proportional representation (as would be the case elsewhere in Europe). Many of the Labour Party saw this, quite rightly, as the first step to a change in the system for voting for Westminster. Callaghan would only promise to bring in a bill with cabinet backing. He would not guarantee that his whole cabinet, let alone the parliamentary party, would back it.

Jo and David argued then – as they were to argue throughout the pact – that the Liberals must be seen to have gained substantial and specific concessions if they were to support what was clearly an unpopular government. The country might benefit from our influence but, without the introduction of specifically Liberal measures, we should not get the credit. The very least we should insist on was PR for the European elections.

The majority, however, accepted the Callaghan compromise and the pact was agreed for the next four months, at least. Jo and David accepted the decision with good grace and David was given the jobs of dealing with all environmental matters (there was no cabinet post for this) and for liaising with Bill Rodgers, the Secretary of State for Transport. It was a substantial brief. Environmental matters covered the role David had been playing on his own initiative until then on nuclear power, while the responsibility for transport would involve him, at least peripherally, in the most tricky of the initial negotiations with the cabinet: the addition of 5½p to the price of petrol.

The problem over this apparently trifling sum was that the Liberals, along with other MPs for rural constituencies, had been campaigning to keep down the cost of rural transport, none more so than David himself. As David Steel was to acknowledge, 'over the next few weeks, David Penhaligon seemed to be conducting regular tutorials with Bill Rodgers whose Stockton-on-Tees constituency provides no background experience of the subject'. Eventually the Liberals got their way: the 5½p increase was taken off in August.

It was not an easy decision, if only because the Liberals felt that in the long run it was essential that the nation should not use up so quickly what was likely to be a diminishing resource. (Any price increase, however, had to be done slowly, without exacerbating the problems of unemployment.) Nor was it for David an easy introduction into the world of government, successful though his negotiations with Bill Rodgers eventually proved. However, over the next year the two men were to forge a friendship that was to make transport policy one of the more productive areas of the pact and was to help considerably over the equally tricky negotiations that lay ahead for both men when they would meet again as members of the Alliance.

12
A TASTE OF GOVERNMENT

'To suggest that David was all laughter and fun would be to lessen this man. He was a deeply serious man who often hid his seriousness and his troubles behind a flippant exterior.' – Bill Rodgers

The new year of 1977 had brought with it the realization that I was pregnant again. We were both delighted and relieved, though we had hoped to have the two children closer together. Indeed, when Matthew was four, and I was still not pregnant, we thought we ought to make a few enquiries to see if anything was wrong. I was, however, rather startled to be told not just 'not to worry', but 'What else can you expect with your husband away so much?' I changed doctor and luck. The baby was forecast to arrive in August.

The pregnancy was inevitably more eventful than the last, as I had constituency commitments now besides the family and the post office. However, the most traumatic period during this time was when I was seven months pregnant and David went down with what was first thought to be flu. The illness continued and David was getting worse not better, and he was suffering from agonizing headaches. We decided it was time to consult the doctor. He called for about a week before deciding he needed tests to see what was causing the problem.

Off we went to Treliske hospital where the medical staff there soon diagnosed viral pneumonia. They also warned me that because David had not been receiving the proper drugs there was a slight possibility that he might suffer brain damage. As if this was not worrying enough, when I entered David's room he asked me if I could see the green men on the door.

Fortunately this state did not last for long, although David was ill and could not work for a month. During that month I had to try and fulfil much of his casework including surgeries. At a time when I should have been resting, I was therefore working very hard, especially as for that short time David lost all his energy and did not show any interest in what was going on around him.

It so happened that his illness occurred during one of the most delicate periods of the Lib/Lab pact. David returned to Westminster at the end of June and it was in July that the Liberal parliamentary party had to decide whether they wanted to continue the pact into the next parliamentary year. They put together a list of ten points they would want included in the Queen's Speech and, with varying degrees of enthusiasm, the majority of the MPs agreed to negotiate on that basis.

Again Jo and David were uneasy. They wanted more. They deplored the failure of the Party to get any credit for what had already been marked improvements in the rate of inflation and industrial relations. Cyril Smith went further. Cyril had in fact initiated the first discussions between the parties but now he felt that the pact should definitely end. Outvoted by their colleagues, the three of them reacted in different ways. David simply accepted democratically his colleagues' decision. Cyril resisted it. He decided that he would no longer support the pact. Jo would support it but was unwilling to continue what had been a fruitless dialogue with Tony Benn, the Secretary of State for Energy.

The formidable Nancy Seear took over responsibility for employment from Cyril, and Eric Avebury took over energy. However, as they were both in the Lords, someone had to handle those matters also in the Commons. David S. asked David to take on all of this in addition to his other duties. David had after all handled employment before and his concern over nuclear power had given him some experience of how Benn worked. A glutton for punishment, David agreed.

David might be prepared to accept the majority vote of his colleagues, and take on even more portfolios to help them out, but that did not mean that he would stop arguing for better terms, especially as the Liberal vote at by-elections had fallen sharply since the beginning of the pact. At one meeting they all had that fateful July, David arrived (as so often!) late. There was at that time one of those recurrent crises in British Steel and in David's hand was a copy of the *Evening Standard*, with the headline 'Steel loses one million a day'. To shouts of laughter from everyone, especially David S., David slapped it down on the table with the wry comment, 'Is that pounds or votes, David?'

In the event, agreement was reached with the government for the following parliamentary year and David Steel received the backing of the Liberal Assembly that autumn. By then, however, something even more important had happened in our lives. Our daughter had arrived.

As I had been exhausted by coping with the constituency

during David's illness, I decided enough was enough and I backed out of accompanying David to local functions until after the birth. I was by this time as large around as I was tall. Although by nature I have never been fat, I managed to put on over three stone in weight by the time the baby arrived. This got me into a lot of trouble with the medics as well as restricting my physical capabilities.

This also meant not only that I grew out of maternity clothes but that everyone was convinced that I was about to deliver from the beginning of July onwards. This was the Queen's Silver Jubilee year and many of my Chacewater customers thought I would qualify for a free shawl from Boots the Chemist if the baby arrived on the Jubilee anniversary. I also grew out of David's beloved Triumph TR6. I could no longer reach the steering wheel or get down to the rather low driving position. Besides that, the car was a two-seater with only a little bench, which was hardly practical in our new circumstances. I therefore sold the car and bought a Triumph saloon. David really knew it was the only practical solution but I don't think he or Matthew, who loved travelling with the soft top down, ever really forgave me.

Only on one occasion did I break my decision to stop attending functions. It was when we received a royal invitation to attend a reception on board the royal yacht *Britannia*, which was calling into Falmouth. I thought this invitation too special to miss and I found myself a long black swirling dress which went a little way to hide my shape. All went well until I had to curtsy. It was more of a droop than a drop! However, it was a great occasion and I was relieved that the baby put off her arrival until the following Saturday.

The birth took quite some time and this time I was grateful for David's company. He stayed throughout and, whilst the records show a perfectly normal birth, we both felt there were some problems. Indeed, when Anna eventually arrived, my doctor felt some concern for her condition and the on-duty paediatrician was called. It was not that Anna was a little weakling – on the contrary she weighed in at 8 lb 4 oz, only 4 oz lighter than Matthew had been, and if anything was short and tubby – but nevertheless because of her prone condition it was decided to take her away to the special baby unit for the night.

We thought nothing of it at the time, nor did we for some time in the future. We simply put our minds to choosing a name. Susannah was my choice and David seemed happy at the time. However, he returned later in the day to say rather diplomatically that the name had not received too much enthusiasm with our relatives, and in any case perhaps Susannah Penhaligon was rather a mouthful. In that case, I decided, Hannah was a good compromise. 'No,' said David. 'We Cornish never pronounce our aitches. I think it had better be Anna.' And so she became Anna Charlotte.

Anna was to prove the perfect baby, quiet, placid and undemanding, quite unlike Matthew! However, after a few months I started to feel uneasy, as it became obvious that Anna was being very slow in making progress. I mentioned it to my doctor, who felt it was too early to be alarmed but that we should monitor the situation for a while. After all, Matthew had been physically very forward, and it was wrong to compare the two, who clearly were temperamentally totally different.

A little while later, however, we were spurred suddenly into action when a doctor examined Anna at the regular

David during his Bosvigo County Primary schooldays.

The Penhaligon family: parents Charles and Sadie, David (top left), older sister Margaret and younger brother John.

The first photograph of David with me, taken at a social evening at the clubhouse at Kenwyn Hill Caravan Site.

Peter, Anne, Clive, Wendy, me and David on holiday at John o'Groats.

David and I leaving St Kea Church, Truro after our wedding.

David is congratulated by Peter Bessell after being adopted as prospective Liberal candidate for the Totnes constituency.

David and I with my parents, Owen and Mabel Lidgey, at a family party.

Talking to farmers at Truro market during the October 1974
General Election campaign.

Visiting Wheal Jane, the mine David was to save.

Addressing the anti-nuclear rally in Trafalgar Square, April 1978.

In his home city of Truro, with the three spires of the cathedral in the background.

With Matthew in his arms, just after hearing that he had won the May 1979 election with a greatly increased majority.

David and I enjoying a cuddle with Matthew and Anna in our newly acquired garden, shortly after moving to Daniell Road.

Among the claypits above St Austell.

With his long-time friend and agent Malcolm Brown, examining the result before the announcement of his victory in 1983.

The Steels and the Penhaligons celebrating David's ten years in Parliament at a constituency dinner.

A round-up of Liberal MPs at the Assembly held at Margate in 1979: David Penhaligon, Stephen Ross, Richard Wainwright, Jo Grimond, Alan Beith, Russell Johnston, David Steel (Leader), Clement Freud, Cyril Smith, David Alton and Geraint Howells.

Three of Truro's past Liberal candidates at a get-together with David at St Agnes: Nancy Seear (1955 and 1959), William Hosking (1964 and 1966) and Michael Steed (1970).

A favourite family photograph, taken to celebrate David's year as Party President.

clinic and made a wrong diagnosis of the problem. He suggested there was some spasticity. This scared the day-lights out of me. David, from 300 miles away, was able to be a little more sceptical. My doctor too disbelieved this prognosis but felt the time was right to look further into the problem.

We were referred to a paediatrician in London, at Guy's Hospital, and for the next four to five years we were to pay regular visits there as Anna's progress was monitored. The diagnosis was, and still is, that she has moderate learning difficulties. That really means that she is moderately edu-cationally subnormal, but what caused her developmental retardation is in my view open to question and always will be.

She is wilful, determined and above all active, which does not make bringing her up at all easy. This has caused considerable heartbreak as well as a lot of hard work and patience, but on the plus side there is not a child around who enjoys life more fully or is more popular and affectionate than Anna. She now attends a special school and is loving it.

Certainly Anna was very special to David and, whilst he and Matthew had a lot of common interests, he always found lots of time to play with her. He was also sensitive to the fact that Anna, by the nature of her problems, was much more demanding of my attention and time than would normally be expected of a child of her age and that he was unable to contribute as much to helping as he would have liked.

It was only after David's death that I discovered how often he would talk of her to his friends at Westminster. It is sometimes forgotten – I forgot it myself sometimes! – that life in London away from their homes for nearly the whole week is as hard on the MPs as it is on their families. David and Alan would spend hours discussing politics but, impatient for release on Thursday night from what David called the Madhouse, they would also spend hours discussing their families and worrying about phone calls from distraught wives over problems that defied solution over so great a distance.

Certainly poor David suffered a regular string of phone calls over the next few years as the children's activities caused me either embarrassment or alarm. Bringing up kids with a part-time father is not easy. Threatening all sorts of punishments when Dad gets back at the weekend does not hold much water if you know that Dad, quite rightly, would never see them through.

On one occasion before Matthew was five his teacher called me to one side, with all the other parents present, to explain that my son had attacked her. Apparently she was playing 'What's the time, Mr Wolf' with Matthew and some of his friends. However, when she got to the bit where the wolf gobbles up the children, my son took her literally and went to the rescue of his friends, knocking the teacher's glasses off. Did my son not know the difference between fiction and reality, I was asked.

'Where have I gone wrong?' I asked myself on the way home. I did not think I was going to get the hang of this parent bit and I was less than five years into motherhood. It was as well then I did not know what further trials and tribulations children can put you through, especially during their teens, but that is a different story.

Of course, by the time Anna was born, Matthew had already spent a term at school. He was, I think it is fair to say, a reluctant pupil, always finding more interesting things to do at home. He was particularly clever at thinking up good reasons why he could not attend and on one occasion he hobbled around on one leg, making out he was unable to pitch on the other, for a day and a half before he lost concentration.

David always had stories to tell about the children, sometimes in the office to Stephen Ross, sometimes to Cyril over the tea kettle. 'David was obviously very proud of the lad,' Cyril recalls, 'but it was Anna he would talk about again and again. He would tell me how she was going on. He would worry about her future. He would become emotionally downcast about her in a way that he never showed about anything else. Obviously he loved her very deeply.' He did.

David returned to Westminster for the new session in October 1977 to find the pact almost immediately facing a crisis of confidence, at least from the Liberal point of view. When it came to a vote that November, almost inevitably too few of the Labour Party supported PR for the European elections for it to get through parliament. So great was the dismay in the Liberal camp that a Special Assembly to debate the pact was called in January. However, as there had never been a guarantee of the Labour vote on PR, David S. got the backing of his colleagues (except for Cyril) in the debate. The Assembly backed him too. Cyril then unselfishly asked his supporters to accept the vote. The pact went on.

However, one phrase – and it was David's – had caught the attention of parliament, Assembly and the press, to be remembered long after all the rhetoric was forgotten. 'Turkeys,' David had said in parliament, 'don't vote for

Christmas.' For him, and for the public, it summed up the logic behind the pact.

David had also caught the attention of the PM. Callaghan knew he was an uneasy ally, but he enjoyed David's style. 'When he rose to speak in the Commons he made the members feel that they were listening to someone who had just got off the train at Paddington and dropped in to give them a piece of his constituents' minds.'

Meanwhile, however, back at Westminster, the show went on. Although, as before, the Liberals got precious little credit for them, a number of the Liberals' favourite causes made progress at last, in particular the one that had brought David into the Party in 1964. John Pardoe reached agreement with Denis Healey on a scheme for profit-sharing. For the first time firms were to be given tax incentives for granting their employees shares in the business where they worked.

What the pact also achieved were some points even less well publicized. Socialist policies were abandoned or, where they were not abandoned, the Liberals stepped in and stopped them in their tracks. David again played a major part in one of these. This was Tony Benn's Electricity Bill. Jo had been briefed on the bill during the one meeting he and Benn had managed to arrange, before Eric Avebury and David took over. Jo in his rather disdainful style had pointed out certain flaws but for the Liberals in general and David in particular there remained a central problem. Benn was proposing a centralist solution, a giant electricity board in the hands of appointed, not elected, members. Jo had not liked it. David hated it. It promised to produce all the problems he had found in the south-west boards, on water and on planning, writ large.

Disagreements were not made any easier by the fact that Tony Benn was violently opposed to the pact. This had led originally to Jo's decision to opt out of the argument. Eric and David could appreciate Jo's problems. David certainly did not get on any better with Benn than Jo had done, especially as they had so often disagreed in the past over the nuclear energy programme.

In a memorable *Observer* article on the row Alan Watkins pointed out that David was 'sometimes called Penhooligan . . . because of his general air expressed in a Cornish accent and in a variety of other ways, of refusing to be intimidated by all this fancy political carry on. He refused to attend a meeting with Mr Benn because he was taking his son to the pantomime. He is unrepentant about this episode, saying that he had exhibited a proper Liberal scale of values.'

What had happened was that we had booked a long time before to see Tommy Steele in *Hans Christian Andersen* at the Palladium. It was a bit of a family joke as I had been a real Tommy Steele fan as a teenager, loving his infectious sense of fun, and I think David felt this pantomime was as exciting for me as it was for Matthew. It was. Such a trip to London in our circumstances needed a lot of forward planning as, at that time, we did not have a proper base and so accommodation needed to be organized as well as everything else. This sort of planning would naturally have been completely lost on London-based MPs. However, David clearly felt that Matthew often sacrificed the sort of home life his friends enjoyed and he had no intention of letting him down over this post-Christmas treat.

The meeting with Tony Benn could have been rearranged for another date. However, Benn was absolutely furious.

The subsequent row is on record – in *Hansard*. The story illustrates, I feel, the considerable change (for the better) in the attitudes of politicians since that time. I cannot imagine any Labour MP now reacting so strongly to a father with real family values. Anyway it did Benn little good. David was not going to be bullied. He would not budge and Benn had to rewrite his bill omitting his brand new Electricity Corporation.

Convinced though he was that this was the right decision, David did not enjoy the exchange. He wanted to see progress, not just control over the wilder socialist ideas. Luckily, because of the range of his responsibilities, he was to see these too, for it was as a result of David's 'seminars' with Bill Rodgers that the government's transport policy now included measures that the Liberals with their mostly rural constituencies needed most. There were subsidies for country bus services and more money allocated for pensioners' bus passes, while the threat of closures for 'unprofitable' rail services was lifted at last.

Until now David had been subjected only to the normal amount of criticism from members of the other parties. With the pact, that changed. He was now, unsurprisingly, fiercely attacked by the Tories, who were frustrated by what they saw as an alliance that robbed them of power. After one particularly fierce exchange when it was suggested that the Liberals should get a new transport spokesman, David responded with pointed emphasis. 'I am very successful in one way as the Liberal spokesman on transport. All I have to do is to get to my feet for five minutes and the Conservative benches erupt with anger and general dismay. I suspect that the truth is that the Conservative members recognize that in the Bill the first real progress has been made for rural transport for many a long year.'

His vision now took on a broader canvass, as he argued for travellers right across the country, but still with a personal touch. 'I claim to spend more hours per week on a train than does any other honourable Member in the House at the moment. I spend about twelve hours a week bumping from here to the south-west and back on British Rail. On the whole, I think the service is good . . . My main criticism is that the trains are filthy. It is time someone did something about it. When I hear of all the fancy investment programmes advocated by some members of the railway lobby in this House, I hope that included in that investment will be a new bucket, spade, bar of soap and a couple of vacuum cleaners for cleaning out the carriages.'

As always, there was a general principle to the particular point he raised. Money was being saved by allowing 'natural wastage' among the lowest paid. The customer was losing out – but so too was the employee, and David was always especially concerned for those in the lowest paid employment. And David, after all, was also spokesman for employment.

Employment and wages were for David the most important issues on which he ever fought. With good reason. In January 1978 Cornwall had the highest rate of unemployment of any county in the UK. Out of the ten employment exchanges in England with the highest level of unemployment, Cornwall had six. Unfortunately, on employment the government had in Albert Booth a Secretary of State dead set against the pact. David from the other side had some fellow feeling with Booth, but for totally opposite reasons. Booth found the Liberals' influence on policy far too great. David found it far too little. David, however, at least accepted that their job was to make the pact work. Booth gave no sign of wanting to do so.

David's Liberal colleague on employment issues, Nancy Seear, was an expert in this field. Nancy had always been one of the Party's most effective speakers and she had something else very special in common with David: she had fought Truro – in the 1950s. Invaluable both for her specialist knowledge of employment matters and for her debating skills, she had been made a life peer. Nancy and David now argued especially for more money to be spent on training – David being able here to congratulate English China Clays on their apprenticeship schemes and to remind his fellow members of how dangerous was the decline in the status and promotion of engineering.

'When I was standing for parliament in my constituency, the other parties were rather worried that I might get elected. In fact, I was more worried than they were. As a chartered engineer, working for Holman's in Cornwall, I remember the final message that went out to deride my efforts. Canvassers said, "Of course, he only works down Holman's, you know. Would you like such a person to represent you in Parliament?" I only just won, but the fact that I was a chartered engineer was of little significance.'

David's concern over the decline in engineering as a career was not, however, just a personal matter. He had two special heroes: Lloyd George, the politician, and Isambard Kingdom Brunel, Britain's great nineteenth-century builder of bridges and ships, and incidentally the man who built the first iron bridge across the Tamar at Plymouth. At that time Britain's lead in the world had depended on the application of its greatest minds to engineering work. In the 1970s this was no longer so and David felt that Britain's survival depended on a revival of the profession.

It was now thanks at least in part to the Liberals' efforts that new orders were made that every company should contribute towards training. David welcomed them. 'It is desperately important that we both increase the status of engineering and bring training and education closer to industry. It is obvious that we must increase the general level of skill available. If we cannot achieve these objectives, all the parliamentary debates and all the industrial levies will be as nothing, because the backbone of our economy will not be there.'

The other major achievement of the pact in this area was a more generous allocation of the small firms employment subsidy. For counties such as Cornwall – and there were many of them – which depended almost entirely on small firms (ECC and Holman's were the exceptions in our area) this subsidy was crucial. Without it there was for most of the young really no hope of employment where they lived, as David had thumped home when once again, in January 1978, he had managed to get an adjournment debate specifically on Cornish problems. 'When a young man comes to my surgery, as often happens, asking for advice on the career that he should pursue, it gives me no pleasure to have to tell him, as one Cornishman to another, "Young man, if you want a career, you had better go to England."'

The subsidy was to be a great help but, even as David celebrated its extension, his own constituency was dealt a totally unexpected blow that threatened at a stroke to double its already agonizing rate of unemployment. The news broke that the two big local tin mines of Mount

Wellington and Wheal Jane were on the point of closing down.

Both mines were comparatively new. Wheal Jane had been opened by Consolidated Goldfields in 1971; then in 1974 the Cornwall Tin and Mining Company opened Mount Wellington, no further than a mile away from Wheal Jane. As an engineer of drilling equipment with at least some experience of how and where tin could be found and mined, David had always been somewhat surprised that the two companies had chosen the sites they had. Still the work had been a godsend to all the villages nearby and to Chacewater in particular. Between them the two mines provided some 750 jobs. Another 750 jobs in other businesses were dependent on them. Now the villages faced disaster.

The major problem was one of water. To keep Mount Wellington open, eight million gallons of water had to be pumped out every day. Now Mount Wellington had reached a point where there was too little tin accessible to justify the cost of pumping. The case for its closure was unanswerable. Wheal Jane on the other hand was profitable. The problem there was that it would be flooded with Mount Wellington's water, once the pumps at Mount Wellington stopped. Consolidated Goldfields, who had been having management problems, proposed to close it down, rather than take on the burden of doubling their pumping costs.

So sudden and urgent was the problem that action had to be taken immediately. Six hundred miners marched on London; the county council, 'not famous for throwing away money' as David said, offered £20,000 to keep the pumps going at Wheal Jane; and David quite ruthlessly set out to exploit the Lib/Lab pact. Of course, he had a case, and a good case too, for government intervention. He made the most of it. He obtained an adjournment debate on 11 May 1978 and he set out what total closure of both mines would do to Cornwall, comparing the contribution of government to the steel and car industries with that to tin mining. What Cornwall needed to keep Wheal Jane open was chicken-feed in comparison.

The minister concerned was Alan Williams, himself from a mining background, the South Wales coal mines, and he was personally very sympathetic to the Cornish miners. Thanks to the pact, David had been able to establish and maintain day to day contact with Alan over the issue. They liked each other and Alan promised to do what he could. It was also clearly in the interests of the Cabinet to do what it could too. The pact was due to come up for negotiation soon and David was known to be the most critical of the Liberal spokesmen. The Cabinet was happy to go along with whatever solution could be arranged between Alan and David.

In his reply Alan committed the government in effect to do everything short of running Wheal Jane itself: it would offer grants to any operator and keep the mine in operation, pending negotiations with a new independent operator. David wanted no more. He certainly did not want the mine nationalized. The question now was whether or not a new owner could be found. There seemed to be just three candidates: Consolidated Goldfields, which might continue if the government would help; Cornwall Tin and Mining Company, which, having closed Mount Wellington, might try next door; and St Piran, the company that already ran successsfully the only two remaining mines in Cornwall and had the expertise to take on another one. In the event, none of them could agree terms.

Rescue came from a totally unexpected direction. David was in his Westminster office one day when the telephone rang. The caller introduced himself as Mr Sprinkel, and and he said to David in an American drawl, 'I believe you have a couple of tin mines for sale.' At first this seemed unreal. After arranging to meet Mr Sprinkel, David hastily set about trying to find out a little bit about this 'white knight', as he would now be described. What David learnt led him to believe that the interest Mr Sprinkel was showing was certainly worth pursuing. Mr Sprinkel had a good track record for spotting opportunities, raising the necessary cash and then finding suitable companies to take over and run the firms he bought. David introduced him to Alan Williams's department, a deal was struck, a geological survey commissioned and within a few months the mining giant RTZ stepped in and decided to run the mine. Wheal Jane was saved.

Ironically, by the time the government's commitment to Wheal Jane had been finally resolved in this highly satisfactory manner, the Lib/Lab pact itself had come to an end. It reached its conclusion in July 1978, only a few weeks after the vital government guarantee on the future of the mine. The pact was not renewed for the next parliamentary session.

The pact can now be seen to have given the country possibly the best fifteen months of government it had enjoyed in the whole decade. Inflation came down from 20 per cent to under 9 per cent; mortgage rates fell from 12¼ per cent to 8½ per cent. Tax incentives were introduced to encourage employers to set up employee shareholding schemes. Rural transport benefited; so too did rural employment. Extreme socialist policies were shelved. There was a lot to shout about and the Liberals did their best to shout about it in their local newsletters. Yet in the national press and media they got virtually none of the credit. That was why all the Liberal MPs – not just Cyril, Jo and David – now decided that enough was enough.

Apart from the gains to the country as a whole, only one of the Liberal constituencies could be said to have got anything specific out of the pact and that was Truro, with the rescue of Wheal Jane. The irony was that it was gained by the MP who had throughout the pact been most critical of what it was doing to the Party. Perhaps it was a form of poetic justice. Certainly Alan Williams thought David deserved his luck. 'In politics no one ever minds someone fighting his corner hard, so long as he fights it cleanly and with integrity – and I never knew David to breach a confidence. I may have told him more than perhaps I should on occasions. In the House of Commons a lot depends on whether you are trusted by the other side, and David would never pull dirty tricks on people, nor pull the rug out from underneath your feet if you told him something that perhaps he could use against you. You always knew where you were with David.'

13
CONSOLIDATION

'I don't know anyone else who in the course of a few minutes could have a meeting laughing with him, and then on the verge of tears.' – Paul Tyler

When David Steel broke the news to Jim Callaghan that the Liberals would not be renewing the pact in October 1978, the country assumed that the Prime Minister would take the very first opportunity to go to the country. The polls were more encouraging than they had been for many months. He had a chance to cash in on the improvement in the country's fortunes over the time of the pact, especially as Labour had shrewdly seen that the improvement had been credited to them and not to the Liberals. On the other hand, he no longer had a guaranteed overall majority, as he had with the pact. If he staggered on, the government would have to depend on the support of whatever minority groups might support it, bill by bill.

David, who was rarely wrong in his predictions, was totally convinced the General Election was coming in October. All the pundits were predicting the same and so 1978 for us was planned around an autumn election. Besides holding regular surgeries, David had now adopted an innovation first introduced to Cornwall by John Pardoe: an annual travelling surgery which visited all the towns and villages in the constituency. This took the best part of a fortnight, with over seventy stops. Generally it was carried out after the annual Liberal Assembly in the autumn but in 1978 David was so sure this would coincide with the election that he did his tour in August. For most of the country this would not be too much of a problem, other than coinciding with some people's holidays, but in Cornwall he had to struggle from one centre to the next on the busiest roads of the year. Nevertheless it was a good way of meeting people, learning of their problems and generally having the time to 'yarn' with everyone who came to see him.

At about this time my parents, recognizing we would soon be facing a difficult and stressful time with a narrow majority to defend, suggested we took a week off together without the children. This sounded absolutely wonderful to me, but not to David. He could not spare the time, he said. Every moment was precious to prepare for the election. Enough was enough. I booked a week in the Scilly Isles, somewhere I had only enjoyed before on the very occasional day trip, and told David I was going and he could come if he wanted to. With a threat like that he came. Indeed, by the second day of our holiday it had become his idea, and a brilliant week we had.

That experience taught me that David would always have to be dragged away on holiday and for the next few years we enjoyed many family holidays in the Scillies. This continued until Matthew reached the grand age of twelve and announced in very deprived tones that he had 'never been abroad. But *all* his friends had.'

I was not allowed to book any engagements for the whole

of October so that David could concentrate on retaining the seat, and then came the fateful day when it was announced that Mr Callaghan would be addressing the nation that evening. Well, it could mean only one thing. We have never worked so hard as we did that day. We set about catching up with every particle of casework, answering every letter and filing every file. With all the work reasonably up to date we sat down in front of the television to hear the announcement of the General Election. We listened. Did we really hear right? Did he really say he was *not* going to the country just yet? It took some time before the penny dropped for both of us and from the reaction of all our friends we were not alone in our surprise. I looked in the diary. It was free. Someone had taken the horizon away and it felt most peculiar. However, it was not long before David showed some relief as he recognized that any delay would be to Labour's detriment and to our advantage.

Amazingly, Callaghan would stagger on right through what would be called the winter of discontent. For the Liberals this was a godsend. We had seen our own support wither through the pact. We had then seen our next Assembly bedevilled by the media's renewed obsession with Jeremy Thorpe, who was on the point of appearing in court on a charge of conspiracy to murder. The more time we were given the better for our frail chances. We were to have till April 1979.

It is at times like this that MPs' minds are wonderfully concentrated on their prospects of re-election. On the face of it, the Liberal MP most likely to lose his seat had to be David. He had a majority of only 464. The Liberals were far less popular than they were in 1974. Yet, the shrewder political analysts were already hedging their bets on Truro.

David had two big advantages over his chief challenger: a large Labour vote that might switch tactically to him and exposure on radio, press and television unique for a Cornish backbencher. One of them might have been enough for him to hang on. Both together were to prove decisive.

There had always been a large Labour vote in Truro. David had plundered it in 1974 but there were still 11,606 Labour voters to go after. Those voters did not like the Tories and they were willing to give David some of the credit for the pact. He had also been an MP of a kind that they had never seen before. He had been very active within the constituency, to the extent that even the traditionally Tory local press had enjoyed his exploits. It had given him coverage the Liberals had never enjoyed before. Our own members had supplemented this. *News from the Liberals* now went to every house in the constituency.

As for the national exposure he had received, although it was nothing compared with what he was to receive later, it would certainly help him considerably when the election came. From his first arrival at Westminster, he had been spotted by the Liberal leadership as someone who had exactly the image they were happy to project. They might watch with alarm his difficulties over procedure in the House but they could see that he had something that very few MPs had got – an ability to express in simple terms what others could only discuss in parliamentary jargon. And he could be brilliantly and effectively funny at the same time.

Jeremy used him twice in 1975 on the Liberal Party political broadcasts. He was also asked to speak to Oxford undergraduates and the Welsh Assembly. He was then invited to make the appeal for funds at the Liberal Assembly of 1975, challenging comparison with the success of Cyril and Clement Freud in 1973 and 1974. He survived pretty well.

Of course, from 1974 onwards he was expected to speak at the Assembly on those subjects he covered in the House. For him this was interesting, though not entirely to his taste. The strange fact was that this new MP, so fêted for his success and for so many years a conscientious attender at Assemblies, had hardly ever spoken there before. He had generally come to listen but not to speak. Ironically at the last Assembly he attended before he won Truro, he did speak – in favour of a referendum on the EEC – and he was booed!

Now he found himself the darling of the delegates – or at least those who agreed with what he said. The others saw him, rightly, as a danger man who could swing the Assembly against them. It was a position of power that he did not always relish and of which he did not always take advantage. What it did, however, was attract the television pundits. Given the chance to interview an MP, they chose David.

This led to an invitation that was to establish David as a media personality rather than just a politician. In May 1978 he was asked for the first time to appear on *Any Questions?*. Over the next eight years he was to be on it on more occasions than anyone else – on average twice a year. On that first occasion *Any Questions?* was held in Cornwall and he was invited specifically to tell the country about the problems of Wheal Jane. After that he was asked whatever might be the current national issue under discussion. Inevitably, that meant that, come the General Election, he would be there to comment from the Liberal point of view.

The election eventually came in May 1979. David did

Any Questions? in Evesham and campaigned in other constituencies at the start of the campaign, but he was able to spend most of his time in the constituency. The old partnership of Penhaligon and Brown moved into top gear. We may have lacked a professional agent but we had a battle-hardened team so used to covering the constituency that we were at least as efficient as in 1974.

The opposition candidates were articulate and concentrated their fire on how little a Liberal could do in a House virtually split between Tory and Labour. David replied by stressing the successes of the pact. That argument ended in a draw. Where David pulled ahead, however, was on local issues. He had not only pursued all the major problems, he had solved one or two of them – and those that were outstanding were ones on which the neighbouring Tory MPs had been involved as well.

There was a threat to the neighbouring Falmouth docks that would add to local unemployment. David offended against parliamentary etiquette by raising this himself in the Commons before the local MP, David Mudd, had done so but he subsequently made his peace with him and they were now fighting a joint campaign. They also combined their forces – though to less effect – against the overfishing of the mackerel.

So too all the Cornish MPs had backed David's long battle against the sonic bangs of Concorde over Cornwall. Some thought the complaints were inspired chiefly by farmers out for compensation, and that both cows and people would grow to accept them. David however stuck at the issue, because he could see that if Cornwall accepted Concorde's bangs it would have to accept others. He even obtained a Commons debate on the issue. It was accepted that supersonic flying over land would make no appreciable difference to the British Airways flight times. However, we would still have problems from the French Concorde as it came up the Channel.

The key issue though, as before, was in the clay district. Here David had been fighting his old opponents, English China Clays and the county council. The state of the roads was appalling. (David had checked them out personally on a sponsored walk.) So too were the schools they served. (David had taken advantage of his empty diary in October 1978 and visited every school in the area.) 'Most of them seem to have been built under either Gladstone or Asquith. Perhaps we shall have to wait for another Liberal administration for their successors.'

David's complaint on these, addressed especially to the county council, was that the whole area 'was being robbed of the wealth it produces'. ECC he had been hammering on quite different issues: first on their failure to control the dust the pits threw up and then on their quarrel with British Rail over who was responsible for paying for new wagons to carry the clay. Here the problem was that BR might close all freight services to Cornwall if this major cargo proved unprofitable.

By the time of the election there were signs that in these battles David was gaining some ground. The local press was behind David now. He was a fighter, and they liked a fighter. So too, however, was the Tory candidate, Rosemary Brown, though she made the great mistake of saying that if she were elected Truro would at least have an 'articulate voice' at Westminster. The electorate rightly interpreted that as a reference to David's accent – she could hardly be implying that he lacked eloquence. The accent was no handicap. It was David's greatest asset.

CONSOLIDATION

Rosemary Brown was all action. She was anxious to put across an image of energy, intelligence and culture – qualities, she implied, that were sadly lacking in David. Some people thought her image was rather overbearing, as did a friend of mine who during the campaign was travelling from St Austell to Truro and at the same time looking out for posters. She and her young son devised a game: as they saw the posters they would shout 'hooray' for Uncle David's, 'boo' at the Labour ones and 'yuk yuk' for Rosemary Brown. All went well until they started their Saturday morning shop in Truro when a lady's foot crossed their path, preventing them from walking on. 'I'm Rosemary Brown,' said the lady. 'Yuk yuk,' responded the little boy.

On another occasion I was furious with David when I saw a local television news item on the Truro campaign. There was Rosemary Brown running from house to house shaking hands and handing out leaflets, a vision of high power. And there was David calmly ambling down a street in Mevagissey stopping to chat to a few voters *en route*, as if he had all the time in the world. 'Why couldn't you look as if you had some energy?' I complained. I was answered the next day on many doorsteps by people who had also seen this broadcast. They were delighted with David's laid-back approach and the fact that he had not played up to the cameras. Well, not much!

David used this opportunity to get across his message in words. 'Our best role,' he said, 'is to stop the nutters of British politics from reorganizing everything in sight, nationalizing everything in sight and taking extreme measures to solve problems. I do not believe that extremism has any vital or important contribution to make to solving our problems – neither interestingly does the great British public.'

The national press again was quotable, the *Guardian* contrasting him with the very different London-based M Ps. 'When he catches the train to Paddington,' it said, 'he is a Cornish rebel going to battle in an alien land, not a carpet-bagger going home.'

In the event, Rosemary Brown was to add 2,000 to the previous Tory vote but on the day the 'Cornish rebel' astoundingly picked up so many extra votes himself, mostly at the expense of Labour, that he raised his majority to 8,708 and ensured that he would be on that train to Paddington for many years to come.

The General Election of May 1979 changed our lives in some ways even more radically than David's initial victory in 1974. In 1974 we had not dared consider what might happen to us in the long run. The margin had been so close and it had been a year that had favoured the Liberals. We might have found ourselves fighting, and perhaps losing, another election at any time, so small was the Labour majority in parliament. If we had lost, David would have had to try to get his job back and the post office would have been even more important than ever.

May 1979 was totally different. In a year in which the other Liberals had done badly, some disastrously, David had hugely increased his majority. What was more, the Tories had won a large majority in parliament and were very unlikely to want another election for at least four years. It did seem possible that David really did have a new career. We had better now work out how we ought to cope with it. Certainly, after another four or five years in parliament he would be so out of touch with the latest developments in engineering that he could no longer assume that he could go back to Holman's. He had better make sure that his political career would keep us and there was no better way of achieving that than for both of us to devote our efforts full-time to keeping him in parliament.

The major change would be in my lifestyle. For almost five years I had been leading a double life. Quite apart from bringing up Matthew and Anna, almost single-handed, I had been both the postmistress of Chacewater and at the same time an MP's aide. Now we decided to give up the post office and buy a bigger house. We would miss the income from the post office but I could give more time to the children as well as having enough space to run David's office.

Since Anna's birth we had outgrown our home and we desperately lacked space. The children were sharing a small bedroom next to our own, the third bedroom having been taken over by David's work. We all shared a fair-sized living room but if David had people in for discussions, the children and I had nowhere to go. We had no garden. When the weather was nice I spent a lot of time taking the children to the local park or for walks. Though this could be fun, it was not always convenient.

I have always suffered from impatience and when I want something I am like the children in that I want it now. I had constantly complained about how impossible it was with all of us living on top of each other and how having David's office on the premises left us no privacy at all. I wanted to move immediately. Virtually the day after David won, I was scanning the local papers for suitable properties. David, however, was more attached to our post office home than I was and he could see no real reason to hurry in giving it up just yet. He eventually gave in in August 1979 but was quite adamant that we should not look at future homes until our own place was virtually sold.

It soon became apparent that we would have no difficulty in finding new owners. Prospective buyers came from all corners of the country. The only difficulty would be over finding ones we thought would be right for Chacewater. It was at a time when there was a boom in the property market and David could see only too clearly that, after all he had said about 'up country people' taking over local communities, he was in danger of adding to the problem himself. Then, just as two or three couples were trapped in a race to raise the capital, a young man who had been brought up in Chacewater and whose family still lived there showed more than a passing interest in the business. He was the ideal man to take over the property. David's prayers were answered.

When eventually I was allowed to house-hunt, properties were being sold almost before going on the market. Indeed that was how we came to buy our present home. As we could find nothing suitable in Chacewater, where we had lived for almost twelve years, I was looking for somewhere in Truro itself. (After all, both our families lived there and it was the political, if not the geographical, centre of the constituency.) An estate agent told me of a client who was just at the stage of talking about selling up. I went straight round. The house fitted our requirements, we agreed a price, and were delighted to get it.

We moved in at Christmas 1979. Well, we took the key then and the builders moved in to make a few alterations including installing central heating. We stayed again with my parents while the work went on and each room was gradually decorated. I did not relish the thought of living in a mess and so avoided it – too long in David's view – and he made it quite clear one weekend that if I had not moved in by the next he was going to. We duly spent the first night in our new home on St David's Day. It was lovely having space at last and a garden for the children. We all loved it then and still do.

The new house, where we have lived ever since, is at the top of Daniell Road, a residential street that clambers up one of the steep hills that enclose the city. It is late Victorian, semi-detached, four-bedroomed, with two large living rooms and an office at the back. The garden is large enough to give the children room to rush about, yet demands a minimum of tender loving care. That suited us perfectly. I am no gardener. David enjoyed looking after our splendid *Escallonia* hedges and the lawn, which he levelled with immense care, but not much more.

David did, however, become intensely interested in growing trees. This began when he and Matthew collected some acorns which David grew in pots in his Westminster office. From the other end of the office, Stephen Ross was fascinated by David's scientific approach to the challenge of growing plants. There were milk bottles and plastic cups all over the place, each of them linked to an intricate system of pipes that ensured that they were drip-fed at the correct rate. The system worked and eventually his oak trees grew so big that he had to bring them home. He was asked to show them to one of the local schools and they even appeared on a local television gardening programme. Some of them, now well over seven feet high, are still behind the house. One has been planted nearby, in David Penhaligon Way, and several in the churchyard near his grave.

David loved the house and I will always picture him at his happiest sitting at his big oak desk, during the summer recess, in the dining end of the big room. The television, tuned to the Test Match, would be moved from its usual position to the middle of the room, its wires and aerial looped across the carpet, a radio on the floor adding to the confusion. The radio was essential. David loved to watch cricket on television but insisted on listening to the radio commentary at the same time.

(Cricket had always been his favourite game and he was delighted when Matthew turned out to be good enough to represent his school. For a while David even became a member of Somerset Cricket Club, which is the closest first-class cricket club to Cornwall. He was only able to go to Taunton once or twice, because political activities always had first priority, but he felt it was only right to subscribe to a game which gave him so much pleasure.)

The desk was always full of letters, the floor covered in bumph thrown there by David, while I kept him supplied with endless cups of coffee. In the middle of this confusion David would be dictating letters into a dictaphone, watching cricket with the inevitable cigarette in his spare hand. It was his idea of heaven but to me it was a nightmare and I constantly complained about the incredible mess. On the other hand, he always caught me out when he went to look for something in a drawer or cupboard, which I never found time to tidy, and would accuse me of only wanting the place to look tidy in case anyone called. He was quite right.

By this time Matthew was seven and a half and Anna two and a half. Matthew fitted into his new school very well. Indeed, it was the same primary school that David had attended many years before. At one stage they even shared the same teacher, Joyce Heather, whom David remembered with great affection. By chance our new neighbours had a son the same age as Matthew, even sharing the same birthday, and Matthew and James spent many hours playing in each other's gardens. During the Falklands war, the gardens would become Port Stanley and the kids did battle royal against imaginary Argentinians. I did, however, find it mildly amusing when, on one of the many occasions these two friends fell out, I enquired of Matthew what the problem was and he announced that James wanted to use nuclear warheads and Matthew did not agree with them. There were the vicar's son and the Liberal MP's son introducing politics into their game and fighting with a passion of which neither of their fathers would have approved.

14
BREATHING SPACE

'We looked on him not just as MP for Cornwall but as MP for the whole of the region. He was wonderful at giving his services to other constituencies.' – Vera Harvey

We not only had a new house in Truro, David had a new House of Commons to cope with too. This was to be as different from that of 1974 as was our new home from Chacewater post office. The most obvious difference in the House of Commons lay in its leadership. From its very first day, the 1979 government was not just Tory but distinctively Thatcherite. The policies were to be totally different from those of Callaghan and indeed from those of Heath at the beginning of the decade. Monetarism was in, along with its consequent cuts in public services and benefits. This would be hard on all local authorities but as David pointed out in *News from the Liberals* it would be especially hard on Cornwall, which was already bottom of the league in public spending.

A less obvious difference, from a national point of view, lay in the composition of the Liberal group, but it was a difference that would mean a lot to David. The Party had done less badly than it had feared in the General Election – thanks largely to Callaghan's delay in going to the country and an exceptionally skilful campaign by David Steel. However, in the country overall the Liberals had polled only thirteen per cent, compared with eighteen per cent in 1974, and there had been shattering losses: Jeremy Thorpe (although he would be found not guilty of conspiracy to murder), Emlyn Hooson and John Pardoe.

The loss of John was a terrible blow to the Liberals of Devon and Cornwall. He had been swept aside by the swing to the Tories. Most of the Liberal MPs (David most dramatically of all) had survived only because they plundered the Labour vote to compensate for the loss of votes to the Tories. John, however, had no more Labour vote to plunder. He had already reduced them to three per cent in 1974. As a result, David was no longer the most junior of the Liberal MPs in the south-west. He was the only one.

This was to add considerably to his responsibilities, or – luckily for other candidates in the south-west – what he saw as his responsibilities. Vera Harvey, the Liberal organizing secretary for the region, who had done so much to encourage him as a Young Liberal and as a candidate, now came to rely on him to encourage and inspire a new generation of parliamentary candidates himself. Over the next few years, he would become the key speaker at the training sessions she ran, as well as at major meetings of the Devon and Cornwall region.

David was also now no longer the youngest of the parliamentary group. David Alton had won Edge Hill in a sensational by-election in early 1979 and held it in the General Election to become the youngest MP in the House. (It is extraordinary how many times the Liberals have had the youngest MP over the last few decades: first David Steel, then David Alton and now Matthew Taylor. The party has always given youth its chance.)

David was anyway no longer thought as of as a new MP but almost as a veteran. So in a way he was. He had already been Liberal spokesman in the Commons for social services, employment, transport, energy and the environment (a portfolio then unique to the Liberals) – and at one time for four of them all at once. He had bargained directly with Cabinet ministers, won amendments, gained concessions and positively Liberalized national policy in these areas. He had also through his first five years seen the fate of the government turn on his vote and those of his colleagues.

After that experience, the new parliament was bound to be something of an anticlimax for the Liberal MPs. There were only eleven of them left and Mrs Thatcher had a large majority. No one needed their votes any more. If they wanted to get something done for their constituents, they would have to cajole, persuade, embarrass the government. They could no longer demand attention.

This of course was nothing unusual for David's colleagues. That was how it had nearly always been. For David, though, it was a new experience. He had, however, already worked out how he should approach it. He had explained his philosophy in a long and well-received interview on the NHS he gave to the medical magazine *On Call* in 1976. 'If you believe in the power of persuasion and argument, then that is the type of role any opposition party can take. It does not really matter whether you've got three members or 314.' He had now to prove that point. He would find it difficult.

In May David Steel asked him to take on energy and transport in the House, so he was certainly on familiar ground. On energy, the Tories in what David dubbed their 'hunger for the grand solution', were if anything even keener than Labour on the use of nuclear power stations, while David had moved by now from scepticism to outright opposition. On transport, the Tories, disappointingly, were rather less sympathetic to the rural constituencies than were Labour. The Labour party had threatened a rise in petrol tax of 5½p in 1977 and only removed it at the Liberals' insistence. The Tories now proposed an even larger increase.

The Liberals immediately moved an amendment to keep the increase no higher than the rate of inflation, pointing out that cars were responsible for only twenty per cent of the oil used in the country. David went further. 'We should,' he said, 'introduce a system that has the effect of charging the owner of a large car that consumes a great deal of petrol a high rate of duty . . . That would encourage the car-driving public to buy economical cars.' One of the major problems was that seventy per cent of all new cars were now bought by companies, who paid for any increase in the cost of petrol. This was all very well for their employees but no comfort for the less well-off and the self-employed in the rural areas, who had to pay it out of their own pockets.

David returned to the subject of the mileage allowance received by MPs. He was given £84 for driving up and down to Truro. It was a temptation – into which he admitted falling on occasions – to drive rather than take the train whenever he had a big bill coming up. So too did everyone else, he said. David had the reputation of managing to remain friends with everyone in the House, however much he opposed their point of view. His attacks on the MPs' petrol allowance, however, invariably sparked off heated exchanges in the House and strained that friendship very close to breaking point. Certainly the Liberals did not win their amendment.

Where they were on the winning side, however, was in a long-running debate on a suggestion that the payment of benefits should no longer be handled by sub post offices. The government claimed that the Prime Minister was the expert on this. Was not her father a sub postmaster? David, however, could claim even more relevant experience and for the first time was free to speak without an interest to declare on the subject, as our sub post office had just been sold.

'This,' he said, 'is one of a series of debates in the House that pose the question "Do we or do we not wish to destroy villages?" I do not. But the government clearly do.' He pointed out how difficult and expensive it would be for most pensioners to travel to the towns and, if they did so, they would buy their goods there. Not only would the sub post offices be ruined but the other village shops as well. He handed in huge petitions not only from Truro but also from North Cornwall Liberals, whose interests he now looked after too. But it was not just a Liberal issue. Robert Hicks was equally against any change, along with many Tory backbenchers. The idea was shelved. 'Persuasion and argument' did not always work, but here they did.

It was at this time that there was a free vote on hanging, the third time the issue had been raised during David's first five years in parliament. On this occasion David voted against its reintroduction, as he had done on the first occasion in 1974. It was not an electorally popular stance but after his experience of the murder trial in Bodmin, he had always been instinctively opposed to capital punishment. In 1975, however, he did vote for a motion calling for further investigation into whether or not it should be reintroduced for acts of terrorism that caused death. It was one of the most traumatic occasions I can remember in our marriage.

At the time I think David probably thought I was suffering a brainstorm. When he arrived home and told me how he had voted, in sheer disbelief I kicked every stick of furniture in the sitting room. He should have felt relieved, because there is no doubt where I would have preferred to have vented my feelings. Anyway, he was also considerably bigger than me!

I had taken it for granted he would vote against. I was never more shocked by any of his political actions either before or since. It seemed totally out of character and a complete betrayal of all his beliefs. He, like me, remembered the hangings that had occurred in this country and the physical revulsion I always felt on such occasions. To me it seemed totally wrong morally for the nation to take a life and I did not see it as a deterrent.

David's reasons for acting in a way I thought totally out of character were quite clear to him. He was not voting on legislation but only on whether or not there should be further investigation. He thought the arguments for and against the death penalty should be subjected to such investigation. It did not mean that he would in the event of proposed legislation vote for it. I can now appreciate the logical force of his argument but the incident did illustrate our different ways of looking at some political issues. I would have voted – and would now vote – against any suggestion that there are any arguments worth investigation for restoring the death penalty in any circumstances. David voted – and would always vote – that any arguments should be subjected to full investigation, however little he liked them.

In the early days David never left the constituency 'unattended' for more than a few days and on only three occasions in all the twelve years he was an MP did we have holidays of a fortnight. David never ever forgot how hard-won Truro was and he was hyper-cautious over doing anything that might lose support. He therefore rarely sought or accepted invitations to join parliamentary delegations abroad. Once he went to Brussels to visit the headquarters of the EEC, once to New York to visit the UN and once he spent an eventful day in Northern Ireland when the MPs were stoned – literally.

However, there were two occasions when he was prepared to take a little longer away. The first of these was directly after the 1979 election. The end of the pact, and of the Liberals' day-to-day involvement in government decisions, had released the MPs to play a larger role in the work of Liberalism worldwide. It was a role that David relished; so he was happy to accept for both of us when he was asked to speak at the Liberal International Conference which that year was being held in Stavanger, Norway. We had a wonderful time exploring some of the spectacular scenery of that area as well as participating in the conference. The highlight had to be a midnight sail around the many islands and fjords near to Stavanger on Midsummer's Night. It was planned to give us the experience of twenty-four hours of continuous daylight and was only slightly spoilt by the fact that the sky was hidden by clouds.

That trip was in sharp contrast to our only other holiday experience of sailing. It was on the Norfolk Broads, soon after we were married, when we went out in a boat with Des and Janice Honey. It pelted with rain the whole way and we got ourselves stuck on a mudbank. 'It's like sailing down a gutter,' was David's verdict. We never tried it again.

The Norwegian boat trip was rather better organized. It was laid on by the local newspaper and we were given traditional Norwegian fare to eat. This included a very salty pork dish which made us all very thirsty and when we were offered beer to drink we eagerly accepted, only to find that our host was a temperance newspaper and the beer was aptly named zero beer. It was ghastly and only David found it funny. Being teetotal himself, he was of course cheerfully unaffected by the party's lack of alcohol.

I particularly remember the trip for two other reasons. One was telephoning home regularly to find out what was happening in the Thorpe trial, as the verdict was expected any day. The second was that one morning we came down to breakfast to find a note from the hotel receptionist which read: 'Telephone Truro police. You have had a thief.'

Horrified, I telephoned home to find that burglars had indeed broken in and ransacked our home, presumably looking for access to the post office money, which fortunately they did not find. The only item missing, according to my parents, was a £10 note left in a pot in the kitchen. However, the police were worried because they could not find my jewellery and thought perhaps this was also stolen. No, they could not have stolen my jewellery I said, as I was wearing it. The police, I think, expected M Ps' wives to own a little more than that.

The second and most enjoyable of all his visits abroad – even including, I suspect, holidays! – was the fortnight he spent following Jimmy Carter's Democrat campaign trail a few weeks before the 1980 Presidential Election. He visited many, many towns and industrial centres as well as seeing rural America at first hand and it left quite an impression on him.

On preparing for his trip it seemed a good opportunity to persuade David to buy a new suit, something he hated doing. I always had to drag him along to the shops for anything like that. In fact once I had got him there I persuaded him to buy two, as I had no idea of when my next opportunity would be. Of course, once he got to America David forgot how many suits he had taken with him and left a brand new one in one of the American hotels! When I first knew him David's mother always made an inventory of everything in his suitcase whenever he went away and stuck it to the inside of the lid of the suitcase. At the time I thought it very funny but now I realized why she did it.

At first David was viewed with considerable caution in the States whenever he was introduced as a Liberal MP – there the term 'liberal' is frequently used as a term of abuse – but he soon won his hosts over. Liberal was not the only word David had difficulty with. Discussing polling day techniques with his new-found friends, he enthusiastically explained that our method of getting out the votes in the evening was by 'knocking up' the voters, only to find that this piece of information was greeted by embarrassed silence. David was then told solemnly that over there knocking up had more to do with sex than votes.

One of the difficulties for any visitor to the States, let alone a politician invited, as David was, to see America as a guest of the country, is that he is always being asked what he thinks of his host's town, house, neighbours, politicians. One American interviewer pressed David to compare the average Briton with the average American. 'Well,' said

David diplomatically, 'I am not too keen on averages. I don't know about the average American, but I can tell you that the average Briton has 1.97 legs.'

'What did the British think of the presidential candidates?' was another favourite question. 'I think they would mostly vote for Carter. There is a fear that Ronald Reagan may be a bit trigger-happy.' 'They are against his policies then?' 'I don't think they know much about his policies. They have just seen too many of his old movies.'

The American press loved him and he loved America. It was not until some time later that I realized just how much he loved it. We were at a party and were asked to participate in a 'Mr and Mrs' quiz, not something I would generally have agreed to do. David, however, said he did not mind, so I gave in. One of the questions I was asked was, 'Where would David like to live other than Cornwall?' Easy, I thought. There is nowhere in the world he would be willing to live other than his beloved Cornwall, but I was wrong. His answer had been America.

With the loss of such brilliant speakers as Jeremy, John and Emlyn, David's skill as a communicator was vital now, as never before, both to the Party as a whole and to David Steel in particular. David found himself employed on most party political broadcasts, a star speaker at by-elections, guest speaker on *Any Questions?* and innumerable television political programmes. As a result he was not only away on foreign trips but also beginning on what would be a major preoccupation of the next few years – spreading the word all round the UK. The responsibility for organizing his diary was mine.

Obviously there was a limited time David could spend either away from parliament or the constituency but invitations were now coming in thick and fast either by post or on the telephone. David was anxious not to overdo the visits but at the same time when approached directly with an invitation would say he would love to come but they had better check with 'the wife'. Indeed I suspect his friendly reply was even more positive than that, judging by the phone calls I received. Most said, 'David promised to come on such and such a date.' When I said that it was not possible, I am sure the people on the other end of the line thought I was being a possessive dragon preventing their dear David from coming when he so obviously wanted to. Whenever I tackled David on this he always seemed surprised that he was so misinterpreted. Rubbish, of course! He just could not say no himself. Indeed he had no need to, as he had me to do that for him.

Another problem we had with the diary was to make sure David attended the various functions in his diary when he was away from home. I always wrote everything down for him day by day, even packing his bag in such a way that he knew which tie to wear with which shirt. Most of this was a total waste of my time as he lost the list and muddled up his clothes. However, he would ring each day for instructions and generally we managed – except on one occasion when he was speaking in Derby.

That morning I told him which train to catch and whom he was meeting. I was therefore somewhat surprised to receive a telephone call in the middle of the afternoon from a sheepish, sleepy David. 'Ah, I fell asleep on the train and I'm in Sheffield,' he said. 'Is that above or below Derby?' I could not believe it – how could he have managed it! 'Catch the next train back,' I said, 'and I'll get a message to the poor souls waiting for you at Derby.' I heard from him again that night. He was in a cheerful mood and said everything had gone fine in Derby. 'What did you tell them about being late?' I asked. 'Nothing,' said David. 'What, you just got off the wrong train, and said nothing?' I asked. 'That's right,' replied David. 'I've found out in this life that if you are going to be late, be really late and they will be so relieved to see you they won't say anything.' And they didn't.

The one compensation for the Liberals' loss of influence at Westminster after the 1979 election was that the Liberal MPs had more time to work in and on their own constituencies. David had certainly established a reputation for being accessible to his constituents in a way no Tory MP had thought to be before but there was always more that he felt he could have done and now he had the chance to get on with it.

By this time the local press was beginning to be a great help to him. Before he had been elected it had virtually disregarded him but over his first few years in parliament it had discovered that it now had a very newsworthy MP. The press in fact was probably quicker than we were in recognizing how unusual an MP he was. We just did what we thought was required and were glad if people seemed to approve. The press saw that the approval was based on an affection that was quite unusual between constituents and MP.

The paper best placed to make this judgment was the *Western Morning News*, which, unusually, had its own lobby correspondent at Westminster. Winston Grant Evans, who died tragically young, early in 1989, held this post throughout most of the 1980s and therefore had the chance to see David at work both at home and away. Winston, like others, was struck by how slow David was to appreciate how popular he was becoming both in and out of the constituency. However, he did find him very interested in how the press worked and happy to cooperate with it.

David was generally happy to cooperate with anyone in his role as MP if he thought Truro would benefit, even if he did not agree with them on other matters. He was for instance an ally of the Bishop of Truro, Dr Leonard, over such matters as the importance of overseas aid. However, David did not agree with the Bishop's conservative views on other matters. David was not keen on high church ritual, and I was strongly against the Bishop's views on the role of women in the church.

In 1980, when Dr Leonard was translated to the bishopric of London, a motion was put down in the House of Commons to congratulate him on his move. David added his name to the motion. A few days later, at the opening of Marks and Spencer's in Truro, we saw the Bishop bearing down on us along one of the aisles between the merchandise. 'Now, don't be a hypocrite,' I whispered to David. I needn't have worried. The Bishop immediately made a point of thanking him for adding his name to the motion. 'Ah, yes,' said David with a grin. 'Of course, I did. I am delighted you are going.'

The move to Daniell Road was a great help to David in his work. Chacewater was right on the edge of the constituency. Truro was more central. At this time too the Liberal headquarters were moved. The association took the big decision to buy its own premises at last and found a suitable building in Charles Street, only a few hundred yards from our new house.

David's chief concern over the next few years was to be

the county council. His major criticisms centred on their meanness over bus passes, their lack of investment in the clay district and their failure to take action over unemployment. The Cornish Liberals had so far failed to win seats on the county council and were not to do so until 1980. With its almost exclusively Independent (Tory) membership, the council had little sympathy with the lone Liberal MP.

'Cornwall is in the scandalous position of being the only county in Britain which does not have a concessionary bus fare scheme for the elderly and disabled in its community,' David said. 'The excuses given for not implementing such a scheme are puerile and one can only assume it reflects the interests of the car-owning county councillors.' It was not surprising that little love was lost between him and the councillors.

What had been happening was that the county had been trying to shift the responsibility on to the other councils. The issue was becoming even more urgent as the Tory government were now encouraging deregulation of services, and the operators, who badly needed the extra contribution for the bus passes, were already tending to cut out their less profitable routes. David was no less critical of the operators. 'A situation in which nobody can get from the main town to one of the surrounding communities after 6.50 is unbelievable. St Austell is not a rural village with one chapel, one pub and a few houses; it is the commercial centre of Cornwall's largest industrial complex and the social centre for a total catchment population of nearly 35,000 people.'

In this industrial complex the condition of the dilapidated schools and roads had improved slightly after David's criticisms in previous years but not as fast or as far as David thought fair. David also deplored the council's refusal to introduce a sixth form college in Truro. If they did not, he said, there could not be a true comprehensive system. Instead they attached sixth form provision to one of the two secondary schools and left the other without.

If relations were generally strained between David and the county council, they were only slightly better when all the MPs combined, and they did so over unemployment. David had already hammered the council over the inadequacy of their promotional budget for industrial planning. Now the other MPs joined him for a meeting with the council. They had good cause for concern. Besides the closure of Mount Wellington and the loss of the ship repair work at Falmouth, English China Clays were cutting their workforce by 800 jobs and the large Rank/Toshiba company in Plymouth where many Cornishmen had worked by even more.

The council were on the defensive. They could not wave a magic wand, they said, and they blamed the government for most of the problems. But there was some slight progress. They at least acknowledged that there were problems and that they were committed to do all they could to help. As one of the Cornish MPs was John Nott, and he was Secretary of State for Trade and Industry, they hoped their own complaints would be noted. David made sure that John Nott would not forget. David had, by chance, just been given yet another change of job. He had handed over transport and was now himself his own Party's spokesman on industry.

In the big unemployment debate of November 1980, he turned to draw attention to the gap on the government's front bench. 'I am disappointed that the Secretary of State for Trade is not sitting in his place, although he has been here for most of the debate. The Secretary is not a "wet". Indeed, I am told that he is so dry on these matters that he is surrounded by deliquescent salts in order to ensure that not a drop of water enters his thoughts. I shall tell the right honourable Gentleman something about the area that he represents, in the far south-west. In Penzance male unemployment has reached 16.5 per cent. In St Ives it has reached 24.7 per cent. In Helston 18.2 per cent. In the right honourable Gentleman's constituency, the largest source of income in the winter months is state benefit. Almost one-fifth of the right honourable Gentleman's constituency is unemployed. Nevertheless we are told that the right honourable Gentleman wishes to pursue such nonsense further.'

The 'nonsense' that David was hammering here was the Tory theory that strict control of the money supply was a sufficient answer to the recession afflicting British industry. David pointed out that the major problems were the high value of the pound and the unnecessarily high price of our own oil. The answer, he said, lay in a reduction of interest rates and the introduction of a prices and incomes policy.

This speech marked for David a major change in how he was seen both in parliament and in Cornwall. He was no longer an engaging and enthusiastic junior MP. With the experienced Richard Wainwright, he was now responsible for arguing the case for the Liberal economic policy. He was a spokesman in what would be the key debates of the next six years and would come back again and again to the message that interest rates were the key to a broad-based industrial recovery. He would be attacked fiercely for his opinions in the House and would attack the government's policy as fiercely in return.

In Cornwall similarly he had with that speech laid claim to the position of the county's champion at Westminster. If Cornwall had a Cabinet minister who would not speak up for the Duchy, David would. Symbolically, within a year David was made a Cornish Bard for 'his services to Cornwall in Parliament'. He was not the first MP to have been so honoured, nor did he speak Cornish, but he was from now on to be seen as the undisputed Voice of Cornwall.

More importantly for David Steel, he also discovered an ability to sway opinion at Assemblies. In 1980, he spoke up for the first time on defence and made the key speech in persuading the majority to accept the philosophy of multi-lateral disarmament at a time when many of his closest friends and greatest admirers were pushing for a unilateralist policy.

David had not intended to speak in the debate but he was in agreement with his colleagues in parliament over the key issues. They were against an independent British deterrent but they supported NATO and were therefore prepared to accept Cruise missiles. The problem for their defence spokesman, Stephen Ross, was that however much they were in agreement few wanted to defend their position in the debate. Desperate for support, he seized a speaker's card and filled in David's name. 'Sign there,' he said.

A few minutes later, David was called to the rostrum. Totally unrehearsed, he decided to ask the unilateralists what they wanted. Were they advocating no Cruise missiles in Britain, he asked. Yes, they shouted. Were they advocating no Cruise missiles in NATO, he asked. Yes, they shouted again. 'In that case,' he told them, 'you are advocating surrender. If you are prepared to defend your freedoms, you will never have to – if you are not, they will be taken away from you.' As for those who wanted a separate European non-nuclear force, they were behaving like 'virgins in a brothel'. It was a fierce debate and for David the first time that he had received a standing ovation there. However, it was also the first time he had aroused equally vociferous opposition.

That Assembly was notable also for another debate. It was not in the main conference chamber – just in a fringe meeting. The speaker was a former Labour MP, David Marquand. He was not very well known to the general public. His style was professorial. His subject matter, however, was explosive. He was talking about the plans of certain Labour MPs to leave their Party and possibly look to the Liberal Party as allies. The Social Democrats were on their way.

15
THE SOGGY DEMS

'He cultivated a faintly prickly image with the SDP but I think it was only skin-deep. On liaison and policy committees he always played a helpful role.' – Roy Jenkins

What eventually became known as the Alliance was to catch the attention of the media and the public to an extraordinary degree over the next six years and was to be a key element in every political issue in which David was concerned. The Alliance, however, was quite unlike David's earlier experience of politics, in that its successes and its failures would depend very largely on the personalities of a very small number of key people: David Steel, Roy Jenkins, Shirley Williams, Bill Rodgers and David Owen. With the exception of his own leader, David knew none of them especially well, yet by 1986 he was to know them very well indeed and was himself seen as the man most likely to succeed them. It was to be a strange six years.

At that 1980 Liberal Assembly there had been a discussion, though somewhat oblique, about the possible formation of the Social Democratic Party – the 'Soggy Dems' as they were at first to be called by many of the Liberals. The SDP had roots that went way back into the troubled history of the Labour Party, springing from the ancient split between its right and left wings. Since the days of Gaitskell, this split had widened, as left and right adopted totally different views on Europe, defence and the economy. Labour had always seen itself as a broad church but by now there were virtually no gods on which its two wings could agree.

This division had led to Dick Taverne's decision to leave the Party and fight – and at first retain – his seat as a Democratic Labour Candidate in 1973. Then, in 1974, a former Labour minister, Chris Mayhew, joined the Liberals. There were other defections too but none significant enough to be called a splinter group and none by a major figure.

When the first major figure decided to act, it was almost surreptitiously. In 1977 Roy Jenkins decided to accept the offer of the presidency of the EEC. At the time this was seen as a graceful departure from politics by a man who no longer wanted to fight. How wrong we all were. Roy had not lost his taste for battle. He was choosing his ground and looking around for allies. In 1979 he made two significant moves. He agreed to deliver the Dimbleby lecture, in which he was to analyse what had happened under the two-party system over the last twenty years, and put the case for a new centre party and proportional representation. This was to start a nationwide debate on the subject. Roy also began that year a series of meetings with David Steel – meetings concerned not with the theory of a new grouping in parliament but with how it might be implemented.

For David S., the invitation came at exactly the right time. He had always been determined to realize Jo Grimmond's vision of the realignment of the left. The Lib/Lab pact had been his first attempt and he had enjoyed the taste of power, faint though it had been. He had now to find some other way to get Liberal policies on to the statute books. A coalition between disaffected Labour MPs and the Liberals might be the answer.

Psychologically, David S. and Roy were ideally matched. In fact, they got on so well that Roy thought he might first join the Liberals and then try to persuade his old friends in the Labour Party to do the same. Aware of what was being discussed, both Cyril and my David were in favour of this solution but David S. was certain that the creation of a new party such as the SDP would attract more defectors – and more enthusiasm throughout the country – than a suggestion that they join the Liberals. After all, the opportunity to join the Liberals had always been there and Labour dissidents had rejected it. Certainly, this was true of the three major figures on the Labour right: Shirley Williams, Bill Rodgers and David Owen.

These three were key to any significant move from the Labour Party. Shirley, though she was currently without a seat in parliament, had a huge following throughout the country. David Owen, who had been the youngest Foreign Secretary of our century, commanded the attention of the media. Bill, though the least well known of what was nicknamed the Gang of Three, commanded the loyalty of a large number of Labour backbenchers. All three were known to be contemplating a split unless their Party's drift to the left were halted. It was not. The Labour conference in October 1980 voted for unilateralism and for withdrawal from the EEC. It was followed by the election of Michael Foot as leader. For the Gang of Three the choice now was plain. They linked up with Roy Jenkins, set up the Council for Social Democracy with its so-called 'Limehouse' declaration of principles in January 1981, and finally broke from the Labour Party by establishing the SDP in March.

The Liberals watched these manoeuvres with feelings that ranged from delight to dismay, particularly because David S. was suggesting that there might be some electoral pact with the SDP. Obviously anything that might strengthen the causes we pursued was welcome and we certainly welcomed any allies in the fight for Europe and electoral reform. On the other hand, as David was quick to point out, our policies on nuclear energy, education and community politics were miles apart from those of the 'Soggy Dems'. Other Liberals, but not David, were worried that the SDP accepted the existence of a British independent nuclear deterrent. The SDP wanted multilateralist disarmament. Many Liberals were unilateralists.

A greater problem was one of ideals rather than particular policies. Might not Liberalism be swamped if we combined forces to create this so-called third force in politics? And anyway were we not the third force already? We had a high vote at General Elections. We might be under-represented within parliament but we were influential in local government. How would we benefit from an electoral pact? And could any pact be made to work? Yes, said David S. Perhaps, said David P.

David was seen as a natural champion of pure Liberalism and it was now, perhaps for the first time, that he realized that his opinion mattered very much indeed to his leader. On this issue, David S. was not looking so much for his support on policy as on strategy. He recognized that David had an instinctive grasp of grass roots reaction in the Party. David also had the ability to put across ideas to the Party as well as the general public. As so often before, David Steel's problems lay with the Party. He needed its support. He could not afford to have David Penhaligon on the other side.

The two Davids had by now appreciated that they had more in common than a love of cars. They shared a love of politics. This, as John Pardoe has pointed out, is less common among politicians than people believe. Most politicians pursue politics as a means to some ends. They find it frustrating, and the frustration shows. Few genuinely love it and have the chance to pursue it at the level they enjoy. The Davids did.

Their ways, however, were very different. David Steel has always relished the large scenario, the rise and fall and manipulation of governments. David Penhaligon loved the battle, the platform, the swing of the votes. He needed, however, to be persuaded that that battle, that platform, those votes, would support the cause he loved. He had, he admitted, come into politics because he too believed in Jo's vision of a realignment of the left. So he told his leader that he would work with the SDP but his first priority would always be the interests of the Liberals. David S. accepted that. He needed a colleague to make the Alliance work but also prepared to be the hard man in any negotiations between the two parties, and the first negotiations would be over seats.

The launch of the SDP had brought them a membership within two months of 70,000. At the first by-election since March, Roy had nearly won Warrington, with a totally unexpected forty-two per cent of the vote. In the opinion polls in September they rated thirty per cent to the Liberals' eight per cent. By October, they would have twenty-three MPs, more than twice the size of the Liberal group. On the other hand, out in the constituencies, it was the Liberals who had the workers and the experience. They had associations which had steadily built up their strength and some of these were now on the point of winning parliamentary seats. Someone had to persuade the SDP that at least the first fifty of these were sacrosanct.

David made this point on his own at the most effective moment. This was at the Assembly of 1981. On the day before the Liberals would vote on whether or not to continue negotiations with the SDP, David turned to Roy, who was at a fringe meeting as a visitor, and drew attention to a rumour that the SDP wanted to stand in half those fifty 'most winnable' constituencies. 'It is not on,' said David, 'and I want you to say now that it is not on.' Rather than risk a row, Roy agreed. Next day the Liberals agreed to negotiate. The Alliance had begun.

In the long term the greatest difficulties for the Alliance were bound to turn on policies. Though both parties agreed on most issues, there would always be some on which compromise or blunt disagreement would have to be tolerated. After all, they were not one party; they were two. At first, however, a far greater cause for concern tended to overshadow policy differences. This was what the Alliance rather grandly called 'seat allocation'. This in fact was the process of deciding which constituencies would have Liberal and which would have SDP candidates in parliamentary elections. David was to be intimately involved in the negotiations, first at the local level and then, at David Steel's request, the national level too.

It would not be easy but it would give David a chance to use the knowledge he had acquired over the years from his interest in psephology. In fact, by a strange coincidence, three of the Liberals who would have the most influence on the negotiations were fascinated by psephology, all knew each other well and were all connected with Truro. In the week before the 1981 Liberal Assembly, a book had been published which provided a computer analysis of Liberal prospects in all the seats in the UK. It was written by Michael Steed, our candidate in 1970, and his assistant John Curtice, who had been on our executive at that time.

The book caused an outcry, as it recommended that the Liberals should in general concentrate their forces on rural seats and the SDP on the urban and industrial areas. Although the authors' analysis was convincing, neither party was keen to be typecast in that way. However, the book was clearly going to be an invaluable work of reference for the negotiating teams. From it both the press and negotiators could identify which were the fifty golden seats that David was determined to keep for the Liberals. As for the other seats, David gave this advice: 'To both sides I say: don't publish any shopping lists. Sit down and talk quietly.'

Generally, this is what happened. Guidelines had been agreed in September 1981, under which detailed negotiations would be left to joint negotiating committees, which would represent the interests of the two parties in areas that covered approximately two counties at a time. It would be up to the members of these committees to persuade those associations that would not be fielding a candidate to accept the share-out.

In the south-west this on the whole worked well, though it would not be until May 1982 that agreement was reached on the last two seats. Our experience was generally typical of that elsewhere, although as our two counties had an exceptional record of Liberal activity, the final decision was that the Liberals would fight nine of the fifteen seats. To prevent what David called 'bunching', the SDP were to fight two Cornish seats – Falmouth/Camborne and St Ives – even though ours was the strongest Liberal county in the country. Conversely, the Liberals would fight one of the three Plymouth seats, though these all had strong SDP memberships.

For everyone concerned these negotiations were an interesting experience. It was the first time they met their new allies and some of those allies initially seemed odd bedfellows. There was David and there as the chairman of the Cornish SDPs was Bruce Tidy, who had been the Labour candidate in Truro in 1979. There too was David Owen, MP for Plymouth Devonport and now one of the Gang of Four, arguing with David, and not for the last time failing to win his argument, that the SDP should have all the Plymouth seats. (Neither David O. nor David P. were on the southwest negotiating teams but they met separately and then briefed their colleagues.) It was the first time that these two had met as allies, though they had campaigned together before as West County MPs with unemployment as a common cause.

At this time, though, it was not David Owen so much as Bill Rodgers that David was most concerned with. Bill was the SDP chief negotiator on the share out of seats. In December, worried by the failure of one or two negotiating teams to reach agreement because of what he saw as Liberal obstructionism, Bill had called a halt to the whole operation. David S. persuaded him to let the talks resume, on condition that difficulties could be referred to two 'firemen'. The SDP chose John Horam, MP for Gateshead. The Liberals appointed David Penhaligon.

'The great placator, that's me,' David laughed, 'the reconciler.' As he pointed out to the press, it was bound to be an agonizing process. There were 250 Liberal candidates who had already been adopted; some eighty of those would be asked to stand down in favour of SDP candidates. 'There are obviously not going to be many volunteers,' David said ruefully. 'Some of them have been carrying the Liberal flag when it has seemed hopeless and they are not going to take kindly to being told to stand down now the prospects are so good.'

If the Liberals were reassured that David would be there, Bill was a little less so. He knew David from the days of the Lib/Lab pact. It was not they did not get on. They did – extremely well, in fact. The problem was that Bill knew that David could be disarmingly effective in negotiation. Bill remembered meetings in his office in 1977. He was then Secretary of State for Transport and had been startled when the Liberal spokesman wandered in with his hands in his pockets, with no papers, not even a brief-case, and just started to chat about Liberal transport policy. David had been quite at ease, despite his lack of experience, and had got his points across without the slightest difficulty. Bill's civil servants could at first hardly take David seriously. He was so unlike other politicians. Bill, though, took him seriously, from the very start. David's suggestions fitted in far better than with Bill's own views than those of the rest of the Labour Cabinet. They went into his White Paper.

At the birth of the Alliance, Bill had warned his colleagues that David should not be underrated. Now here he was acting for the Liberals in key disputes about the seats. As it worked out, it worked extremely well. By the first deadline of March 1982, 505 constituencies were settled, leaving

122 to be settled in the next few weeks. Obviously there was disappointment, even indignation, in several associations. How could it be otherwise? Liberal associations are independent of Liberal headquarters and cannot be told what they must do. They can only be persuaded. They were persuaded.

When all the negotiations were complete, it could be seen that, with the odd exception, the Liberals had kept their fifty golden seats and the SDP had the best of the next 150. Honour was satisfied all round. Yet always at the back of their minds the SDP were a bit disturbed. The Liberals had given up so much, it was true, but it was equally true that the Liberals still had the best of the prospects overall. Had the two Davids been all too shrewd for them?

There was locally an unusual complication, in that Totnes (which David had fought in 1970) was about to be split and a new constituency of Teignbridge would be created by the next election. The man who was eventually to be chosen as candidate was a friend of David's, not a long-time politician but a policeman – John Alderson, Chief Constable of Devon and Cornwall, and the great advocate of keeping the local bobby on the beat. This 'community policing' was very much in line with Liberal thinking. John was typical of the new type of candidate attracted to politics at this time, a man of experience who hoped that his experience could be of value to the House. David was delighted when he stood, would have liked to see many more such candidates, and had great hopes that he could win.

That January David had every reason to be optimistic. The polls were giving us as good a chance of forming the next government as Labour or the Tories. The Alliance had won the last two by-elections, with Bill Pitt in Croydon and (especially important) Shirley Williams at Crosby. Then in March Roy Jenkins also got back to the House when he won a storming campaign in the unlikely setting of Hillhead, Glasgow. David spoke at all three by-elections and for the first time he felt that he was at least on fairly friendly terms with all the Gang of Four.

Relations between most of the Liberal MPs and the leaders of the SDP had so far been polite rather than close. All the initial negotiations between the parties had been conducted very much by David Steel and his advisers, most of whom were outside parliament. One or two of the Liberal MPs knew one or two of the SDP from their policy discussions in the days of the Lib/Lab pact: David knew Bill Rodgers, for instance, and Alan Beith knew Shirley Williams. Otherwise they had surprisingly little in common. The Liberal MPs tended to congregate within the House, typically in the tea room or the dining room. The SDP and David Steel tended to conduct their discussions over private dinner tables. The by-elections brought them together.

With all this euphoria, the great hope was that even more Labour and Tory MPs would join either the Liberals or the SDP. There were by now twenty-eight SDP MPs from the Labour Party and one from the Conservatives. Several other Tories were known to be discussing the possibility of a move. Among them was Robert Hicks of Bodmin. For Robert the temptation was to join the SDP. He was not a Liberal but he might well see himself as a member of the SDP in alliance with the Liberals. The idea was not so bizarre. He had been in alliance often enough with David, and never more so than over the last few years.

16
FRIEND OR FOE?

'*There are two characteristics that all politicians would like to have. The first is political nous, a gut feeling for what people are thinking about; the second is an ability to find a solution that people can associate with. Many politicians don't have either; a few have one. David certainly had them both.*' – Robert Hicks

Robert Hicks and David were close friends in a way that occasionally, but only occasionally, occurs between members of opposite parties. After all they spent more time together than many members of the same party. They would travel up together on the train from Cornwall, always in the same carriage – they were both incorrigible smokers. What was more, they very seldom found themselves opposing one another, certainly on Cornish issues.

They felt the same over unemployment – that all governments underrated the problems peculiar to Cornwall. They felt the same about sub post offices and had won that one. They felt the same about the price of petrol, Robert making himself very unpopular with his colleagues by joining the Liberals in voting against a further increase in the tax proposed in the 1981 budget. That one they lost.

Robert and David also felt the same about fishing. Looe,

in the Bodmin constituency, suffered even more than Mevagissey in our own from overfishing by the Scots and from the Russian factory ships. It was in response to a concerted campaign by Robert and David that in the end the Tory minister laid down a quota for fishing ships off Cornwall. David at first had written off the government inspectors' efforts as 'an abject, miserable farce . . . Is the minister aware that the White Fish Authority's current paper indicates that last year Britain succeeded in exporting twice as much mackerel as it succeeded in catching? . . . Limiting fish on a tonne-a-day basis is no good. Fishermen seem to have difficulty in counting beyond a certain number. Some have difficulty in weighing the fish they have caught, except when they come to sell it, when inspiration suddenly returns.'

Eventually in 1982, the EEC agreed to a 'mackerel box' that gave some protection to the Cornish inshore fishermen. The monitoring was improved and David then accepted that the quota system was a help. The Russian factory ships sailed away, and so did the Scots, who found the quota too small to justify so long a voyage. As a result today there are still some 1,000 handline fishermen making a living from the mackerel. David and Robert had at least restored the status quo. It was an example of how backbench MPs can use the parliamentary machinery to real effect – even if it did take them some eight years to get action!

It was over fishing that David first crossed words with the new Prime Minister. He was particularly irritated by her attitude to the Russians over the Moscow Olympics. 'I cannot understand why Mrs Thatcher has made such hysterical attacks on the Russians when we all know that Britain still does a great deal of business with that country. I see no verbal attacks or any emotion being shed over the Russians destroying people's livelihoods on our shore-lines.'

David enjoyed teasing Mrs Thatcher on her double stan-dards over the Russians. Much later he discovered that we had been buying TNT from them. 'Is the Prime Minister aware,' he asked her at Question Time, 'that a current Ministry of Defence order for 17,000 artillery shells is being fulfilled by a Belgian-based company which appears to be using Soviet TNT, because it is the cheapest. Can the Prime Minister let the House know what assurances have been given of continuity of supply in the event of hostilities between East and West?'

David and Robert felt the same over Concorde too. Both of their constituencies suffered from supersonic bangs. The government reaction was unhelpful, even farcical. David was asked to note the identification numbers of the planes – ten miles up, flying at supersonic speed?! For some time David could not even discover whether the planes were British or French. The government could not say. British Airways had announced that they were not theirs and that BA would not overfly England at supersonic speed.

That was fine but the bangs persisted. They still persist. Dogs bark, houses crack, the cathedral glass is monitored for damage. Now it is admitted that the bang comes from the French Concorde which turns towards the Charles de Gaulle airport out in the Channel opposite the Cornish coast. Now, when one Cornish constituency complains, the flight path is slightly altered and another constituency is affected. So the problem persists but at least the com-plaints of the Cornish MPs have established a vital prin-ciple: British commercial planes do not overfly British land supersonically. When all planes fly supersonically, that will be a principle that not only Cornwall will need to invoke.

Most importantly of all, David and Robert felt the same over nuclear power. They first came together on the subject on their knees in a Whitehall office. They had been invited by the ministry to discuss certain Cornish sites proposed by the CEGB for nuclear stations in the south-west. Some of the sites were obviously unsuitable. The most likely one was slap on the border of their two constituencies. The map on the wall stretched from Bristol to Land's End. Cornwall was right at the bottom. David and Robert knelt before the map. 'It is yours, David.' 'Oh no, it's not. It is yours, boy.' It was Robert's.

The rumour had been that it was to be at Bugle in the china clay district. It was as if David's constituency had been selected deliberately to punish him for his opposition to all nuclear power stations. In fact it was a few miles east at Luxulyan. The consultants had found it easier to pronounce Bugle! Of course, it made little difference to David. This was his cause just as much as Robert's. He was the man who had campaigned now for five years against the spread of nuclear power stations. He would not opt out of this one, especially as they both could see that the power proposed for this station was three times what was required in Cornwall.

David set out to fight against it with all the fury that he would have shown had it been in Truro itself. 'If Mrs Thatcher is so sure nuclear power stations are safe,' he said, 'let's build the next one on the vacant Battersea power station site opposite her Chelsea home.'

There was a very big rally in Truro in July 1980. I particularly remember it because we all demonstrated, including the children, joining Liberals from all over the county in an attempt to show our solidarity to the cause. At a guess the march was for a couple of miles ending at Boscawen Park, a park next to the river where everyone could rally and listen to the speakers of the day, who included David. I well remember that the Olympics coincided with that rally. Someone had brought a portable TV, and the platform speakers had to tear themselves reluctantly from the television to make their speeches – none of them more reluctantly than David.

That was the day on which we were first introduced to Linda Norton, who was a member of South-East Cornwall Liberals. Malcolm and ourselves spent some time together with her on the walk and afterwards we invited Malcolm and Linda back to our house for tea. Of course, it was only when we got to the end of the march that we realized neither we nor they had been wise enough to leave a car there; so we had to walk the two miles back again with me pushing Anna in a pushchair. I never was keen on more exercise than was necessary. Malcolm and Linda already knew each other and over the next few weeks and months we were to see their friendship develop and we were very thrilled when they asked David to be the best man at their wedding in 1984.

Support for the campaign came too from the local councils, in a way that would have been unthinkable a few years before. The reason was that the councils themselves had changed, dramatically. In 1980 the county council with which David had such trouble had not a single Liberal councillor. By 1982 it had sixteen and it carried overwhelmingly a motion declaring total opposition to the building of any nuclear power station in Cornwall. The motion was proposed by Joan Vincent and seconded by John Hurst of Truro. Joan we had recruited from the clay villages only a few years before. John had been part of David's first campaigning team in 1970.

On Restormel District Council the campaign was led by another stalwart with an even longer history of commitment to the Liberal cause: our former candidate, William Hosking. Though William had decided back in 1966 that he could no longer stand for parliament, he had since found time and energy to go into local politics, where he is still a major force. It was the energy and commitment of such councillors that were now to give David the support he needed. He was no longer on his own.

In some ways the campaign was harder for Robert. It would be Robert who obviously would be the more unpopular with Whitehall. He was a member of the ruling party. No matter. Together, he and David took the case to parliament. Together they supported a protest group who camped on the site to advertise the strength of popular feeling and who attracted much the same publicity as the women of Greenham Common. Together too in the end they were able once again to celebrate success. In November 1982, after being subjected to two years of persistent protest, the CEGB decided to abandon the idea and look elsewhere.

One other joint campaign they fought was for very different reasons. In 1981 the Boundary Commission came up with a plan for reorganizing the Cornish constituencies. Truro was bigger than the other four constituencies and reorganization was obviously overdue. Everyone agreed on that. A few agreed with the Boundary Commission's solution, which was to give St Austell to Robert's constituency, while he lost Bodmin to North Cornwall. Robert did not agree. Neither did David. Robert did not want St Austell. David did not want to lose it.

It was not simply a matter of where the votes lay – though both were very conscious of that. The Boundary Commission's proposal would split up what had become a natural community of interest between Truro and St Austell, and also divide many of the clay villages from St Austell, their local town. Several members of that community who had no political allegiance objected also. So too did the local councils.

In the end, a simpler solution was approved. Robert still lost Bodmin to North Cornwall, and gained Fowey, St Blazey and Tywardreath from us. We also lost a number of villages to Falmouth/Camborne but we held on to St Austell. What that would mean when it came to the next election we did not know; neither did Robert. What, however, we did know by then was that Robert would not be fighting on our side. He had not joined the SDP. Nor had a number of other possible recruits from among the Tories. Instead we had a national crisis. The Argentinians had invaded the Falklands in April 1982 and the political world had been turned upside down. Any hope of recruits from the Tories had sunk alongside the *Belgrano*.

In March 1982 the Alliance and Labour shared first place in the opinion polls with thirty-three per cent and it was in March that Roy achieved his victory at Hillhead. It really did look as if Britain had accepted the third party as equal and possibly preferable to the two old parties. The Alliance seemed to have broken the mould for good. But it was in March too that Argentina invaded the Falklands, and the Falklands would shatter our dreams.

The British people responded to the Falklands crisis with a wave of patriotism and it rewarded the government for its successes with a complete reversal of the political spectrum. Although in Truro we did well in the local elections in May, nationally they did not go as well as we had hoped – and by-elections through the next six months went even worse. It was now clear that Mrs Thatcher would go for an election as soon as she decently could after the return of the Task Force. Eventually she chose June 1983. In the meantime the Alliance did its best to polish up its image. To take maximum advantage of Roy's prestige and experience, it was suggested that he should be named as Prime Minister designate, while David Steel should be leader of the election campaign.

This had a lot to recommend it. Roy carried great weight with the media; so did he with his fellow MPs. David certainly held him in great respect, not only then but in the more difficult years to come. When asked in 1986 whom he admired most in parliament, David responded bluntly that it was a difficult question to answer. 'I've got to know them too well. I used to admire them more before I got elected than I do now.' However, he did make an exception in the case of Roy – 'a man of great substance'. It was an interesting choice, since in 1983 he caused a major storm when with equal bluntness he advised the Alliance to choose David S. and not Roy as PM designate. He put it bluntly too. He pointed to the MORI poll, where fifty-two per cent preferred Steel and only fourteen per cent Jenkins. 'Age may be the factor now,' he said. 'David Steel is forty-four. Roy Jenkins is not exactly geriatric, but he is not too young either.' Roy was sixty-three.

This kind of bluntness was very typical of David's approach to such matters. It was how he would express himself, for instance, at the Liberal MPs' weekly meetings when they would discuss tactics in and outside the House. David's friends have told me that he would generally keep silent while the others pushed their points of view, then if he disagreed he would move in with some remark such as, 'That's plain stoopid. No one outside this madhouse [his favourite description of the House of Commons] will understand what the hell we are up to.' Amazingly he managed to do this without affecting his friendship with the other MPs, partly because they saw there was nothing personal in his criticism, but also because they knew that David's great strength was that he knew instinctively how the British people were likely to react.

If his Liberal colleagues were used to David's bluntness, however, the SDP were not. There was an outcry. They rallied to Roy's support and, rather than rock the boat, David Steel refused to let his own name go forward. It was a decision David S. would himself regret and in the middle of the election campaign when our poll ratings remained obstinately stuck in the low twenties he tried to reverse the decision. By then, however, it was too late.

David was not involved in the grand strategy of the election campaign but he did see something of how it was going, as in this election he took a little time off from Truro to speak for candidates elsewhere. He also was inevitably involved in broadcasts and television programmes around the country. He had first appeared on *Question Time* just before the Hillhead by-election and was to be asked back once a year. On *Any Questions?* he was an even more frequent guest and he would also be in demand for programmes geared specially to the south-west.

I very seldom could join him on his visits to the studios and generally made do with seeing and hearing the programmes. I found the other day an interesting comment in the *Western Morning News* by Sarah Foot, who had made a critical assessment of the *Any Questions?* team in 1982. '*Any Questions?* panel are show-offs. If not, they are not much good for the job. David Penhaligon is a pleasant kind of show-off. He likes giving views on many subjects and does it succinctly and intelligently. He doesn't ramble on about things he may be interested in, but no one else understands. As well he is relaxed enough to crack a few jokes, sound breezy and effortless but nevertheless make one or two serious points that give you something to think about afterwards. One of the audience said: "He often puts across what hundreds of ordinary people are thinking."'

I know now from all the letters I have received how much those programmes were enjoyed. That is a great comfort because I also know how much David enjoyed himself. Of course, they needed preparation and he took them seriously but for him they were also fun. David enjoyed life. That enjoyment, it seemed to me, came across in such programmes.

Paul Tyler, who worked alongside David on so many campaigns and sat beside him on so many platforms, summed up David's style perfectly, when asked of his abiding memory of him: 'That moment when he was about to tell a joke in a big meeting and you could just see a twitch around his mouth, because he was going to enjoy it too. He knew what was coming; it was his joke. He enjoyed it as he enjoyed everything he did, but he particularly enjoyed making other people enjoy themselves, and that's very important.

'He had an enormous power over an audience and, having known him for a fair amount of time, I found it fascinating to see how he not only grew to be able to do that but grew to realize that he could do it, and how invariably he did it not only to good effect but to good purpose.'

For David it was to be a very strange election. From his travels around the country, he could see what disappointments awaited his fellow candidates if the Alliance rating did not rise above thirty per cent but there was nothing he could do about it. The irony was that he could also see that exactly the opposite was likely to happen in Truro. He would probably win by miles. For us everything was – almost wastefully – going in our direction.

Not one of our opponents of 1979 was still in the field. The Tories had lost the energetic Rosemary Brown, found a new candidate, lost him, found another, lost him too, and now had their fourth candidate in four years. Bruce Tidy, Labour's candidate of 1979, was now in the SDP and canvassing for David. His successor was a newcomer. Dr Whetter, the Cornish nationalist, had gone off to fight North Cornwall, on the grounds that for the nationalists Truro was a closed shop, as 'Penhaligon is a good Cornishman, and a good constituency MP'.

Since the last election too, the Liberals had had a run of almost unbroken successes in local elections. There was a large band of councillors on all the local authorities. Although we did not control any of the authorities, we now outnumbered the other political parties and were beginning to introduce much needed Liberal reforms. In 1983 there was at last a Liberal feel to the whole constituency.

It was also a great help that so many of the councillors now knew so many of the electorate personally. Doris Ansari, who remembered first getting on the Truro Council in 1971 by a few votes, when her local council estate had been awash with red posters, had seen that same estate change colour gradually till now only day-glow orange could be seen. In June a *Daily Telegraph* reporter came to Truro to go out with our canvassers, to get a feel of how the vote might go. Doris suggested that the reporter chose which road they should canvass, then took the reporter from door to door. The response was always the same. 'I'm voting Penhaligon.' 'You must have fixed it,' said the reporter. 'You chose the road,' said Doris, 'but it would have been just the same wherever we had gone.'

She was right. Despite the loss of some 10,000 constituents, because of the boundary changes, David won by 10,480, by far the biggerst Alliance majority in the country. That was one election count I almost enjoyed, as I could go down to the count in the morning knowing that we must have won comfortably. Even so we had one cause for concern. The returning officer might be on the point of declaring a huge victory for D. Penhaligon but there was no sign of D. Penhaligon himself. David had spent the night in the ITN studios as a commentator on the results as they came through. ITN were sending him back in a car, in which he could get some sleep, but it only arrived just in time for the declaration. We nearly had Hamlet, without the Prince of Denmark!

17

HEIR APPARENT

'I learnt my politics from David. What he had done in Truro was always a beacon for people like me who felt that was the way to go about politics.' – Paddy Ashdown

That 1983 election was a terrible disappointment for the Alliance. Yet probably after the Falklands adventure there was no way we could have pushed our vote over thirty per cent, the magic figure at which we would have begun to gain seats in proportion to our vote. As it was, our twenty-five per cent of the popular vote gave us only twenty-three seats. This result could not have illustrated more starkly the injustice of our electoral system but that was not much comfort to those 300 Alliance candidates who came second.

Neither was it much comfort for David Steel. His search for the realignment of the left seemed to have hit a wall. He had known the wall was there, of course, but he also knew that with only a few more votes he could have breached it. He had not, however, and there are no rewards for those who come second, let alone third. For him too there was a further blow: Roy had decided to resign the leadership of the SDP.

Where the Liberals had done disappointingly, gaining just five seats and losing one, the SDP had done catastrophically.

They had gained only one seat and lost twenty-five, including those of Shirley Williams and Bill Rodgers. Roy had held Hillhead but he thought it time to stand down as leader. David S. could hardly lecture him on that. Had he not asked Roy only a few days earlier to give up the prospect of Prime Minister designate? For David S. the problem was that David Owen, Roy's successor, was all for the Alliance but most definitely not for what most of the other MPs wanted – a merger of the two parties. David S. decided to go home and think about it – and there he was to stay for the next three months.

Quite suddenly we had a most extraordinary situation. Here was the Alliance, which had achieved a higher vote than any third party in history, in total disarray. One part of it was reeling from an appalling loss of seats, while slap in the middle of the other was a vacuum, and as every schoolchild is supposed to know – but most surely never did! – nature abhors a vacuum. The media, on the other hand, adore it.

Until now there had been little speculation about a successor to David S., either in the media or even within the Liberals. He certainly had his critics in the party – many Liberals resented what they saw as a habit of manipulating and overriding opinion. However, there was no one who was able, or even apparently wanted, to rival his standing within the country. He had been by far the most admired of the party leaders for almost every year of his leadership. What was more, he had shown no sign of wanting to give up the job.

Now everything was changed. The leader had said publicly that he wanted a rest and would then decide whether he would carry on. What if he decided he had enough? Who would succeed? As deputy leader, Alan Beith was in charge while he was away and had to be the most likely to succeed. At the same time, though, people began to speculate about David's chances. David himself dismissed any suggestion that David S. should resign, or that he might succeed him. He was asked by the media what he thought of the election and what now should be done. We should have had Steel in charge, he said, and we should now recognize that the grassroots of both parties favour merger and get on without delay.

As it turned out, David S. returned from his sabbatical full of determination to take up the reins once more. However, things could never be quite the same again. Once speculation is raised it never goes away for good. It would recur whenever David S. had a rough time either from his fellow MPs or from the Assembly, and he was to have a rougher time from 1983 than ever before, especially as David Owen refused even to consider merger. Such speculation was to be something with which David S. had to live with and with which his possible successors had to live also. Inevitably, it was to affect both David and myself, though probably less than people thought.

It would be wrong of course to suggest that the idea of David leading the party had never occurred to us before. Geraint Howells had repeatedly said to David, almost from the time he first entered parliament, that the time would come when he would be leader. Geraint of course was not wholly unprejudiced. He, like David, was a Celt and intensely proud of it. He thought he was too old to succeed David S. and so put all his hopes on his young fellow Celt. Still, Geraint had not been thinking of 1983; neither had David.

David certainly did not seek the succession then, nor would he later. However, he now knew he might be urged to stand if David S. did go, and he had to work out whether he would take it if it were offered. In discussing the chances of possible contenders in 1984, *Liberator* described David as the outsider, dismissing him as 'the party's funny man who fancies his chances. Shrewd electoral tactician . . . has yet to overcome country yokel image.'

Liberator tended to support those Liberals who were unilateralist and most suspicious of the SDP. It had always been ambivalent over David, because of his commitment to multilateral disarmament, but its comments, if prejudiced, were themselves quite shrewd. David certainly had a country yokel image. That was not so surprising. He had cultivated it. He might modify it but he had no intention of 'overcoming' it.

David was then on the point of celebrating his first ten years in parliament. He had learnt a lot in those ten years and he had changed a lot. He had for instance reached the most reassuring of positions in the House, achieved by very few: he was a popular speaker. His fellow MPs genuinely looked forward to his speeches. That meant he could be as critical as he wished without being in danger of being shouted down. If he was interrupted or heckled, he revelled in the repartee. He had in fact become an accomplished parliamentary performer.

In parliament his accent had been an asset, as Emlyn Hooson noticed. 'He reminded me of Nye Bevan. Nye had a stutter which he used marvellously as an aid to his speeches. Nye had to stutter but he was able to stutter in exactly the right place, to keep everybody in suspense. Now David, it seemed to me, learned to use his accent in the same way. He could lay it on thick at exactly the right place and the House loved it. The House has always loved a fellow who was different, and David was certainly different.'

David had also become an exceptionally effective, and very funny, speaker outside the House, whether on the platform, on television or the radio. This was not just a matter of natural ability, though it was very much a reflection of how he looked at life. He could always see the funny side as well as the serious one. It had taken practice too. Occasionally, he had made mistakes: he had dropped clangers, made bad speeches, had not done his homework, misread the mood of the audience. I have seen him deeply depressed when he got something wrong. Yet he always learnt from the experience. Being amusing on a platform does take planning and David would take immense trouble to discover how best to put across his argument.

'I do believe,' he said, 'that if you can think of an amusing way of making a serious point, you can make it far more effectively in that manner. I think one of the problems politicians have in Britain is that people never listen to what they are saying. They are talking away but no one is ever listening. And it is not that there is a lack of merit in what they are saying but they present it in such a flat, boring way that the good, sane, British public thinks, "I wonder what's on the other channel."'

It was not only *Liberator*, however, but some of his friends, who thought he overdid the Cornish rustic style on such programmes. Vera Harvey, who so many years before had awarded him his first cup for speaking, would warn him if she felt he was going over the top. He would nod non-committally, think about it, and she would notice a slight modification next time he appeared. However, it was only a slight modification, for a very good reason. David was Cornish, proud of it, and had no intention of ever changing his accent. After all, his great hero Lloyd George never lost his Celtic accent. If the Liberal Party ever wanted him as leader, they would have to take him as he was.

By a strange twist of fate, it was at this time that David and one other possible successor were to be brought very close together. In fact they were to share an office. For much of his parliamentary career, David had mostly enjoyed the luxury of a room to himself. Stephen Ross had moved on, and the next occupant of the second desk was the Northern Irish MP, Frank Maguire, who was chiefly famous for not attending the House. The only equipment that Maguire had on his desk was a phone that never rang, its messages automatically switched through to the parliamentary answering service. There was a light on the machine to show that there were messages awaiting. As he never came in, the bulb would burn out and every now and then a telephone engineer would appear to replace it.

Frank Maguire came to Westminster on only three occasions. He voted against abortion and against the death penalty for terrorists. He also came to Westminster in 1979 when Callaghan appealed to him to attend, in the hope that his vote might save the government. He duly flew from Belfast, only to abstain. The government fell. Frank Maguire returned to Belfast and that was the end of what must have been one of the quietest parliamentary careers on record.

Over those years David and Frank Maguire's office was certainly the quietest in the building, as David was notorious for very seldom being there during working hours. He was the despair of the Whip's Office who could very seldom track him down. If he were not working on the committee stage of some bill, he would be off doing his own research in the library or seeing a pressure group to pick its brains on issues he had identified as 'interesting' – in other words, likely to be of concern to his constituents.

On the other hand, he was just as likely to be in the Whip's Office itself. He would wander in, perch on a desk and distract the staff with stories of this and that. The Whip's Office was in effect the nerve centre of the Liberal MPs. The Chief Whip and his staff would make sure that there was an MP to put the Liberal point of view at debates, would warn of vital divisions, would, if there were time for it, prepare briefings for speakers. There were far too few employees to cover all the work that needed doing, but that was the problem throughout the Liberal Party. One of those employees was Andrea Hertz. Andrea had come from America to learn how the British system worked, liked it and stayed. They had a no-smoking rule in the office at the time and no one was more stringent over enforcing it than Andrea. Somehow when David arrived the rule went out of the window. She decided that he cheered them up so much that they could stand the smoking after all.

From 1979 to 1983, apart from the short time when Bill Pitt shared his office, when he won the by-election in Croydon, David's office remained as quiet as ever. Then in 1983, when Bill had lost, the situation changed dramatically. Instead of a faintly clicking phone at the far end of the room, there was the newest, sharpest and probably the noisiest of the class of 1983, Paddy Ashdown.

It was not that Paddy was renowned for the noise he made personally but he came equipped with machines that rattled and whirred. He also came with a team of volunteer researchers who dashed in and out with briefings and reams of figures. (I hasten to say that this is Paddy's own description.) David in contrast was almost totally self-sufficient. Engineer though he was, he made no use of computers. He did his own research. He did not hold meetings in his office. He had oak trees and plants instead.

What was more, he and Paddy lived to totally different clocks. Since 1974–79, when every vote was marginal and every debate fought out long into the early hours, parliamentary business had become less hectic. It might still go on after midnight but not so frequently. David, however, an incorrigible night owl, would still stay on and do much of his correspondence in the office before going home to the flat that we now had in Dolphin Square. Paddy would then arrive at 8 a.m. David would eventually wander in late in the morning, knowing that all his own work was complete, and amble through to see if Paddy had any coffee on the boil. That would be a prelude to putting his feet up on Paddy's desk and a discussion of what was really significant in the latest news.

'It was so rivetting that you had to put everything down,' Paddy recalls. 'He had the most extraordinary capacity, and one that made me boggle-eyed with admiration, to see the very centre of any political problem, without any clouds, without any complications.'

With David S. back at the helm, David was perfectly happy to soldier on alongside him but he had one problem. Being now just one of an Alliance team dealing with employment in the House, he himself felt underemployed. It was a bit of a change from those early days of the Lib/Lab pact when he had handled four portfolios all at once. David S. now took advantage of David's energy, asking him to take on a job for which he was very obviously better equipped than any of the other

Liberal MPs. He was to be chairman of the by-election unit.

By-elections require skills of every kind and David did not pretend to have them all. What he did have, however, would prove invaluable. David had an almost encyclopedic knowledge of the voting patterns throughout the UK. He loved figures. Just as once he could quote all the Olympic records, he now could quote the majorities of parliamentary constituencies. If ever the Whip's Office could not find *The Times Guide to the House of Commons*, Andrea Hertz could be sure that David had walked off with it. He would then startle his opponents in the House by reminding them of the exact size of their majorities, with a jocular warning that they might well find them under siege.

David was also an expert on campaign leaflets. He already had a reputation for approaching by-elections in a rather more down-to-earth manner than did other MPs. They turned up to canvass and address meetings as required. So did he but he would also have on board his car the Truro offset litho printing press. This he would then assemble and use to run off whatever leaflets were required. Usually too the press would misbehave as it always did at home – we never could afford a new one – and David Penhaligon MP would appear on the platform with his hands black with printer's ink. It never seemed to put him off, nor the audience for that matter.

This new job brought him back alongside an old friend of ours from the very first days we attended Assemblies. This was Andy Ellis, with whom we had often sat up until all hours discussing the finer points of community politics and how we were going to put the world to rights. Andy had settled initially for putting Newcastle to rights and had made his name by winning our first county council seat in what was thought to be England's most unpromising area for Liberalism in the 1970s. He was now the Party's by-election manager.

David's job was to chair the committee meetings that would decide the by-election strategy. Andy would then carry out that strategy. In practice, however, David spent days at the by-elections himself. One activist, Hugh Warren, recalls helping in an election when David had come up to speak. 'After the meeting David returned to the campaign headquarters where activists were folding election addresses and stuffing envelopes. David joined in. There was a lot to do and we went on into the early hours. Knowing that David had a hard day, and was probably to have another hard day on the morrow, the person next to me said something to the effect that folding and stuffing was probably not the best way for the Party to make use of its MPs. "No," said David, then added with a grin, "but it is still quite effective. I know that as long as I stay here folding and stuffing, none of you activists are going to go home, are you?"'

Although David was responsible only for by-elections at that time, there was another set of elections that did much for his morale, and for his reputation as an expert in the field. In the county elections of 1985, the Alliance made substantial gains throughout the country but nowhere did better than the south-west. Cornwall's total grew that year to twenty-eight and the only other county in England with more Alliance councillors was our neighbour Devon.

The European elections fell at that time too. As always, ever since our failure to get proportional representation for them from the Lib/Lab pact, we were doomed to do appallingly. We would get a lot of votes but not a single seat. David nevertheless had agreed to speak for the candidate in Birmingham. That was fine. However, he was not pleased when he was asked to come early and speak to the 'masses' from a landrover.

The local chairman, Blair Kesseler, remembers meeting David and driving him to the venue where the candidate was hard at work speaking to an audience of pigeons. 'I don't like doing these things so far from home,' complained David. 'No one knows me here.' This said, he got out of the car. Immediately an elderly gentleman rose from a bench and approached him, saying, 'It's nice to see you in Birmingham, Mr Penhaligon.' David swore it was a put-up job. It wasn't. He had no idea of how widely he was known from the BBC programmes.

The most important by-election at that time was the last before he gave up the job. It was at Brecon. The canvassing returns showed that it could be desperately close and Andy Ellis can still remember the wave of disappointment at our campaign headquarters when they saw copies of the *Mirror*, due to be published the following day. 'Its headline trumpeted the news that Labour was still clearly in the lead. They quoted the result of a poll based on interviews in which the Labour candidate was indeed ahead. They also added that, even if this were combined with the result of another, more recent, telephone poll, Labour were still ahead.' How could we counteract that?

'At that point out came the Penhaligon calculator. "Got it," he said. "You know what that really means? It means that we were in the *lead* in the telephone poll and that they did not dare publish it. We shall. I have just worked out what it must have been. We have got our last-minute leaflet." And so we had. It was "Liberal in the lead in final poll". We went on to win the seat by less than 600 votes. Still, win it we did, and Richard Livesey holds it still.'

David stepped down from that post a fortnight later but only to take on a rather more uncomfortable task. He was to chair the Liberal team in negotiations over the re-run of the seat-allocation competition. It would be another chance for him to use his psephological expertise. The one cheering element in what would have to be a difficult few months was that the chairman of the SDP group was his old ally Bill Rodgers.

Most of the seats had by then been settled. The Liberals had insisted this time around that the first efforts to reach agreement should be left to constituency associations. That had generally worked well, as Liberals and SDP had already fought one election side by side and could agree on what to do next time. What were left, however, were the difficult cases where one of them thought it was time for a change.

Matters were made no easier by the fact that the new SDP leader, David Owen, was set against the most natural way in which such difficulties could be resolved: joint open selection. This allowed both Liberal and SDP members to decide on their candidate at joint meetings in which every member had a vote. To David Owen that smacked of something far too close to merger, and he was right against that. It did not help that David Penhaligon was known to be the most determined of all the Liberal MPs that merger should come, and come soon.

In the event, David Owen had to give way over joint open selection, if only because Bill Rodgers agreed with David that it was in some cases the only possible solution. There were those then who wondered if David Owen might not in the end give way over merger too. If he did not, David said, there would be another shambles in the next election.

18
RECREATION

'It was all my doing really. I was always complaining that all my friends went abroad, and we never did.' – Matthew Penhaligon

Holidays are special for all families. Certainly ours were but some were more memorable than others. The one we took in 1984 was one of those, largely because it took us right away from David's job.

Over the years it had become more and more difficult to have holidays at home. Inevitably, if we had a holiday in Cornwall people would come up and ask for David's opinion or advice – or even for his autograph. David and I had to accept it as part of our life. It was impossible to say to someone, 'Please go away. We are on holiday.' The children really hated it and Matthew was eager to go abroad for a change. So we did.

When we decide to do something as a family it seems we tend to go rather over the top. The holiday we had was, according to David, akin to one of those holidays that used to be advertised by coach companies many years ago – you know the kind: 'Nine countries in seven days' (or vice versa)! It was a tour organized by a tour company, where they booked the accommodation and we travelled by car. It should have worked quite well, only we never dreamt the tour company would have us travelling over 500 miles a day between hotels! Fortunately we were to have a week in a chalet on the Italian Adriatic coast to build up the stamina for the ride home!

The first night after disembarking from a ferry at Calais was spent at Strasbourg. It was delightful as we spent the evening and next morning sightseeing in the old town. Then we were into the car, into Germany (and quickly out of it again) and on to Innsbruck in Austria where our second night was booked. And so it went on.

Our drive through the Brenner Pass into Italy was spectacular. However, David decided we were not seeing the Dolomites as he felt we should and so he suggested I navigate us on a more interesting route. Although I did this reasonably well, I have a terrible fear of heights and for me our tour turned into a funfair ride without the fun but with the sound effects. I don't think I did much for David's confidence as I moaned and groaned at every sharp corner he steered us around – and there were an awful lot of them.

It was during this journey that we stopped for a snack. It was a very beautiful, hot day and David decided he needed a cup of tea. I was irritated by this, thought cold drinks were quite sufficient and was afraid that our magnificent detour would make us very late in reaching our destination. However, it was three days since David had a cup of tea and he was getting withdrawal symptoms.

Out came a Gaz heater and David set about lighting it. Unfortunately we had borrowed the heater and had not checked to see if it worked. It didn't. 'Okay,' I said. 'Have a Coke and let's get on.' I don't know if it was my words that made him bloody-minded, or if he was really desperate for that cup of tea, but he was not going to be so easily defeated. He found the problem was the lack of a washer. 'Where's a pair of scissors and some thick cardboard?' he enquired. Rather ungraciously I found the equipment for him and he set about meticulously making the necessary washer. Triumphantly he assembled the heater and got it working.

'Only put on enough water for one cup,' I said impatiently as I saw other people stop, have a quick drink and leave again. I was not going to give in and have a cup with him now, and in any case I had not seen a loo in ages. Out came the teapot, teabag (which he usually hated) and milk. His face was something to be seen when he had the eventual satisfaction of pouring himself out a cup of tea. At that moment Anna got too close to the Gaz burner. Fearful that she might burn herself, David put down his mug and went to catch her. His foot hit his cup and over went his precious tea. Too afraid to laugh, we all climbed back in the car in total silence, and in silence we drove on. It was some miles before we all together saw the funny side of the incident and fell about laughing.

We had a lovely week on a lovely campsite. Our chalet was very close to the private beach and the children loved the sand and sea even though they see it more often than most children in this country. I was very eager to visit Venice and eventually David and the children gave in and off we went. If you have visited Venice on a hot and sticky August day with three people who are only there under sufferance you will know why one day I will return on my own.

The weather was even hot enough for David to don a pair of shorts. Matthew took one look at his father about to join him on the beach in shorts and ordinary black lace-up shoes and black socks, and that was enough. Matthew is not renowned for being a fast mover but he was across that beach in no time at all and David was sent packing back to the chalet to change into more appropriate footwear.

It was later the same day that Anna, who was tailing her father towards the beach, became inexplicably lost. Not worried for the first ten minutes, we looked in all her favourite places. For one and a half hours we scoured the beach and every bit of the campsite getting more frantic by the minute. Eventually David went along to the reception headquarters and a Tánnoy message was relayed in Italian, French, German and English (although we were the only English family on the site). Within ten minutes a very nice German lady turned up with Anna by the hand. She had recognized Anna by her description but was rather puzzled as to why when she asked Anna if she was English Anna emphatically answered no. Perhaps we should have described her as a Cornish child, not English.

After our week on the coast we set off to travel across Northern Italy back into France through the spectacular Mont Blanc tunnel and eventually came to rest in Annecy. From there we went on by way of Geneva (for the kids to add one more country to their tour) to Paris, where we were staying for a couple of nights. It was for all of us our first visit to Paris and we all loved it tremendously.

For Anna the Eiffel Tower had to be conquered. Try as he might, David failed to persuade her not to go up so that he and Matthew could do it on their own without the encumbrance of a little one. There was no way I could go. I felt dizzy looking up. However, I thought I was being very helpful when I pointed David in the direction of the smallest queue at one of the legs. After David had spent some considerable time before reaching the front of the queue he then learned too late why there was less interest in that entrance than the others. There was no lift.

He, Matthew and Anna had to climb quite a portion of the total 984 feet before reaching the lift to take them up the final stage to the top look-out platform. Then they had to come down the same way. By the time they got to the end it was not only Anna who was having difficulty walking. That evening when we went out to eat, Anna kept taking her shoes off because she said they no longer fitted. The truth was her feet were absolutely killing her.

It was in Paris that Matthew, who by then had completed his first year at the local comprehensive school, managed his first French into English translation. Unfortunately it was a rather dubious lady telling a gentleman – to quote Matthew – it was 60 francs for a massage. However, we were pleased he had at least learned something!

Though holidays like that in 1984 were rarities with us, it would be wrong to suggest that David never had time to relax. It was just that his idea of recreation was very much his own. He could enjoy himself anywhere and everywhere, especially in the House.

David's ten years as an MP had made its mark on Truro. It had also made its mark on him. So had Westminster. He was now, though far from being a veteran MP, an exceptionally well-known personality there. And, of course, he had come to love the place.

Geoff Aver, David's old friend from many of his election campaigns, was now a headteacher and would, like many schoolteachers, bring pupils up to London on school journeys. The tour of the House of Commons, personally conducted by David, was always the highlight of the visit.

On one occasion there was such demand that he found himself bringing thirty children. He knew that there would be difficulties, as the maximum size of any party at the House was sixteen. He would never get passes for thirty at short notice. At first David agreed that they would have to settle for a quick tour of Westminster Hall, then he said: 'This is crazy. They have come all this way. They deserve to see more. Let's have a go. Forget about passes.' Whereupon he marched off past the attendants like the Pied Piper with all thirty kids chasing after him.

'Most of the attendants were too surprised to protest,' Geoff recalls, 'but one hurried after us and caught me by the arm. "Can I see your passes please?" he asked. I gawped at him wordlessly. "Is anyone showing you around?" he went on. "We are with Mr Penhaligon," I replied weakly. His eyes rolled up to heaven. "Ah, it's Mr Penhaligon, is it? OK." Then he added, before retreating to his box, "Mind you, you will have more fun out of Mr Penhaligon's tour than you would if you got tickets for *Cats*." [*Cats* was then the hottest ticket in town.] And he was absolutely right.

'That kind of tour can be very boring for children of ten, but not with David. He made it absolutely fascinating. We did the whole division lobby thing. He got the children to improvise a mini debate of their own, choose their own tellers and then march off into the appropriate division lobbies. Then he explained that the one thing they were not allowed to do was to sit on the benches in the House. "That's a pity, I know. I reckon every one of you would like to say you had sat on a bench in the House of Commons, wouldn't you? But of course," he went on with a twinkle in his eye, "if you were to sit when I wasn't looking, I wouldn't know you had done it, would I? Now I am just going to have a look at that picture over there, and I don't want to find any of you sitting down when I come back." Off he went, then turned slowly round. Not a child was sitting down. "That's very good," he said.

'A high point of the tour was when he showed them the statues of all the famous prime ministers, with the gap still waiting for that of Winston Churchill. "And whose statue do you think is going to be there?" he asked. As one they shouted, "Yours." David rocked with laughter. "You go and tell Mrs Thatcher that," he said. "You tell her."

'The extraordinary thing was that, although he broke all the rules, he was so very clearly universally popular and trusted by all the attendants. Also, although he kept the children in gales of laughter with his stories about the oddities of parliament, they came out with an immense respect for what they had seen.'

Geoff is right. David used to call it the madhouse but he loved that building and by that time it was not only the attendants who were prepared to forgive him his eccentricities. Phil Middleton, who worked for some years in the Liberal Whip's Office, wrote in *The Radical Quarterly*, 'his personal charm took a very Liberal form. He was absolutely no respecter of people's positions. Everybody from "the person in the street" (or the committee room) to the leader of the Liberal Party inclusive received the same mixture of cheerful abuse and genuine concern. David was held in very high regard by party staff for this very reason. He was never stuffy, never dismissive and he never succumbed to the Westminster disease of acting as if being an MP set one entirely above and beyond the concerns of normal human beings.'

His style of cheerful abuse was accepted by both friend

and foe at Westminster, largely because he had a reputation for never bashing his opponents just for the sake of it. He might insult them to their face but never behind their backs. This had been especially noticeable in election campaigns, when he used to argue that you were always better off putting forward your own views than attacking your opponent.

His 'rustic' style of speaking in the House had remained peculiar to him but now it had that practised air that comes from confidence. He knew that the members would certainly listen to what he said and that they would enjoy it too. David once gave another Liberal candidate, Harry Warschauer, the recipe for making a speech: 'Tell them what you are going to say, then say it, and finally tell them what you have said. That should do it.' It is an old formula. It sounds mechanical – the least likely adjective for a Penhaligon speech. What few knew, however, was that, however spontaneous a Penhaligon speech might sound, it would generally be based on most meticulous preparation. David was forced occasionally to make spontaneous unrehearsed speeches, and he managed them better than most, but generally the spontaneity lay in its presentation, not in its content.

David would prepare a speech by writing down each point he wanted to get across on a separate piece of notepaper along with any details or statistics he might need. There might be as many as thirty sheets of these. He would then memorize them and all he would take with him would be a list of half a dozen major headings, sufficient to remind him of the notes he had made. The time he spent on each point would depend on the mood of the audience or on what had gone before. That is where the spontaneity was vital and the humour could have full rein.

Certainly not all the subjects David pursued in the House were of the kind that would usually raise a smile but he always tried to do so nevertheless. It was, he found, the best way to attract the interest and support of members to causes that he held dear – and these causes could be fairly obscure. One was the control of noise at work. 'I suspect that some Conservative members who have spoken in this debate would not recognize a decibel if it walked through the door of the Chamber. In a previous incarnation I worked for a company that manufactured rock drills. At one time, as an employee of that company, I had to measure the noise level of a rock drill in what is called a closed end in a hard rock mine. We recorded 132 decibels. Many of the people with whom I worked had put up with that degree of noise for a decade or more. They insisted they were not deaf, but you had to shout to make them hear. Legislation is required and compulsion and pressure must be imposed.'

He championed too the cause of the scientists who were developing what was called the Cornish Hot Rocks project, through which it is hoped that the heat given out naturally by underground rocks can eventually be used for domestic heating. David had of course by now become known for his concern for the mines, especially those in Cornwall. When on *Question Time*, he was asked his opinion on the Channel Tunnel, he solemnly suggested that if they wanted a tunnel they should buy some from Cornwall. The mines were full of them.

David was known at Westminster for his ability to make time for other people and other causes. Stephen Ross well remembers a time when a delegation came from the Isle of Wight and the Liberal spokesman for the subject that concerned them was too busy to see them. David made time for them instead.

At Westminster, he was, in Jo Grimond's words, 'the politician of the crumpled smile above the crumpled suit. He looked like a bitter-sweet apple. And that is what he was. It was a delight to meet him shambling around the lobbies, never in a hurry, ready with a few pert observations on life, always willing to be helpful, never giving more than a rueful aside to his own troubles.'

Matthew too became a familiar figure around the Palace of Westminster. From a very young age he would spend his school half-terms with David, based at the flat at Dolphin Square. Much of the day Matthew would be either in David's office or in the Whip's Office. When David could get away, they would wander off together to visit the Science Museum (or the Tate Gallery, but only if I was there), go shopping, eat huge meals in Macdonalds, then after midnight when the business of the House was over walk to Trafalgar Square 'to see if the lions were still there'. For them it had become a ritual ever since the day that David had assured him the lions were taken in at night. Somehow they always arrived and left before that magic moment came! Then they would wander back to bed, to sleep on through to midday and breakfast in the House. It was the night-owl pattern being passed on from father to son. I notice it persists!

19
PARTY PRESIDENT

'He had an intellect that could cope with anything if he put his mind to it' – Alan Beith

When David gave up his chairmanship of the by-election unit in 1985 it was not just because he had to help out with the seat allocation. He had landed two other jobs as well: one that he had deliberately sought himself, and one that David S. had thrust upon him. He was to be President of the Party for 1985/6, and he was to take on the major Liberal spokesmanship within the House, that of treasury spokesman. For years he had been underemployed; now he was in danger of being swamped.

When David S. chose David as Treasury spokesman, most of the press greeted the announcement with reactions that varied from polite surprise to outright scepticism. Penhaligon was fun, they felt, certainly refreshing, but hardly Chancellor material. David had become a victim of his own media myth.

He had been happy to go along with the image of the simple country lad with a funny accent, a fund of good stories and a nice line in homespun rustic philosophy. He had even cultivated it. The fact that he was also a deeply serious politician with a first-class brain and original ideas on the economy was therefore known only to his close friends. Alan Beith had known it for a long time, David S. for less long. He had come to realize it later than he might but now he was determined to give David the chance to show what he could do. It would take a little time but his faith was to be justified.

Relations between the two Davids had grown significantly closer over the last few years. David continued to play the role of the members' shop steward but David S. found a new mateyness had crept into their exchanges. 'David would sidle up during a late night division and say, "'Ere, gotta moment, 'ave you?", and off we'd be to my office for a heart-to-heart.

'On one of his last visits to my office he was, as usual, smoking, and I said, "Haven't you seen the no-smoking stickers in the outer office?" "Yes," he said, "but you've got none in here, and don't tell me that you don't have the odd cigar in here." "Well, yes," I said, "but the staff decided to make it a no-smoking zone, so kindly desist." After our meeting I left him chatting with the secretaries and went into the chamber. When I returned later I saw one of the anti-smoking stickers on the polished oak of my door. "Who put that there?" I asked to a chorus of giggles. Then I looked closely. In unmistakable Penhaligon writing were the words, "Including cigars". He always got the last word.'

The appointment was made in the summer of 1985. Richard Wainwright had been treasury spokesman since John Pardoe lost his seat in 1979. Richard planned to retire in 1988 and felt that his successor should be appointed in 1985 to prepare policy in good time for the next election. David S. chose David because he wanted not only new ideas but also a higher profile for party policy. David had the highest popular profile of all the MPs.

The first publicity, however, could hardly have been worse. David's approach to the job was quite unlike that of other treasury spokesmen. He publicly expressed doubts of his own ability, admitted gaps in his grasp of economic theory, asked questions rather than proclaimed solutions. His first speeches on the economy were judged to be lightweight and incomplete. Hugo Young in the *Guardian* considered his performance inadequate. It seemed as if the media's initial scepticism was justified.

What in fact was happening was that David was feeling his way towards a new approach to economic policy that in normal circumstances would have required time and a team of economists. Unfortunately David had neither the time nor a team and the circumstances in which the Liberal MPs worked were, by any business standards, anything but normal.

Their problem lay simply in the poverty of the Party. They had none of the research facilities available to the larger parties. The leader had a small staff, scarcely adequate to deal with his duties. The Whip's Office generally had only two members of staff, who carried out what research they could when they were not making sure that the MPs knew what debates were coming up, what votes were important and who was to speak on what. Otherwise the MPs were dependent on volunteers, their secretaries/assistants and their own initiative. David, with his secretary in Truro, did all his own research, as well as handling his own post. He was also almost impossible to track down in an emergency.

David could hardly carry out his new job on his own in conditions such as that. He had to have some help. It was found from the Rowntree Trust. It gave sufficient money for him to employ an economist and one assistant. Compared to the expertise available to the Conservative and Labour spokesmen it was minuscule but in Liberal terms it was wealth indeed. The economist was Harry Cowie. Harry had been an adviser to the party in the 1970s, had left to work in the City and now ran the *New Democrat* magazine. He found that David had very definite ideas on what solutions the Liberals should pursue. What he needed was an economist on whom to try them out. Their discussions would be Socratic in style, with David asking questions and Harry giving him the classic economist replies.

The strategy that David was pursuing was to differ from that of his predecessors in one marked respect. He accepted, as they did, the need for a prices and incomes policy and for the UK to join the European Monetary System. He also believed in an investment-led recovery, with the government investing in a renewal of the country's infrastructure. However, he felt that this must be combined with a growth in the private sector.

Interest rates were the key element in this strategy. David had always fought for low rates ever since he had first had the trade and industry brief in 1980. Now he got Harry to work out what impact various lower interests would have on the economy, allied to greater investment in training and a rather lower level of public investment than the Liberals had previously recommended. These projections were then tested by computer on the Treasury model. The results were sufficiently encouraging for them to be confident that the new strategy could work.

Also involved in this shoe-string experiment was David's new research assistant, Matthew Taylor. Matthew was then fresh down from Oxford where he had been President of the Students' Union. At his interview, David left most of the questions to the rest of the panel but came in at the end. 'I see that you went to school in Truro,' he said. 'How was that?' Matthew had a pronounced Oxford accent. 'I lived there as a boy,' Matthew explained. 'A pity about the accent,' said David. But he gave him the job.

David set Matthew to research such matters as the projected oil revenues and what would happen if privatization were stopped and what it would cost to renationalize. Too much, he thought. Also, knowing that Matthew had parliamentary ambitions, he involved him in his work within the House. Matthew found that in discussions and committees David spoke surprisingly little. He would ask others to speak. He would listen, occasionally comment or interrupt with the words, 'What does that mean?' Although he was extraordinarily sharp with figures and lethal in the House if the Chancellor got a statistic wrong, he knew very little economic jargon. What was more, he never pretended to understand a word if he did not and was totally unembarrassed by having to admit his ignorance. Even on social occasions, David could see no point in the kind of small talk that hypocritically implies knowledge of a subject. He would always say if he did not understand something, and that could disconcert and irritate others, especially if his blunt question caught them out.

His colleagues now discovered a new side to his personality, one that they had perhaps always known was there, but they had never felt the full force of it turned upon themselves. This was his ruthless determination that they cut the suits of their political dreams strictly according to the very limited cloth available in the national economy.

'Between you and me I believe this to be quite the dottiest document presented yet,' he wrote of one of the Liberal blueprints to the parliamentary spokesman involved. 'I hope you can persuade your specialists that a twenty-five per cent increase in budget would be very difficult to find.' The style might sound breezy but the message could be as cold as any iron chancellor of the past.

Gradually during 1985 and 1986 the new economic strategy was built up, tested and publicized. In the media, the initial scepticism subsided. Perhaps Penhaligon had more to offer than they had thought. Then late in 1986 David delivered two speeches of a kind quite different from his usual style, one in the House and one in Plymouth. They ranged not just over domestic problems but worldwide. It was not just the content of the speeches that impressed. There was a change of style. David still spoke from what seemed to others to be the most rudimentary notes but there was now a very carefully planned structure to his speeches. He was certainly a chancellor in waiting, and perhaps much more.

David's other major role at that time was as president of the Party. To be elected president is perhaps the greatest honour that can be given to a Liberal but it is also a very exacting job. The president is seen as the guardian of the constitution, and so of the soul, of the Party. Although the Party is of course theoretically a massive iceberg of which the MPs and councillors are merely the visible tip, inevitably the health of the Party is felt to be linked to the fortunes of the MPs. After the 1983 election there was increasing concern over what was seen as a dangerous gap between the MPs and the rest of the Party. David sympathized with this concern and decided that he could close that gap if he himself took on the job of president.

This was a revolutionary proposal. Never before had an MP been president, partly because no MP had believed he could spare the time to travel all over the country and partly because there had always been a 'them and us' division between Westminster and the rest of the country – them were working on bills and so forth, us were working the grassroots. David wanted to show that it was a false and dangerous distinction. David also felt that it was time to show that he had considerably more to offer the Party than had been asked of him so far.

In fact, David had been toying with the idea of standing for the European Parliament. He felt it was vital that the British Liberals have at least one seat at Strasbourg and knew that the best chance lay in the Cornwall/Plymouth constituency. Malcolm and I, however, were right against this, as we could see that his Truro constituents would feel that he was letting them down, for they would no longer have a full-time MP at Westminster. On the other hand they would feel as honoured as himself if he were president of the Party. As it happened, we very nearly won the Euro seat and with David as candidate would probably have done it. It was a hard decision.

David's name was put forward at the Assembly of 1984. (As the Liberals always picked their president one year in advance, the election was for the year 85/6.) Traditionalists were shocked that an MP should be proposed for a post they saw as the members' champion. Pressure was applied on his supporters. Would David stand down in favour of Des Wilson and perhaps think about it for the following year. No, he could not, was the answer: 1986/7 might well be an election year.

At the Assembly, a Young Liberal, David Senior, stood against him on the grounds that MPs should leave the presidency alone. The vote was restricted to Assembly delegates, many of whom disagreed on principle with an MP taking the job and even more of whom disagreed sharply with David on unilateralism. Nevertheless David won by a huge majority. Now in 1985 he had to justify his claim that he could unite the Party.

His year began at the close of the 1985 Assembly at Dundee. David had always had rather a love/hate relationship with the Assembly. He felt that major decisions were taken in far too cavalier a fashion. He preferred fringe meetings, where the delegates explored ideas rather than made policy on the hoof. When he was asked by the *Guardian* to give his impressions of the Assembly programme in 1985, the piece was headed 'How the Fringe gives the Party sparkle'.

'Politically, parties are part tribe, part family, and the annual pilgrimage to the Party conference is rather like visiting your aunts and second cousins who live hundreds of miles away. Quite enjoyable, but a week is long enough.

'Conference has during my years become one of the annual media events and I am not quite sure who is taking the mick out of whom. I remember one of my colleagues, David Alton, actually undertaking an early morning swim for the *Today* radio programme which included the sound effects of the gasp on entering the pool and the roll of water against his flesh. The media must find a story – they are there in their hundreds with deadlines to meet, expense accounts to justify and salaries to warrant. The consequence of all this is that every story is written up with a series of adjectives which often suggest that the Party has split, the leader is about to get the sack or the economy will collapse. Then just occasionally when something actually happens there are few if any adjectives left to use.

'The conference has changed. It used to start on a Wednesday and finish on Saturday; now it seems to start on one Saturday and roll on to the next. Delegates also find that every lunchtime and evening is filled with fringe meetings, making conference more fringe than set piece, with caucus meetings of Liberal councillors, parliamentary candidates and Young Liberals being a familiar part of the whole. I see on Monday Simon Hughes MP is addressing two meetings at the same time at different hotels and on different subjects – that is productivity for you.

'On occasions, fringe can be more important than the main. Roy Jenkins' speech to the delegates on the pier at Llandudno was just such an occasion. The applause and warmth of response was more powerful and enduring than any show of hands after a set-piece debate. Here was the realignment of British politics. After years of praying, hoping and campaigning, the aeroplane had taken off.

'A study of fringe meetings over the years demonstrates how the Party has changed and grown. Meetings entitled "Inner City Problems", "Campaigning against Labour", "The Furore of London's Local Government" and "Ethnic Minorities" tell one that Liberalism is strong and growing in the city centre. That certainly was not true twenty years ago. The 2,500 elected councillors have grafted their hard-earned experience on to the conference to give it a degree of reality previously missing.

'Party conferences have an element of the absurd. We try in a few minutes to consider and amend and eventually commit the party, and all in it, to some blueprint for the future. "Housing" is to be a 43-line, 60-minute debate; "Opening-up Education" an 85-line motion to be discussed in 75 minutes, and "Preparing for Government" just 60 minutes. I cannot help but feel it is going to take a little longer. By training I am an engineer, and I've felt for some time that the quality of debate and the value of conclusions reached could be improved if only a microchip genius could invent a display board which would automatically indicate the cost of various proposals.

'"Free public transport," declared a colleague a few years ago, and after a twenty-minute debate the "Ayes" had it. As spokesman on transport at the time, I naively asked my colleague whether that included buses, the Underground, trains and air flights."Only within the UK," he kindly replied. Fortunately, a couple of conferences later clarified the position by restating its long-term willingness to give subsidies where a social need existed.

'Conferences are a great talk shop. Politicians by nature like the sound of their own voices. Put 2,000 together for just one week a year and the talk is ceaseless. In hotel lounges up to two or three in the morning it goes on and on. Swapped stories, experiences, disasters and successes are a vital part of the learning process. Balance of power, budget problems, relationships with the Social Democrats, or how do we handle the maverick group member, will be discussed *ad nauseam*. A lot will be learned and implemented when the delegates go home; and it is this part of the tribal gathering that does so much to shape the nature of the Liberal Party. Swapped leaflets are clutched enthusiastically and taken home to be plagiarized during a new campaign. The sheer encouragement given by success elsewhere and the general realization that if he or she can win, then we should be able to do the same, have quite dramatic effects.

'It is the activists' week and there is usually one debate which can best be described as "The Activists' Revenge", a sort of annual shot across the bows just to make sure the leaders do not forget they want something to lead. Indeed, conference week is about the only time of the year when the leader actually appears nervous. But come the big speech we will all clap and clap until our hands ache. It is a lot easier to grunt "'ear, 'ear" a few times in the House, but we will all clap because in the end it is our speech, our justification for continuing the battle and, of course, the television is still on.'

That article is more unusual than it may seem. David was unlike most MPs, in that he almost never wrote articles. It was not that he disliked writing them. If he were asked to write one he would do so and was meticulous in responding to any such request from the Cornish papers. After all, he had practice enough in writing for *News from the Liberals*. So if the *Guardian* wanted an article he was happy to supply it. If he were not asked, however, he would never bother.

He was not much better over press releases. Janet Bawden, who was his expert and devoted secretary for so many years, working always from the dictaphone tapes he sent down from London, was for ever urging him to supply her with press releases. They were always the last of his priorities. That was perhaps for historical reasons. When he and Malcolm first organized their campaigns, the press were never interested, so they left to last the chore of writing out press releases which would probably never see the light of day. That habit had persisted.

The other Liberal MPs worked on a totally different principle. They wanted to publicize their views. David Alton was in fact so successful in this that for some time *Liberal News* became known as 'D. Alton's Weekly'! David was instinctively oral and would remain so. That, for certain, was to be the mark of his year as president.

At Dundee, David took over the presidency from Alan Watson. David had begun the week badly, being reported as saying that the odds were still on Margaret Thatcher winning the next election. In fact he had merely pointed out that she would have to lose some eighty seats, as the Ulster Unionists would probably keep her in power if she lost fewer than that. It was true but the Alliance at that time was once again in the lead in the polls and a dose of realism was distinctly unwelcome.

Of course, when it came to David's speech, all was forgotten and forgiven. He was once again the darling of the Assembly. For him, too, there was a special personal pleasure in the ceremony in which the presidency is passed on. Each new president signs his name in a copy of Milton's *Areopagitica*, presented originally by the great Celtic Liberal, Isaac Foot. As David said, 'I suspect he would probably enjoy seeing a Cornishman receiving this book as president of the English Liberal Party in Scotland.'

The year that followed was appallingly exhausting for David, yet he somehow thrived on it. What he would do was to take several days off to tour constituency after constituency in one area of the country. As this meant losing time at home, the family would sometimes go too. Matthew was now old enough to enjoy the change of scenes. It required a lot of planning and long drives but it gave Matthew an opportunity to meet an immense variety of interesting people and see the country in a way that few boys of his age could.

David's visits went very much to a pattern – not one that he chose but one that the constituencies evidently found most convenient. There would be a tour of a part of the area where there was some local campaign under way. There would be a gathering where the faithful could meet their president and tell him what they thought. There would be a public meeting at which David would speak, probably alongside the leader of the council group and the parliamentary candidate.

David's message would also follow a pattern – in this case because there were three basic points David always wanted to get across. First, that the MPs needed the members and the MPs could help the members. Secondly, that the Liberals needed the SDP and the SDP needed the Liberals: 'There can be no Liberal success with SDP failure; there can be no SDP success with Liberal failure.' Thirdly, that anyone can win if they work hard enough. He would quote the reaction of an enthusiastic chairman who managed to respond to one such speech by saying: 'It is quite clear that if Mr Penhaligon can win, anyone can.'

If that makes his year of office sound repetitive, even boring, it should not. The settings and the message might be the same but the differences from one place to another were always fascinating. Everyone had an individual problem or success to talk about. David gained as much as he gave. The experience broadened his grasp of what we should be fighting for in parliament and gave him instances to quote in his speeches, which until then had been based almost entirely on cases in the south-west. For his hosts, he in turn was translated from a telly personality into someone who had experienced and was still struggling with the same problems as themselves.

Des Wilson who was to succeed him as president vividly recalled one of David's 'vintage performances' of that time. It was at a candidates conference. David opened the conference. The next speaker, David Owen, was late. 'David revelled in the opportunity, combining humour with passion so that at one moment he had candidates falling about with laughter and the next cheering him to the echo. Many would recall him waving the draft of *Partnership for Progress* at his audience and saying, "They say we have no policies . . . we have hundreds of policies, and what's good about this document is that most of them aren't in it."'

This practical approach to politics was also appreciated by David Owen. 'David Penhaligon was always very interested in the polls and far shrewder than his colleagues in interpreting what they really meant. He was a Celt first, a Liberal second, but after that he was a real pragmatist.'

His other duties were more managerial. First, he had to chair Party Council. This was an elected body that met some four times a year and dealt with matters of policy that could not wait for the following Assembly. It had a membership of about 200, which made it none too easy to control. David managed it better than most presidents, partly because he had himself been a delegate there since the sixties and knew how to cut short some of the less inspiring debates with a joke.

He also had a weekly meeting with the leader and the Party's chief officers, most importantly the chairman and the secretary general. At one time there was the happy prospect that David's would be the year of the 'Cornish Mafia', as the chairman was now Paul Tyler and until the autumn of 1985 the secretary general (managing director of Liberal headquarters) was John Spiller. John had been agent for years in North Cornwall and had been a great source of support in our Young Liberal days. Sadly, just before David took office, John had to retire through ill-health. The compensation was that his successor was Andy Ellis; so David and Andy were to have another year of working side by side.

Those weekly meetings were to do much to strengthen the ties between David and his leader. They still did not know each other personally as well as they should. Although they met regularly at the meetings of the MPs, the atmosphere there was more of a team discussion led by the captain. At the Party meetings, however, their roles were of equal importance and they had to get to know each other well for the Party's sake. As a result they developed not only a friendship but also feelings of much greater mutual respect than before.

It was sad that the last few days of David's presidency should see them united, but only in despair. The Eastbourne Assembly of 1986 was to provide in its defence debate one of those PR disasters to which Liberal Assemblies are always prone. Much of the fault in Liberal eyes lay with David Owen, who had refused to accept a joint policy worked out between experts of the two parties. He and David S. then cobbled together a compromise policy that merely provoked an even less well thought out amendment from the unilateralist delegates.

Neither David nor David S. spoke, unwisely assuming the less said the better, and the amended motion became official Liberal policy, although it did not bind the parliamentary party. The row that resulted from this would bedevil the Alliance for the next three years. It was as if all David's worst fears over Assemblies had come home to roost to spoil the last days of his presidency. 'What I cannot understand,' he groaned, 'is how anyone could be so *stoopid*.'

20
FACING THE FUTURE

'Who could be luckier than to be paid fairly well, which to be honest MPs are, for pursuing their hobby? That's what politics is.' – D. P. on *Desert Island Discs*

David was at first very depressed after the Eastbourne Conference. He lost a confidence in the national party that I do not think he ever really regained. He had seen opportunities disappear overnight and began to wonder if he would ever have the opportunity to be anything other than a good constituency MP. He had done that now for twelve years and, whilst his constituency was of paramount importance, there was also an extremely tiring and repetitive side to it. The demands on someone like David who was extremely conscientious were enormous; the endless travelling on its own was exhausting and he was allowed little time to himself.

'Do I really want to be a member of a minority party in parliament for the next twenty years?' was the question he would occasionally pose to me and a few very close friends. I must admit I did not take him too seriously, as I knew he would continue for as long as he could. However, David was one of nature's optimists and it was strange to see him so fed up.

In October, during the children's half-term, we took off to

Portugal's Algarve for a week as we had not taken any family holiday because David was travelling around the country so much in his presidential year. That helped, although the Algarve was rather like being at home in the height of the summer, only considerably warmer. We met lots of people from Cornwall and most of the British people there recognized David. However, we all had a super rest and the children loved having David to themselves.

Anna as always made lots of friends, especially on one occasion when we thought she was with Matthew and he thought she was with us. When Matthew turned up without her all three of us set out searching the very large hotel. First place to look was the hotel's two pools – a sigh of relief when she was clearly not there. We looked everywhere. Half an hour later, now very worried, David glimpsed our errant daughter in one of the three lifts and eventually we caught up with her. She had clearly spent a good hour riding the lifts and as each floor was decorated the same she could not recognize our floor. However, she clearly had not put this time to waste as next morning when we came down to breakfast one by one nearly everyone greeted her with a 'Hello, Anna'. She had obviously introduced herself to everyone using the lifts with her.

David returned to Truro very much more himself again, if only because it was good to be at home, dealing with the problems he still cared most about. From 1984 to 1986, David may have been dashing around the country as the by-elections supremo or on presidential progressions; he may have been, in some people's eyes, Liberal chancellor in waiting or Liberal crown prince. However, from his constituents' point of view, he was simply their MP. That was how they saw him and that was his priority too – as it had always been.

His most essential work was there at home. So too were most of our friends – Malcolm in particular. Malcolm had remained his closest friend as well as his election agent. Malcolm was now a senior planning officer on the county council. He had begun his professional career in local government in Cornwall and there he had chosen to stay. So had Linda.

Each weekend David would come home to his family, his own county, his familiar friends. He also came home to equally familiar problems. It seemed at times as if the problems never changed. In 1984 Truro celebrated his tenth year in parliament. We had a 'Hope Supper', when the members were asked to bring their own contributions and we hoped there would be enough for all. There was. The great thing about this kind of occasion, which David loved, was that it suited every member regardless of their income. That year too David Owen came over to speak. David Steel came down later for a special dinner attended by 311 members.

There was certainly cause for celebration. Thanks to David's campaigns, the threat of a nuclear power station had gone; the Russian factory ships were no longer a major threat to the fishermen; bus services had survived, so had the train service; there were still sub post offices. Yet David felt that the whole decade had been spent in holding back threats to the county. He had been unable to generate substantial improvements, especially in the area that most concerned him – in employment.

What was worse, in 1985 Cornwall suffered two further blows – one to the mining industry and the other to David's original employers, Holman's. Wheal Jane had been saved in 1978 but now it was hit by a catastrophic drop in the world price for tin. So too were Cornwall's other two remaining mines of Geevor and South Crofty.

Tin mining in Cornwall has never accounted for a vast number of jobs but the mines have always had a symbolic importance quite out of proportion to their impact on the labour market. In all, the three mines employed directly only about 1,000 men but this latest threat to their survival at a time when Cornish unemployment was approaching record figures sparked off the most amazing reaction in Cornwall. There was a joint rally of the miners addressed by the three MPs concerned. There was a miners' march to Westminster. There was a parliamentary debate, transmitted by the new, influential, Radio Cornwall.

David inevitably was the major spokesman. David Harris and David Mudd were equally concerned but embarrassed by the government's unwillingness to help and even more embarrassed when David pointed out that the government was showing more interest in those who had lost money on their investments in tin than in those who worked the mines themselves. As a result, Geevor had to stop mining and has never resumed. Wheal Jane and South Crofty cut staff but survived.

Almost sadder for David was the destruction of Holman's. It was bought by another company and within a few months was reduced to a shadow of its former self. Camborne was not in David's constituency but he returned as a former employee to speak and march alongside those with whom he had worked himself.

This was as bad a time for Cornwall as David was to see. Every major industry seemed either in danger of closing or at best to be running on smaller staffs than ever before. Even those who were in work were earning wages far lower than elsewhere in the country. Yet paradoxically, if this was the worst of times, it was also the best of times. Hope was on the horizon.

Back in 1981, in an effort to persuade government to pay more attention to the peculiar problems of Cornwall, David had commissioned a survey by the Low Pay Unit. Its conclusions were that wages in Cornwall had remained consistently lower than the national average, while there was no evidence of lower living costs to compensate. David of course already knew this but he needed evidence from an independent survey if he were to persuade the government to intervene.

In the event the government had remained unmoved but some of the Unit's further findings would help in the longer term. In particular, the report stressed that Cornwall's problems were largely linked with the high incidence of low-paying industries, such as agriculture, tourism, fishing and forestry. To correct the imbalance it would be necessary to encourage the growth of higher-paying industries.

What was reassuring for David was that on that march in Camborne he had by his side the planning chairman of the county council, who was quite unlike her predecessors in that job. She too had grasped the importance of bringing into Cornwall higher-paying industries. It was hardly surprising she and David saw eye to eye, for this new chairman was our long-time friend Doris Ansari. The Liberals were now running the county council.

Doris has had a tough time as planning chairman, as she has advocated and pushed through the creation of a development company that involves both Devon and Cornwall, both private and public investment. Cornish nationalists are shocked – and so are a few Cornish Liberals – but it is an effective body. New business has come into both counties. It is also classic regionalism of the kind that David and the Liberals were advocating for years.

David was Cornish from the soles of his shoes to the rapidly thinning hair upon his head ('My Dad's hair is very precious to him,' Matthew had shrewdly written long before in a junior school essay) but he never believed that Cornwall could solve its own problems. Certainly he would have preferred that Cornwall have its own development company but if that was impossible he was prepared to work with the rest of the country – and that included those strange folk just the other side of the Tamar too! At least the plans were now being made by elected councils, not by civil servants sitting in Bristol.

What is even more encouraging now is that there are signs of another of his dreams coming true. For long David's chief complaint was that Cornwall supplied the raw material – the fish, clay, tin, cauliflowers – for which it was paid the lowest rate, while others made the big money out of processing and packaging them. Why should not Cornishmen also develop these industries and form cooperatives to ensure that they control the price of what they produce? That was what was happening over the Channel among our Celtic cousins in Brittany. We should do the same.

The secret of the Breton success lay in the special interest rates afforded such cooperatives there – as low as three per cent with fifteen years allowed to repay the loan, compared to UK rates of some thirteen per cent with only three years for repayment. It was further evidence for David of the importance of low interest rates. Although the county council, and all local government, is starved of funds, there are signs that cooperatives might be established here too. Certainly the will is there.

In 1986 David was content to see at least the will at work. It was for him a fulfilment of the dream he, Malcolm and I had back in 1970, when we had returned from that Assembly fired up to bring Liberalism to Truro. The route we had taken was different from that in other associations, who had looked first to take control at local level. We had got the MP first, then gradually Liberalized all the local councils.

The Liberals are now the largest group on both Restormel and Carrick Councils, and on the county council. David had seen old friends honoured too. William Hosking, for whom we had campaigned for back in 1964, had been mayor of Restormel. Doris Ansari had been mayor of Truro. The way the councils were run had been transformed. Meetings now are open to the public, councillors report back to their constituents, membership of committees is based on pro-portional representation. Of course, the councillors make mistakes, as David made mistakes, but it is now in public and the mistakes are caused not by a refusal to act but in a determination to achieve something new.

By the end of 1986 David and I knew we were about to reach a major turning point on the road we had taken when we first walked into the Truro committee rooms back in 1964. David had travelled a long way since then. He was no longer simply a local activist, nor simply a backbench politician working away at the problems of his constituents. He was those still, of course, but he was now seen as something more.

He was the only MP to have been president of the Party.

He held the senior spokesman role inside the House, and outside it he was one of the Party's most popular representatives. (In November 1986, he was one of three MPs who took over the *Jimmy Young Show* for a week apiece. He loved it.) He had also become the Party's answer to any crisis that might come along. Not that there was any particular crisis at that time, beyond the general discomfort between the SDP and Liberals since the defence debate in Eastbourne. That was quite enough.

However, 1986 marked the tenth year of David Steel's leadership of the Liberals. He showed no signs of wanting to quit but he had served notice that he would consider quitting at this stage and the question of the succession was now publicly discussed. It was also privately discussed – for the first time – between David and David S. himself. David S. recalls that he made the point that David's year as president had been very good training for the leadership role.

'David replied that in some ways that was true, but that year had also shown what a hellish life the leader of the Party must have and he was not sure that he could cope with it! Although he made a joke of it, we then had quite a serious talk about how he would cope as the father of quite young children, especially with Anna's problems. So I cannot say that he would have been a candidate. What I can say is that had he gone on through the next election and the merger process he would have been the preferred choice of the members of parliament, and had he stood I think he would have been elected. I don't think he would have leapt at it but I think he would have accepted it.

'We missed him very badly in the last election. I think too his ebullience and commonsense approach would have

277

helped us through some of the tangles we got into on the merger process. He was very critical of me for accepting the concept of joint leadership, and accepted that merger was the logical necessity.

'If he had agreed to be leader, he would probably have had a difficult three years. It is as I know very difficult to establish yourself in parliament as leader of a third party until you have fought your first election. But then he would have done brilliantly in the next General Election.'

David Steel's assessment is very close to that of David's other colleagues. It was also typical of the kind of opinions that were being expressed in 1986.

David's concern about the family was understandable. The last three Liberal leaders had all found that their public life had some damaging impact on their families and politicians as a breed are anyway notorious for the instability of their family life. Much of this is due to the time that MPs spend so far away from home but there are other strains that any politician's family has to cope with all the time. As David and I had chosen together to go into politics, and continued to share all its excitements and its strains, there was never any argument between us over his career, only over the day to day details it involved. We were in it together. For the children, however, it was different. We might find the number of functions we had to go to every weekend exhausting. The children found them boring. We might not mind every trip in and out of town being interrupted by people coming up with their problems. For Matthew it was agony. (David even relished it, though often he would promise to send constituents information without being able to recall their names. Rather than admit it, he would then have us all searching through his files like detectives in search of clues.)

David was well aware that his own career could make life difficult for his son. On the other hand Matthew would not complain now that having a father as an MP was always a problem for him. Apart from the mistaken assumption that he must be rich if his father was in parliament, his schoolfriends thought him no different from themselves. It helps that he is in fact very much the same as most of them – fairly intelligent and fairly indolent as well. He can boast he was more successful than both his parents in his first exams – not that that was much of a standard!

It is easy now to assume that with so much speculation rife in the Party and press we must have discussed the leadership at length at home. We didn't. This was not all that surprising. David and I shared a certain fatalism in our approach to life. We knew that when David S. stood down, David would be a likely successor and that we would have to decide then what to do about it. There was, however, little point in worrying about it now, and no point at all in deciding now on whether or not he should stand. We would take that decision when the time came, and for both of us the major factor would certainly be how our family life would cope with the inevitable strains.

Meanwhile, there were always more immediate matters to absorb our attention – fulfilling longstanding engagements, for instance. It was in pursuit of one of these that David and I found ourselves towards the end of 1986 bound for Conway in North Wales. David had promised to address a Liberal dinner on behalf of the candidate, the Rev Roger Roberts, whom David much admired. There was something on in parliament on that Friday morning; so it was decided that David would stay in London and I would travel up by train to meet him. He came and met me that

Friday afternoon and we spent a leisurely few hours before deciding on finding somewhere nice to eat.

Usually my trips to London were mid-week, and then for convenience we ate in the House, but this time we had a whole evening before us and we decided to make the most of it. Worried about David's choice of restaurants, which generally veered towards a steak house or a Chinese restaurant in Gerrard Street, to which Emlyn Hooson had introduced us many years before, I suggested we try somewhere different. The choice was mine and we found a rather pleasant restaurant not far from Sloane Square called Joe's Cafe – it certainly did not resemble the establishment with a similar name nearer to Truro. David was a bit dubious about the stylish interior but was prepared to give it a try, if only to keep the peace. We had a super time, just the two of us.

Next day we set off up the M1 reasonably early for North Wales, thinking this was a good opportunity to put in a spot of shopping for the Liberal Christmas Fair which was taking place the following Saturday. Our Liberal fairs were, and still are, among the largest single fund-raising events for our Party throughout the country. We are fortunate in Truro to have a City Hall right in the middle and as Truro becomes more and more popular a shopping centre so have our fairs thrived. Generally all of our many branches bring stalls and these stalls have been worked on for many weeks before. At that time the fair was raising around £3,000 and David's tombola was an important part of the fair. We tried to make the stall attractive and varied, which meant finding good-quality expensive items as well as lots of eye-catching cheaper ones. We stopped at Walsall where we saw a street market and had great fun findings loads of cheap and cheerful Christmas gifts to pad out the stall alongside the ever popular House of Commons bottles of booze. As we left Walsall, this time with me driving and David about to drop off to sleep, he said, 'Do you realize we haven't had a conversation with anyone other than ourselves for more than twenty-four hours – must be a record.'

He slept most of the rest of the journey and as I drove into Llandudno, where we were staying the night, I woke him for the address of our hosts. 'Where are we?' he asked. 'Llandudno,' I answered. 'Oh no,' he said, 'we are meeting the people at Conway.' 'But surely we are going to the house first to get changed?' 'Oh! Never thought of that,' said David. 'I told them we would go straight to the hall.' And so on a cold late November evening I had to get David to drive up a lane while I changed out of my day clothes into an evening skirt and top, and then even more skilfully applied make-up in the dimly lit car. We arrived at Conway to a very warm welcome and as we were meeting all the guests coming to the dinner I put my hand to my back, only to find to my horror that in my hurry to dress I had failed to do up my zip.

It was during that weekend that David persuaded me to come up to London again on 18 December to attend the Alliance ball. We had been every year but this year it was, in my opinion, too close to Christmas and in any case it was clashing with Christmas visits I had already arranged for David to attend on the next day. David on the other hand felt very strongly that it was an occasion that raised substantial sums of money for the Party and that MPs should attend. So, although it certainly was not a cheap event – well, not by Cornish standards – and it was a long way for me to go just for a party, I rearranged his diary.

We went to Hamley's on the Thursday afternoon to buy some Christmas presents for the children and when we came out I could see he was dying to get back to some work, especially as beyond Hamley's there was no other shop that interested him. We met up later and, as always, we were then in a tearing hurry to get ready, having left ourselves very little time in which to do so. In the event, we were in good time and enjoyed meeting up with old friends before the dinner.

David had been asked to auction a number of items including cases of wine, a magnum of champagne and various bottles of brandy and whisky. He, as always, was employing his dry sense of humour to elicit large sums of money from those bidding. Part way through, when the bidding for, I believe, the magnum of champagne had reached nearly £60, I put in a bid. David's face contorted into an expression of disbelief, as he pleaded with his audience to outbid his 'poor' wife. Fortunately, as always, it worked and the bids continued to rise. He was on good form that night and really enjoyed his evening.

The next day we caught the Cornish Riviera from Paddington to Truro and had a good welcome from the children who, of course, were well aware that some of the boxes we were carrying were for them for Christmas. David held a surgery in St Austell and returned to a lovely supper cooked by my mother. My parents had sold their house and were living with us while awaiting the key to their new home.

David was tired but especially happy that weekend, as Malcolm had heard that, following David's request to David S., he was to be awarded the OBE in the New Year's Honours list, in recognition of all he had done for the Party. No one could have deserved it more.

On the Saturday David visited old people's homes for his annual Christmas visit and he came back very tired. Unfortunately he had to go out again that evening but I consoled him with the thought that he had a free day the next day. 'Free day?' he questioned. 'With all the letters I've got to sign and write?'

As was usual on Sundays, I cooked a traditional Sunday roast lunch whilst listening to the *Archers* and David stayed in bed until quite late. I had also decided to have my first real attempt at making saffron cake. My mother was showing me how to make it and as always did so without a written recipe, which I found disorientating. By tea-time the first of the large tea treat buns were coming out of the oven, making room for the larger cakes.

David had a lazy day and he and Matthew decided to round it off by watching a video. Afterwards they joined the rest of the family for a cup of tea and a tasting of my buns. Tea treat buns are large and generally can be cut into four. David, however, picked a whole one up in his hands and was about to take a bite from it when I slapped his wrists. Everyone was in high spirits, and I was getting both rude comments and compliments on my cakes.

We decided to go off to bed in good time, as David had to be up well before dawn next morning in time to pay his annual visit to those sorting the Christmas post in St Austell. As I was going to bed, David decided to at least sign his letters, as he confessed that he had been very lazy. 'I've really enjoyed today,' he said.

EPILOGUE

David Penhaligon was killed at 6.45 a.m. on 22 December 1986, on his way to thank the postal workers dealing with the Christmas post in St Austell. He died after a van careered out of control on a hill and crashed almost head-on into his car. He was forty-two years old.

After his death Annette Penhaligon received over 3,000 letters – from his friends and colleagues, from royalty and VIPs, from many people too whom she and David had never met. All of them did much to help her and the children. A few are reprinted here.

Dear Mrs Penhaligon and family,

I am unknown to you and have no politics, I think I am only one of . . . millions who are weeping for and with you tonight – please excuse my writing on the only paper I have. I *loved* Mr Penhaligon! I saw him only on TV and heard him on radio, but I loved the way he always seemed to be smiling – kind and reassuring. There was *NO ONE* so lovable or fine on the screen, and his way of speaking was *just* very, very good and attractive. He is the *LAST* person we should have lost . . .

Miss Mary G. U. Aitkenhead, BA, Hollin Hall, Oldham, Lancashire

Dear Mr Steel,

I heard of the death of Mr Penhaligon today on the one o'clock news with a great feeling of shock. I am not a member of any political party but would like to express my deep sympathy to you and your colleagues, and to his family.

Seeing and hearing him on television and radio the impression I have gained of him has been that he was not just down-to-earth but very much a man who liked his fellow human beings – he seemed to enjoy people, politics and life . . .

P.E. Burchill, Gillingham, Kent

Dear Mrs Penhaligon and family,

. . . To be truthful, I never knew the name of the man who, whenever I heard his voice on the radio, or saw him on television, I just used to stop and pay attention knowing I would find him amusing and interesting.

I was aware he was a member of Parliament and came from Cornwall but that never mattered, his personality was uppermost and I knew he would be entertaining and informative. He must have had the same effect on many people.

Of course you are all very sad, but as you have said, what lovely memories you have to help you all through this time. Remember – some folk have never had happiness to make those memories . . .

Mrs Brenda Woollett, St Leonards-on-Sea, East Sussex

Dear Mrs Penhaligon,

. . . I know this may sound a little odd, but your husband (although we never met him) seemed almost like a family friend. He made such an immediate impact on radio and television that you felt, somehow, that you *knew* him and could enjoy his warmth and wit . . .

Philip and Sue Hinchliff, St Albans, Hertfordshire

Dear Mrs Penhaligon,

I am not at all interested in politics, and most politicians bore and annoy me. Your husband was quite different . . . Rotten bad luck . . .

Adam Hart-Davis, West Yorkshire

Dear Mrs Penhaligon,

. . . I knew David Penhaligon but had never met him for, you see, it was not necessary to *meet* him in order to *know* him.. . .

Anon

Dear Mrs Penhaligon,

. . . Yesterday whilst visiting family in Barnet, my sister-in-law commented on a young lad in her office who was shattered by your husband's death. Apparently this lad would take his lunch to his car just to listen to your husband doing the *Jimmy Young Show*. A show not usually too popular with youngsters. It was this lad's respect and interest in what your husband had to say which drew him to the car radio . . .

Mrs Shirley Hopkin, Irchester, Northamptonshire

Dear Mrs Penhaligon,

I heard the news on my car radio this morning and I was so distressed that I pulled into the side of the road and did not resume my journey for several minutes.

It is the measure of the man that I, who had never met him, could be so deeply affected by the cruel tragedy of his death . . .

Arthur Parsons, Barnet, Hertfordshire

Dear Mr Steel,

I'm not a member of the Liberal party; in fact I'm not a member of any political party . . . David Penhaligon has always been one of my favourite politicians, not so much because of his political views, as his warmth and sense of humour. He often had me laughing which isn't bad for a politician. Often they are enough to make you want to cry!

I am sure he will be missed by many, many ordinary people, whether they vote for the Liberal, Labour, Tory or Monster Raving Loony Party! Such politicians who can cross the political spectrum like David Penhaligon did are rare and precious.

Although I never met the man I feel I have lost a friend and I'm sure thousands more feel as I do . . .

Chris Seall, Reading, Berkshire

Dear Mrs Penhaligon,
   This is my ninth attempt to write this bloody letter.
   I am so, so sad.
   I have never shared your husband's company nor his politics, but I was sick to my stomach when I heard the radio announcement.
   There have been so many tributes cliché packed, that I can find no original way of expressing myself. Your husband was an honest man who was not afraid to kick the buggers up the ****. I will not forget his honesty and openmindedness.

Dennis May, Chudleigh, South Devon

Dear Mrs Penhaligon,
   In so far as I take an interest in politics, that interest is entirely due to men like your husband, who managed to make complicated issues entirely comprehensible to ordinary mortals, he had no pretensions about himself or the job, and who, above all was blessed with great good humour, and a sense of service.
   Though, to my shame, I have only visited Cornwall once, many years ago, I feel that I have lost a representative of my

views on all kinds of matters, local and national and international, and my sense of loss is keen . . .

Michael Magrett, Crawley, West Sussex

Dear Annette,

Forgive my use – for we have never met – of the familiar salutation; I never met your husband, either, but if I had, I would not have hesitated to address him at once as 'David' . . .

Richard Phillips, Petersfield, Hampshire

Dear Mr Steel,

. . . He was a great Cornish person and a fine champion of progress in the world.

One always recalls his tale of a Cornish fellow asking him, 'Where be this Common Market, m'dear?'

''Tis the other side of Plymouth!' replied Mr Penhaligon.

'Oo-ah,' re-joined the Cornish fellow; ''tis about time us were gettin' on better with they!'.

The stage of State, both in Cornwall and throughout the UK, shall be the poorer for his passing . . .

George Carter, Wolverhampton

Dear Mrs Penhaligon,

. . . Although we have only ever seen him on television, he will always remind us of our honeymoon in Perranporth.

After our wedding in June 1983, we drove from S. Wales to Cornwall intending to book in at a guest house for a few days. It was election week, and we chose a guest house displaying your husband's election poster (voting Liberal ourselves!) . . .

Caroline and Neil Evans, Glastonbury, Somerset

Dear Mrs Penhaligon,

. . . He gave Cornwall, and the Cornish people credibility to those outside, and to break through that 'London barrier', with its sometimes rather patronizing and impatient attitude to Cornwall, was indeed, a remarkable and very valuable achievement.

Many, many Cornish people will be feeling very bereft – and insecure at the moment, and I know that they, like me, will be selfishly thinking, 'What will we do now?'.

Well, I can imagine what David Penhaligon would say to us – 'you must get on with it' – and so, as Cornish people, our lasting tribute to him, must be to keep his achievements alive, and to keep on working for what he wanted–; for haven't the Cornish always shown great strength to carry on in the face of tremendous adversity? . . .

Kay and Nigel Smith, Newcastle upon Tyne

Dear Mrs Penhaligon,

. . . During my short time actively working in the Liberal Party I only met David twice . . . On both occasions I was struck by his ability to talk with people, rather than to people, to listen and then to explain complicated issues in such simple language . . . In Knowsley, I was fortunate to do some canvassing with him on a very cold evening. His fun and sparkle kept us on the boil right to the end. His enthusiasm was infectious but, above all, his politics were realistic and, like mine, of the old fashioned liberal school. I wish I had known him better . . .

David Ridgway, Huddersfield

Dear Mrs Penhaligon,
    . . . On the first of these visits he came to our house to have a brief supper with my wife and myself, and both of us were struck by the extent to which his personal thoughts, as soon as he could relax in privacy, went back to his home and family. As he talked of you and the children, it was obvious how close you all were together . . .

David and Sue Rendel, Newbury, Berkshire

Dear Annette,
    I'm sitting eating smoked mackerel pâté, a recipe from 'Lobby Fodder' bought at the Conference in Harrogate where David was kind enough to encourage me as a first time delegate to make a speech from my wheelchair in the poverty debate . . . your husband was kind enough to spend time helping me overcome my fear and I feel I would not have succeeded without his help . . .

Pat Durie, Barnsley

Dear Annette,

 . . . Literally hundreds and thousands of people must have their own 'snapshots' in their memories of David.

Mine is of David, you and the children at Leamington Spa. David was the guest speaker at our conference. He made everyone laugh and, of course, punched home his serious message – ('We can't afford to do half the things you lot keep promising we'll do').

It was my job to offer you all suitable hospitality. But David standing beside you and the children in the middle of this milling, welcoming throng was quite firm. He wanted to get back home and preferred a pizza/take-away/motorway cafe with his family to anything we might offer . . . I shall treasure my particular 'snapshot' for a very long time.

Phoebe Winch, Bristol

Dear Annette,

 . . . I first met David when I was about 13 years old when he used to come out to Goonhavern to play 'Table Tennis' for Truro Conservative Club, and in between games he would canvass for the Liberals. Since those days of some 26 or 27 years ago David's path and mine would sometimes cross, being the person he was he never altered, he was always the same, he couldn't be any other really because he was one of us . . .

David White, Goonhavern, Truro

EPILOGUE

Dear Mrs Penhaligon,

... I had the pleasure and privilege of hosting David when he visited the North-East in June. I was terrified not just of David but because we were using his visit to cross a communication barrier between our local Liberal councillors, the largest group and the chamber of trade. What a marvellous success that morning was! And how we have built on it ever since. Yesterday three members of that chamber phoned me to offer their sympathy and to pledge their support to a party that could produce such as he. He was so tolerant and patient with all our local foibles – especially with me because I kept stalling the car.

It may have been an attempt to calm me – or just because he loved you all so much but he talked with such loving pride of you and your children. I believe Matthew had just been selected to play, I think cricket for his school team and David talked of him as 'my boy'. He asked after my children and as I stalled the car yet again, I took a deep breath and braced myself for the usual reactions as my 10 year old Daniel is mentally handicapped. I now know that David understood fully my feelings because of Anna. There was no patronizing sympathy just a realistic understanding of the problems we faced as a family.

He also talked of you, of the type of support you have given him, and how much he depended on you. It was no throwaway line but rather a statement of his philosophy of life.

Today, I saw other friends and councillors and of course we talked of him and of course we laughed but I remember how much I understood what he said.

Thank you for sharing him with all of us.

Sarah Mitchell, Northumberland

Dear Mrs Penhaligon,

   . . . We were so honoured last year when he came to speak
to Stratford Liberals and stayed the night at our home. We
anticipated he would be tired after a day in the House, a 100
mile drive, and would wish to go straight to bed. Not at all;
he chatted in an animated and fascinating way half the night
and ended up choosing a second-hand car with me from the
local press, in our bathroom at 2.45 a.m.! (I went and
bought the car next day and still have it).

   I have never taken a more instant and thorough liking to
any man; he was able to establish in an hour a rapport which
it takes most people years to establish . . .

Gordon Brace, Stratford-upon-Avon, Warwickshire

Dear Mrs Penhaligon,

   . . . We were very fortunate to have David visit and speak
to the Association twice, most recently at the beginning of
his presidential year. I have a memory of that occasion as he
walked down the centre aisle of the meeting to the platform
carrying a small tray with a pot of tea on it, having just
arrived off the train from London, in that very human and
unpompous way he had.

   On that and many other occasions he gave an example of
how to hold public office while remaining approachable and
with an everyday humanity which I and many others will
remember and hope to emulate. He gave a spark to our lives
which touched us all and will remain.

Roger Hargreaves, Liss, Hampshire

Dear Mrs Penhaligon,

  ... Bridgwater Liberals mourn the loss of David as a man, as a Liberal, as a wit and as a friend. There is no other Member of Parliament, of any party, who was as welcome at any gathering as David.

  His advice, 'If you've got something to say, write it on a bit of paper and stick it through the door', will be quoted for many a year ...

Frank Connolly, Bridgwater, Somerset

Dear Mrs Penhaligon,

  ... David was a leading member of our rock drill engineering team and we worked together for several years in the early 70s; he had made this subject very much his own and it was undoubtedly a set-back for Holmans' when he won the Truro seat in 1974 – but offset by the tremendous gain for Cornwall and for Parliament at Westminster.

  His personality, warmth and sense of fun which I had experienced at Camborne seemed quite unaffected by his being catapulted into the national scene, and that alone speaks volumes for his character and genuineness of spirit.

Phil Harris, Helston, Cornwall

Dear Annette,

  ... The waiting in the Cathedral before the [Thanksgiving] Service was again an opportunity for memories and listening to the memories of others. The one that came back to me many times was when David, myself and several others had spent *many* hours delivering, knocking doors and spreading the word in the local council election in Truro East ward and eventually tired, well soaked but pleased with progress we returned to HQ at Nan Hurst's at about nineish. David then decided the night was young so Malcolm, David, me and a few others went up to the printing press at Kenwyn and spent ages working the duplicator. It would be more honest to say that we tried to work it and David fixed it after rough handling! . . .

Alastair Holman, Cardiff

Dear Mrs Penhaligon,
   . . . During the seven months I worked for him I felt that he became a friend whom I will always value having known.
   . . . His warmth and compassion also made a deep impression on me, even to the extent of his rescuing discarded plants from dustbins and attempting to revive them in his office . . .

Jonathan Manning, Cambridge

Dear Mrs Penhaligon,
   . . . I have no direct contact with any of the political parties; but have always been pulled towards the centre . . .
   . . . I first came across David Penhaligon in a debate about the planned development of a PWR at Sizewell in about 1980 at Ipswich Town Hall. I was 17 then, I think what impressed me most was what seemed to me to be the

inherent truth of what he said, but more than that the complete conviction with which he said it all.

It may sound corny but I felt he was a sort of beacon, a man who stood out amongst a mass of MPs – he made a big impression on me . . .

Julia Last, Ipswich, Suffolk

Dear Mrs Penhaligon,

I am writing on behalf of Teignbridge Constituency Labour Party . . .

. . . Despite the fact that our political views conflict in many ways with the Liberal Party policy, our respect for David, and our shock at his accident, transcend party political limits. It is almost true to say that we did not mind David holding Truro for the Liberals; he was always a genuine spokesman for the interests of local people; he was an individual and, though loyal to his Party, he did not allow his loyalty to prevent him from speaking out when he felt that other members, or the leadership, were moving in the wrong direction; and he gave people credit for being able to reach sensible decisions if presented with the necessary information. At a time when people are increasingly disillusioned about the ability of politicians of any party to solve the nation's real problems, he offered them some hope that the democratic process would allow their opinions to be taken into account. It is an indication of his outstanding abilities that a politician of such independent outlook could achieve national status . . .

Bob Kennedy, Chairman, Teignbridge Constituency Labour Party, Teignmouth, Devon

Dear Annette,

We confess to canvassing against your dear late husband – the colour of the ink [red] will tell you the party. We met him several times and always shook hands. You have lost an irreplaceable man – so has the country.

I could write a thousand plus words in his praise but let him be remembered as the only true Cornishman who represented Cornwall.

Brian Snowling and Maureen Meekins, Colchester, Essex

Dear Mrs Penhaligon,

I am an aged dyed-in-the-wool Conservative but I am SO SORRY about the loss of your husband.

We are all the poorer.

Mrs Dorothy Dennier, Whitby, North Yorkshire

Dear Mr Steel,

I was so shocked and upset to hear of the death of David Penhaligon MP. Even though I am an SNP member, I thought that his brand of Liberalism was wonderful. If Cornwall was an independent state, he should have been its President . . .

Name withheld at correspondent's request, Edinburgh

Dear Annette,

. . . The regard with which David was held locally and nationally must be of great comfort to you. This became very apparent to me on Saturday last while at the Albert Hall for a briefing for a Youth Band Festival when a representative from an Irish Youth Band approached me and extended his sympathy at the loss to Cornwall and the Country.

Christine Penhaligon, Truro

Dear Annette,

. . . Like many other people (I suspect) I can now see that I had underestimated greatly the extent to which David had become a national political figure – as witness the recent media coverage. He was always so accessible and down-to-earth that one tended to forget his wider role. One of my memories is of coming to a coffee morning at your house and getting involved in a discussion with David and another man about recent developments in table tennis styles! . . .

Peter Mitchell, Truro

Dear Mrs Penhaligon,

It was on Kensington Station that I read of your husband's tragic death in the *Standard*; I have never felt such a sudden feeling of loss in all my life. David was to me like other boys have football heroes. In politics it was him I wanted to be like. I think that your husband could have done so much for this country had he remained alive, and although I'm only sixteen, I hope that one day I can begin to achieve some of what he would have achieved were he still alive . . .

Jonathan Oates, London EC4

INDEX

INDEX

INDEX